Strong Female Character

What Movies Teach Us

STRONG FEMALE CHARACTER

Hanna Flint

FOOTNOTE

First published in 2022 by
Footnote
www.footnotepress.com

Footnote Press Limited
4th Floor, Victoria House, Bloomsbury Square, London WC1B 4DA
Distributed by Bonnier Books UK
Owned by Bonnier Books
Sveavägen 56, Stockholm, Sweden

First printing
1 3 5 7 9 10 8 6 4 2

© Hanna Flint 2022
The right of Hanna Flint to be identified as the author of this
work has been asserted in accordance with the
Copyright, Designs and Patents Act 1998.

All rights reserved. No part of this publication may be reproduced, stored in
a retrieval system, or transmitted in any form or by any means without
the written permission of the publisher, nor be otherwise circulated in
any form of binding or cover other than that in which it is
published and without a similar condition being imposed
on the subsequent purchaser.

A CIP catalogue record for this book is available
from the British Library and the Library of Congress.

ISBN (paperback): 978–1–804–44000–1
ISBN (ebook): 978–1–804–44005–6
Cover design by Anna Morrison
Typeset by Bonnier Books UK Limited
Printed and bound in Great Britain by
Clays Ltd, Elcograf S.p.A.

MIX
Paper from
responsible sources
FSC® C018072
FSC
www.fsc.org

For Monica and Wendy

Contents

Preface

Do you. It isn't easy but it's essential. It's not easy because there's a lot in the way. In many cases, a major obstacle is your deeply seated belief that you are not interesting. And since convincing yourself that you are interesting is probably not going to happen, take it off the table. Think, 'Perhaps I'm not interesting but I am the only thing I have to offer, and I want to offer something. And by offering myself in a true way I am doing a great service to the world because it is rare and it will help.'

– Charlie Kaufman, film-maker, 2011[1]

---

[1] Kaufman, Charlie, 'Screenwriters' Lecture' (30 September 2011) https://www.bafta.org/media-centre/transcripts/screenwriters-lecture-charlie-kaufman

Part One

Origin Story

Chapter 1

'By order of the Princess!'

– Aladdin (1992)

IT'S A QUESTION AS old as time (well, as old as The Walt Disney Studios): 'Which Disney Princess are you?' has been a formative inquiry for most little girls around the world, long before it became a BuzzFeed quiz. For a minority of us, however, that question wasn't the most, shall we say, aesthetically fruitful. And by 'minority' I mean, non-white ethnic minorities.

I am an ethnic minority and the result of a holiday romance that probably shouldn't have progressed further than the summer it took place. My British mother Caroline Flint met my Arab father Saief Zammel while on a girls' trip to Sousse, Tunisia, in 1985. He was tall, dark and handsome with a strong tache. She was a raven-haired beauty whose dance moves caught his attention. His English wasn't bad, certainly better than her French (and non-existent Arabic), but they were fast becoming fluent in the language of love. Nothing like the romantic possibilities of a Maghrebi love affair to heat up the life of a local government worker from the cold shores of England.

In 1986, Mum gave birth to my older brother Karim at a Hammersmith hospital. By the time I was born eighteen months later, she and my father had tied the knot, but the culture clash, among other things, soon turned the relationship sour. In

February 1989, Mum was a single mother-of-two living in a rented two-bed flat in Chiswick and my father had been deported back to Tunisia. Divorce shortly followed and all I had left to remember him by were a few pictures and the colour of my skin – and it certainly wasn't 'as white as snow' like Disney's first princess.

Snow White and the Seven Dwarfs was a landmark film. The first feature-length animated movie ever made, it established Walt Disney's position as a groundbreaking, innovative film-maker and paved the way for animation as a serious art form that could inspire as much awe, intrigue and cinematic nourishment as any live-action endeavour. It also underpinned one of the most ridiculously unrealistic beauty standards ever invented. Adapted from the Brothers Grimm fairy tale, Snow White reinforced the idea to little girls that in order to be 'the fairest of them all' your skin needed to be whiter than white. There's no escaping that expectation – it's literally in the title – and since 1937, generation after generation of young girls of colour watching that film, and its various live-action adaptations, have been indoctrinated with the idea that their darker skin tone is ugly in comparison. It certainly made the younger me resent my skin and I'm at the lighter end of the melanin spectrum. But, of course, back in the mid-nineties when I was first discovering the Magical Kingdom, I didn't understand why this messaging was so discriminatory. I only saw Snow White, and the alabaster princesses that would follow, as aspirational.

We had most of the Disney classics on VHS with *Cinderella* and *Sleeping Beauty* being an integral part of the collection. Just a couple of young blonde babes looking for a charming prince to whisk them away from the evil treatment of two older women. In hindsight, the films' messages of female empowerment were about as pale as Cindy and Aurora, and yet we lapped it up. Every time Mum or I popped those videos in the VCR, I felt a contact high as I sang along and absorbed this particularly addictive brand of fairy-tale romance and femininity. Subconsciously I was telling myself whiteness was

6

synonymous with beauty. Then came the Disney Renaissance and it was over for those hoes . . . you know, respectfully.

Cinderella? Never heard of her. Aurora? Of whom do you speak? My allegiance was now pledged to *The Little Mermaid* (1989) and *Beauty and the Beast* (1991). One of the first dolls I ever owned was an Ariel one. I can still remember the excitement of going to the old Disney Store in Hammersmith's Kings Mall with Mum to buy Ariel a fancy iridescent tail to replace the basic green one it came with. Oh, did I love that shop. They used to have a giant centrepiece filled with soft toys of every character and I felt an urge to dive in every time I saw it. Mum would take us there as a treat every now and then, mostly to browse, but sometimes we'd get to take something home for a birthday or Christmas present: like that tail, an Eric doll to make an honest woman of Ariel, or a pair of Little Mermaid roller skates that I rocked every Saturday at the roller disco hosted by Brentford Leisure Centre.

One time, I got a *Beauty and the Beast* magnetic folding notebook. Do you remember the ones? It made me feel like a fancy young woman with places to go and people to see. It had a notepad, a calendar – to detail your busy social schedule of play dates and birthday parties, obviously – and an address section to list your three pals' landline numbers. My affection for Ariel soon transferred to Belle; when you only have white characters to represent you, you quickly look for small ways in which you can see yourself and *this* Disney Princess had brunette hair and liked to read many leather-bound books. I didn't have leather-bound books – just a growing Josie Smith collection and weekly issues of the *Dandy* – but the bookworm in me felt that little bit seen. And you know what they say about beggars and choosers.

I had the lyrics to both films memorised. I still do. 'Part of Your World', 'Kiss the Girl', 'Be Our Guest', 'Beauty and the Beast'. I sang them so often throughout my childhood, adolescence and into adulthood, that a few Christmases back my Mum and 'step' dad Phil (see Chapter 4) got me a Disney singalong CD. At the time, I told her to return it, taken aback by the shame I felt for my continued obsession with these kids' movies. But who was I kidding? My Spotify playlist features an embarrassment of Renaissance hits. What can I say? Alan Menken and Howard Ashman sure knew how to pen a banger. With the global successes of *The Little Mermaid* and *Beauty and the Beast*, Ashman – the New York playwright, lyricist and director behind *The Little Shop of Horrors* – helped to revive a directionless Disney Studios, suffering an eighteen-year slump in commerciality and creativity after Walt and Roy Disney's deaths, by reminding the new people in charge how much of a match made in heaven animation and musicals could be. He also reminded them that people of colour exist.

If Disney's animated films ever portrayed non-white characters, they mostly appeared in animal form with *Fantasia*, *Dumbo* and *Lady and the Tramp* serving up some of the most racist characterisations ever committed to animation. *The Little Mermaid*'s Sebastian was less offensive thanks to the crab's Trinidadian accent being delivered by a Black voice actor, but nonetheless it was still pretty odd given the film's said-to-be Danish setting. I'm not sure you'd find that many flamingos and tropical lagoons in Denmark, but given how white the humans and merpeople are it's clearly not the Caribbean. Well, unless Prince Eric is a coloniser and, you know, there is historical precedence.

Speaking of colonies, and to quote Mickey Mouse, *oh boy* did the Native American community have their ups and downs with Disney. In *Peter Pan*, the 'Piccaninnies' were pretty awful caricatures, especially Tiger Lily who, for some reason, *doesn't* qualify as a Disney Princess. *Pocahontas* managed to drum up some good will in 1994 with its more dignified depiction of the Powhatan people in a story based on a real woman, and its use of indigenous actors to voice the Princess and her tribe. I have to admit, my heartfelt adoration for this film and the song 'Just Around the Riverbend' was shattered during my first year of university. In an American History class, I was confronted with the harrowing truth that the story of Pocahontas was not, in fact, the romantic white saviour epic that Disney had us believing. That lecture was the equivalent of Laurence Fishburne in *School Daze* screaming 'WAKE UP' in my face. *Pocahontas* is the third most betrayed I've ever felt about a movie. Denis Villeneuve's *Dune* is the second. *Aladdin* is the first.

Ashman birthed the idea for an Eastern-inspired musical the same year Mum gave birth to me, in 1988, though the final film wouldn't be released in the UK until a year after its 1992 US release, just before my fourth birthday. (Kids, you don't know how good you have it these days with simultaneous global distribution strategies.) Specifically, he pitched a musical based on the folk tale introduced to the Western world through *Arabian Nights*, a collection of mostly Middle Eastern stories – collated during the Islamic Golden Age between the eighth and thirteenth centuries – which went by the title *One Thousand and One Nights* when it was first translated into English in the 1700s.

French translator Antoine Galland added the story of *Aladdin* (or *The Wonderful Lamp*) in 1710, citing a Syrian scholar he met in Aleppo as his source. Or so he claims; no one had been able to verify this assertion so people just took his word for it. More recently, however, in a memoir credited to Syrian Antun Yusuf Hanna Diyab, the author claims he told several stories to Galland in 1709. This verifies Galland, but also speaks on the long history of white men erasing people of colour by not giving Diyab due credit and, in the retelling, likely sprinkled his own European ideas into it. The Middle Eastern influence is inescapable, though. It features Arabic words and names, like Princess Badroulbadour, which means 'full moon of full moons', as well as the use of 'Sultan' to describe her father's position. But while the antagonist sorcerer hailed from the Maghreb region of North Africa, Aladdin was originally Chinese, with most of the action taking place in China too.

It's a story that reeks of what Palestinian academic Edward W. Said called Orientalism (see Chapter 14); a term he coined in 1978 to describe, in the most basic sense, the practice of European and American scholars, colonists and explorers returning West with exotic stories that mash up the cultures and customs of different Eastern regions with a big, fat, one-size-fits-all 'Orient' label. You'd think 278 years later, more progressive artists in the West might choose to course-correct some of these problematic depictions when retelling antiquated Orientalist stories, but that was just too inconvenient to their vision. As historian Krystyn R. Moon wrote:

> Aladdin [. . .] was one of the more popular nineteenth-century productions set in China because of its romantic and moralistic storyline and its potential as a spectacle . . . Composers and librettists sometimes chose Persia as the setting for the tale because One Thousand and One Nights was from that region of the world and, like China, was a popular imaginative space for Americans and Europeans.[1]

So, taking its cues from the original text and the 1940 film adaptation *The Thief of Bagdad*, Ashman pitched a forty-page treatment. It was rejected at first, but after a long development process with changes to the script and his untimely death in 1991, *Aladdin* was eventually released in cinemas to tell the story of the eponymous street urchin, the Genie and a couple of non-human sidekicks who would fight against an evil sorcerer in order to protect the kingdom of our hero's beloved Princess Jasmine. A world of little brown girls *now* had someone to see themselves in and with a name rooted in Middle Eastern history:

---

[1] Moon, Krystyn R., *Yellowface: Creating the Chinese in American Popular Music and Performance, 1850s–1920s.*

> The word *jasmine* comes from the Persian word *yasmin*, or gift from God . . . Jasmine, first imported from Andalucia in the sixteenth century, is Tunisia's national flower . . . In the 1980s, foreign journalists began referring to the Tunisian Revolution as the Jasmine Revolution.[2]

It was a major awakening. Sometimes you don't know what you're missing until it's right in front of you and here Jasmine was, in vibrant colour, confirming our existence. I wouldn't say it was exactly like looking in the mirror – I was still a child and she is meant to be a teen, plus animator Mark Henn is said to have used his sister's yearbook photo and Jennifer Connelly for inspiration. But even with this white man's idea of an Arab woman, I finally saw a Disney Princess with my olive skin, my brown, almond-shaped eyes and black eyebrows, even my larger nose, reflected back. I could see the similarities between Aladdin and my brother Karim too and we both became obsessed with the film and its sequel *The Return of Jafar*. Now, when I played with my girlfriends at sleepovers, in the park or in the playground, I had a Disney Princess to pretend to be without anyone questioning whether I was light enough to play her.

'Posh', episode six in season one of *PEN15* – a US sitcom written by and starring Maya Erskine and Anna Konkle playing versions of themselves as teenage outsiders in the year 2000 – is a properly honest depiction of what it feels like to be told you're too dark to play a white idol. Except, they use the Spice Girls when the half-Japanese Maya wants to be Posh Spice, but is told she must play Scary Spice, the only woman of colour in the girl group. 'Because you're different from us, you're, like, tan,' a mean girl tells her, using the classic casual racism excuse that ethnic minorities can only play ethnic minorities (even if the people in question is a girl of East Asian descent and a woman of African heritage). A version of this 'Spice Girl

---

[2] Masri, Safwan M., *Tunisia: An Arab Anomaly*.

11

tokenism' happened to me until Jasmine turned up. At least this Princess had a similar racial background to me compared to Melanie Brown – well, as much as a fictional character can when they are concocted in a room of white writers. Which Disney Princess are you? I was Jasmine and she was mine, and very much the only positive representation of an Arab woman I would see for years.

I was aware that my biological father was from a country called Tunisia but as I had never been, nor had any sort of contact with him, and Mum wasn't exactly talkative on the subject, it was as much of a foreign concept as Agrabah. For many years, that fictional city was a stand-in where I could pretend I came from, a place where I could insert my father and let my young imagination wander through the palace where I would secretly fantasise my royal family awaited. Kids with absent parents love to do that. Invent a fantastical backstory because the idea that their mother or father didn't want you is just too hard a pill to swallow. And a palace was certainly an upgrade from the small flat our family of five lived in, where my brothers and I shared a room with a bunk bed for me and Karim and a cabin bed for my brother (Dad's son) Nick. That's the other thing about the early Disney Princesses; they either become immensely wealthy through marriage or are wealthy by birth and stay that way, with the story ending once they get their man. Sure, we see the likes of Snow White, Cinderella, and Aurora doing various bits of housework, and I guess Belle manages the home she shares with her inventor dad when she's not reading, but Jasmine doesn't lift a finger. Hardly the most enterprising role model, is she?

But being a lady of leisure is not the most problematic thing about Jasmine. This Arab princess was overtly sexualised in a way that her white predecessors were not and even in the nineties it didn't sit right with me. When Ariel is half-naked with just a bikini top and tail to protect her modesty, it all looks rather innocent. Even the 'Kiss the Girl' sequence is awkward and endearing but Jasmine's turquoise costume seemed solely designed to titillate. Her breasts, as well as other exotically presented female background characters, are bulging in a way that Belle's and Aurora's do not. Par for the course for women of colour: we often get hypersexualised at an earlier age than our white counterparts. Jasmine is meant to be fifteen going on sixteen, but depicted as a full-bodied woman with white voice actor Linda Larkin delivering her lines with a lower-pitched, sultry American accent. Then there are the 'come to bed' eyes Jasmine is often animated with when in conversation with the men around her. But the real 'wowzer, are we really doing this in a children's movie?' moment is the sex slave narrative. When Jafar takes power he forces an arranged marriage with the princess and dresses her up in an even more provocative, red version that could give Princess Leia's gold ensemble in *Return of the Jedi* a run for its money. Bourenane Abderrahmene reflects in 'Authenticity and Discourses in Aladdin', the princess is victim to the Orientalist trope whereby Middle Eastern and North African (MENA) women are sexually exoticised:

> Jasmine is represented according to a Western imagination of the oriental female figure; she is over-sexualized through the belly dancer outfit that she wears all over the film and she is confined in the palace until her decision to escape. Jasmine is presented with a tiger pet in an attempt to push the limits of oriental exoticism and danger.[3]

Once in the sexy number, Jasmine uses seduction as a distraction tactic despite being a sheltered fifteen-year-old whose life has been rigidly structured by her overprotective father. The assumption here is that sexual promiscuity is an inherent trait. Jasmine isn't alone in this treatment: *The Hunchback of Notre*

---

[3] Abderrahmene, Bourenane, 'Authenticity and Discourses in Aladdin' (1992) *Journal of Arab & Muslim Media Research*, https://www.researchgate.net/publication/344682480_Authenticity_and_discourses_in_Aladdin_1992

Dame's Esmeralda is a sixteen-year-old of Romani heritage but written as a male fantasy, who dances for money, with a pole at one point, and is trapped in the Madonna and the Whore binary because of the respective attractions of Quasimodo and Frollo. In the DVD commentary, director Kirk Wise admitted she was designed to look like she'd 'been around' and it's precisely this overly mature characterisation that led to her being de-crowned: Esmeralda's Princess status was removed due to low doll sales because, apparently, parents weren't comfortable with the adult themes she's associated with.[4] Way to slut-shame your own creation, Disney!

The company slowly got better with their Princess of colour representation. Mulan, and Tiana of *The Princess and the Frog*, weren't bogged down as much by problematic stereotypes and had more explicit feminist motivations that aren't simply the vague need for freedom. Mulan takes her crippled father's place in the Chinese army and becomes the Emperor's champion while Tiana actually has a job and dreams of opening her own restaurant. These girls had independent spirits, and were not afraid of getting their hands dirty for what they wanted. Nor were they solely relying on a Prince Charming to achieve it. Tiana did, unfortunately, have to kiss a frog to free her man and his ethnic background is as much of an Orientalist mess as Aladdin's. That being said, the fact that Prince Naveen is lighter skinned than Tiana is a significant break from the colourist attitude towards dark-skinned Black and brown women who are still today often overlooked as desirable romantic interests. Both these films, like *Pocahontas* and unlike *Aladdin*, hired relevant people of colour to voice the characters too and that push for authentic representation became the new standard.

But it wasn't just in casting voice actors, like Pacific Islander Auli'i Cravalho as Moana and Scotland's Kelly Macdonald as

---

[4] Disney Princess Fandom at https://disneyprincess.fandom.com/wiki/ Esmeralda

Brave's Merida, who shared their characters' backgrounds, but in the world-building too. The original folk tales weren't treated as simply a jumping-off point, but served as the foundation that grounded the subsequent layers of storytelling and songs in the specific cultures. *Moana*, especially, has rightly been celebrated for how much respect and effort has gone into reflecting Polynesian history and communities in an empowering way. And like Ashman and Menken, Lin-Manuel Miranda, Opetaia Foa'i and Mark Mancina penned some massive hits – 'Where You Are' has been my get-up-and-go anthem ever since 2016.

I went to see *Moana* on my own at West India Quay's Cineworld and I'm not ashamed to admit that I wept at several moments, specifically when her grandmother gave her a third-act pep talk. To be fair, I cry a lot during movies but I think I was also shedding a tear for the little girl in me who didn't get to see this sort of Disney Princess when it would have had the most positive impact on how I saw myself. It's why I was excited at a live-action remake of *Aladdin* following the box office successes of the live-action remakes of *Cinderella* and *Beauty and the Beast*. Maybe now they could offer a version of this story that would right the stereotypical wrongs.

Disney did and it didn't. It still hired as white a creative team to fill the significant behind-the-scenes roles and heads of department, with Guy Ritchie, a director who has made a career of failing upwards, at the helm, sharing co-writing duties with John August. The producers did, however, bring on casting director Salah Benchegra for its global search to find authentic MENA representation for Aladdin and Jasmine. Casting calls were said to have taken place across the Middle East as well as North America and Europe, but while they hired Egyptian-Canadian actor Mena Massoud to play the eponymous hero, the princess role went to Naomi Scott, of Indian, not Arab, descent.

Now I can totally understand why Scott would have gone for this role, as the original film copied and pasted a couple of Indian motifs onto this fictional Arab world set on the shores of the Jordan River. The Sultan's palace was a rip-off of the Taj Mahal and Rajah, Jasmine's pet tiger, is native to the Bengal region. When she was watching *Aladdin* as a mixed kid like me, no doubt she saw herself in the princess too.

I empathise. However, producer Dan Lin promised this remake would be 'culturally authentic',[5] but without an Arab actress playing Jasmine it was not. Instead, they made her dead mother South Asian and added a Bollywood musical influence to make Scott's casting less jarring because the film-makers were happy to conflate Indian and Middle Eastern cultures again. Ritchie calls Agrabah a 'slightly broader world, a hybrid world,'[6] which is white man speak for we haven't done the work to give this a distinct Arab identity, but it does cover our backs when we situate Agrabah on the Silk Road merchant route, and cast Black, South Asian, and East Asian dancers as background characters.

That Scott is also lighter-skinned than the character in animation form also sparked criticisms of the casting reinforcing a white Western standard of beauty in characters already coded as American. Film critic Roger Ebert noted the awkward Western vs Middle Eastern characteristics in his review of the 1992 film:

One distraction during the film was its odd use of ethnic stereotypes. Most of the Arab characters have exaggerated facial characteristics – hooked noses, glowering brows, thick lips – but Aladdin and the princess look like white American teenagers. Wouldn't it be reasonable that if all the characters in this movie come from the same genetic stock, they should resemble one another?[7]

[5] Leadbeater, Alex, 'Producer Dan Lin Interview: Aladdin' (11 September 2019) https://screenrant.com/dan-lin-interview-aladdin-producer/

[6] Sinha-Roy, Piya, 'A whole new world: First look at Guy Ritchie's live-action remake of Disney's magical classic *Aladdin*' (19 December 2018) https://ew.com/movies/2018/12/19/aladdin-first-look-ew-cover-story/

[7] Ebert, Roger, 'Aladdin' (25 November 1992) https://www.rogerebert.com/reviews/aladdin-1992

Preach, Roger! And yet, the live-action remake doubled down on the Americanisation of its romantic couple leads: Aladdin and Jasmine still have generic American accents – Scott's natural accent is actually English – as does the Genie, played by Will Smith, and his love interest Dalia, played by Iranian-American actress Nasim Pedrad. Meanwhile the MENA characters played by Dutch-Tunisian actor Marwan Kenzari (Jafar), Iranian-American actor Navid Negahban (The Sultan), Turkish-German actor Numan Acar (palace guard Hakim) and Arab-Israeli actor (market seller Jamal) all have 'foreign' accents that Others them in what is meant to be an authentic Arab story. And maybe the less we talk about the reports of white extras being fake-tanned to look darker the better because the remake does have some redeeming qualities.

The barbaric characterisation of the Arab world had been established in the 1992 movie's opening number, 'Arabian Nights', with the lyric 'where they cut off your ear if they don't like your face.' Although the American-Arab Anti-Discrimination Committee campaigned to change it to a less offensive line ('Where it's flat and immense and the heat is intense')[8] a market seller's threat to cut Jasmine's hand off for stealing an apple stayed in the final version. The 2019 remake instead uses the less offensive version of 'Arabian Nights', – awkwardly sung by the non-Arab Smith – and improves the market stall scene to have Jamal attempt to take Jasmine's bracelet for payment instead.

The Disney princess has had quite the revamp herself. Jasmine is given a more feminist makeover where she's less sexualised, with her midriff-baring ensemble replaced with brightly-coloured gowns, corsets and trousers that cover her body. Although, once again, her style leans more towards Scott's Indian background rather than Jasmine's Arab heritage. Still, the character overcomes the old 'oppressed woman' stereotype

---

[8] Fox, David J., 'Disney Will Alter Song in "Aladdin"' (10 July 1993) https://www.latimes.com/archives/la-xpm-1993-07-10-ca-11747-story.html

often forced upon Middle Eastern characters. While the original movie focuses on Jasmine not wanting to get married, the live-action version includes a plotline about her ambition to become Sultan that comes with far more agency. It's a message that really hits home when Jasmine sings her brand-new solo song, 'Speechless', a powerful anthem about raising your voice and speaking out. Scott might not have Jasmine's heritage but she certainly has the pipes.

This Princess Jasmine was no longer the poster child for the Exotic Other. I know young me would have been a fan and I am sure many brown girls look up to this version now too, especially as it's currently the only major studio movie to feature a predominantly MENA cast and not be about terrorism. We have slim pickings, even after three decades where, in that time, racial representation has improved more quickly for other ethnic minority groups. But Jasmine is still a cinematic construct with more in common with her Western creators than the foreign Arab world she's supposed to be from. Law professor Khaled Beydoun wrote for Al Jazeera:

> [T]o some measure, the demand to cast Arab actors to play the lead roles in Aladdin amounts to an endorsement that Agrabah is indeed an Arab land or an accurate representation of the Arab world.[9]

A mystical world that in the last twenty years has been victim to Western violence on a traumatic scale that the casual cinemagoer rarely bats an eyelid at unless there's a dead refugee toddler covering the front of a newspaper. And let's be honest, if Jasmine was real she would have had her asylum application rejected while trying to escape an Agrabah where Jafar had succeeded in his coup.

---

[9] Beydoun, Khaled A., 'It doesn't matter that an Arab will play Aladdin' (19 July 2017) https://www.aljazeera.com/opinions/2017/7/19/it-doesnt-matter-that-an-arab-will-play-aladdin

As a vocal advocate for MENA representation, the conflicted affection I have for Princess Jasmine leaves a bittersweet taste in my mouth. And when I think about the recent female characters of *Encanto* and *Raya of the Last Dragon* fame, there's certainly an argument that these Colombian and Southeast Asian women better reflect me than the supposedly Arab one. Why try and find yourself in a Disney Princess that doesn't even reach the lowest threshold of authenticity? Until Disney puts the effort in with the Arabs, this Arab is no longer willing to be pacified with an Orientalist princess for the sake of the bare minimum of nuanced representation.

Which Disney Princess are you? Yeah. I'm good, actually.

Chapter 2

'They let you pick any name you want when you get down there.'

– Superbad (2007)

WHEN I SAT DOWN to interview Jeff Goldblum and Mamadou Athie about *Jurassic World: Dominion*, the first thing Jeff asked was if we'd met before and what my last name was. Once I told him, he began waxing lyrical about it. 'That's a great name, I wish my name was Hanna Flint. I might have gotten a lot further along than I am now,' he said. 'Hanna Flint, now that's a movie star name!' When he brought up the spy series *Our Man Flint* it reminded me of that time Vincent D'Onofrio tweeted me saying my name sounded 'smart & intriguing. Like a secret agent [sic].' This still might be the most randomly nice thing someone has said about me on that website even though it is completely unearned. That's not to say I don't think of myself as being smart or intriguing, but a name is certainly not indicative of that. And in my case, the name Flint, Hanna Flint isn't the one written on my birth certificate. That name is Hanna Ines Zammel. I wonder if the actor Vincent D'Onofrio would still think my name sounded like a secret agent had my handle been @HannaZammel.

According to the website Forebears, 'Zammel' is the 2,091,648th most common surname in the world and worn predominantly in Africa, 'where 49 per cent of Zammel are found' and most commonly pops up in Tunisia.[1] It might look exotic through Western eyes, but to Tunisians it's about as mundane a surname as 'Flint'. I've often Googled it, or popped it in the search bar of various social media platforms, in my search for answers about my Tunisian heritage and mused about the possibility that any one of these people might be a relation. Or not. Though if the Tunisian long-distance runner Ahmed Zairi Zammel, who competed in the men's 5000 metres at the 1968 Summer Olympics, turned out to be a distant relative I wouldn't mind those bragging rights.

The minute I started primary school though I'd go rigid at the beginning of each term as soon as the teachers read my name out. You see, for some reason, even though the school – both my London and Doncaster institutions – were aware that my mum's name was Caroline Flint, and my brother and I went by Flint too, they would sometimes use the names listed on our birth certificates when putting together a class register. So occasionally, a wave of hot shame would wash over me as I heard its nasal pronunciation ricochet off the walls. My eyes would dart nervously between my classmates as I shuffled to my new teacher's desk to remind them that, no, I've never actually gone by that and would they please refer to me by Mum's surname instead, staying next to them until they crossed out Zammel and inserted Flint. The damage was done though; certainly, in the earlier days of school when specific boys were just maniacal in their cruelty, I'd have to suffer the derision of being called 'Hanna Smell' until the novelty wore off, or they'd find some other insult, or sadly a new target to torment. All I wanted to do was assimilate and make people think that my mum and dad were both my biological parents. More importantly, I hated the idea that Mum and I weren't fully connected on paper even though, technically, she didn't share her mum's last name either. My grandmother Wendy Beasley had my mum out of wedlock at seventeen and a few years later married a Peter Flint. He adopted

---

[1] Forebears, 'Zammel surname', https://forebears.io/surnames/zammel

Mum, she took his name and soon she had two younger half-sib-lings to love. When Wendy and Peter split up, Mum chose to keep Flint so she and my aunt and uncle would continue to belong to one another. I wanted to belong to Mum too, but my father's surname suggested I belonged to him and he was a stranger. Egyptian writer and scholar Nawal El Saadawi, in her 2009 article, 'Why to Write and Why', recalls the moment at school when her teacher told her off for writing her mother's name 'Zaynab' as her surname. Her mother had been the greatest influence on her life, who taught her how to use her voice, read and write, so her first thought was to reflect that in her identity rather than a name she shared no affinity with:

> El Saadawi was a foreign name to me, the name of a grandfather who had died before I was born. I never liked the name El Saadawi; it was like a foreign body attached to me. [. . .] From childhood I kept a secret diary on which I wrote my real name: Nawal Zaynab. I felt a strong urge to write. I wanted to erase the false name imposed on me.[2]

That's exactly how I felt. My resentment for my Tunisian surname only grew because it created a gap between my mum and me. Its presence also hindered my efforts to fully pass for white so that people wouldn't ask questions about my heritage that I just didn't have the answers for. And it definitely didn't help that most film and TV characters with foreign names were regularly the butt of jokes or mocking racial stereotypes.

Take The Three Stooges' 1949 short film *Malice in the Palace* and its 1956 feature-length remake *Rumpus in the Harem*, where white actors Vernon Dent, George Lewis and Frank Lackteen are playing violent Arab thieves who are called, respectively, Hassan Ben Sober, Ghinna Rumma and Haffa Dalla. Writer Felix Adler used the same racist, juvenile humour to invent Arab names similar to the one those schoolboys conjured up for me. 'It was a different time!' I hear you cry. What about

---

[2] Saadawi, Nawal El, *The Essential Nawal El Saadawi: A Reader.*

The Simpsons and the nonsense last name they gave to Apu. Staff writer Jeff Martin has claimed 'Nahasapeemapetilon'[3] was inspired by a college friend apparently called Pahasadee Napetilon. I mean, if the person existed surely they would have shown themselves by now, to at least exclude themselves from the narrative. Or maybe they changed their name because it sounds as made up as the gobbledy-gook they labelled Apu that seems very obviously designed to make fun of the length of South Asian surnames. Pull the other one, Jeff!

My brother had it worse than me. At least my first name, written in the French-Arabic way, was English passing. Though people still today get the spelling wrong by putting an 'H' on the end. If I had a penny for how many times I have received emails saying 'Dear Hannah' despite the correct spelling of my name being right there, in my email address, I'd have been able to pay off my student loan ten times over. Anyway, Karim had to deal with being called 'Kream egg' and other such insults as well as the constant mispronunciation. In Arabic, his name means 'generous' and he lived up to that adjective every time someone called him 'ka-rim' and not 'ka-reem', even after he told them the right way of saying it. He still comes across that problem as a screenwriter trying to find his place and his voice in the writers' room without risking his position or opportunities in the face of microaggressions. That's if he gets in the room. Mum liked the idea that our middle names would match, so Karim's is Iskander, the Arabic form of Alexander (al-Iskandarīyah is the Arabic name for the Egyptian city of Alexandria). He started to use it in the early days of his career when pitching for work because 'Karim Flint' wasn't getting many responses. Alex Flint, on the other hand, was getting answered more frequently.

Many screen stars, like Oscar Isaac, Chloe Bennet and Mindy Kaling, had to de-ethnicise their name in order to get a foot

---

[3] Arjun, Sajip, 'Much Apu about nothing' (27 October 2017) https://www.telegraph.co.uk/tv/0/much-apu-nothing-calling-simpsons-racist-misses-point/

through the door. Before becoming an icon as Rita Hayworth, the Hollywood star was known as Margarita Carmen Cansino who was American on her mother's side and of Romani descent on her Spanish father's. When she first got her studio contract as a teenager with the then 20th Century Fox, the actress went by Rita Cansino. But her Mediterranean features meant she became the go-to for exotic characters: in 1935 she appeared as an Argentinian girl in *Under the Pampas Moon* and an Egyptian girl in *Charlie Chan in Egypt*. So, she whitewashed herself. After dying her now trademark hair red, undergoing electrolysis to raise her hairline and using her mother's name, Margarita Carmen Cansino emerged as Rita Hayworth and became a cinematic legend.

While he didn't go to that much physical trouble, F. Murray Abraham came to a disheartening realisation about his Middle Eastern identity. The Oscar-winning star of *Amadeus*, who has appeared in *All the President's Men, Scarface, The Grand Budapest Hotel* and, a recent favourite, TV series *Mythic Quest*, is Syrian-American on his father Farid's side. Farid went by the Anglicised name Fred too – he emigrated with his family from Muqlus, Ottoman Syria to Pittsburgh, Pennsylvania – so when Abraham became an actor, unhappy with the unremarkable combination of his own government name, wanted to add his father's to it to make himself more intriguing. However, going by Farid would create obstacles. As he told David Copelin in *Cinéaste* in 1989, when asked about the abbreviated first name:

> When I first began in the business I realized I couldn't use Farid because that would typecast me as a sour Arab out to kill everyone. I would be consigned to bit parts. With the name Murray Abrahams, oddly enough, I was able to play many roles. As F. Murray Abraham, I had talent. As Farid Murray Abraham I was doomed to minor roles.[4]

---

[4] Copelin, David, '"F" is for Farid' (1989) *Cinéaste*, https://www.jstor.org/stable/23803059?read-now=1&refreqid=excelsior%3Ab8d9c93f7878defea8f-5b1771f890df6&seq=2#page_scan_tab_contents

In the same interview, Abraham says he didn't feel like he had been discriminated against because of his Arab heritage, but also lamented the frequency of villain roles he was being offered. In Lebanese-American writer and lecturer Jack G. Shaheen's groundbreaking tome, *Reel Bad Arabs: How Hollywood Vilifies a People*, he posited this about villains:

> Beginning with *Imar the Servitor* (1914), up to and including *The Mummy Returns* (2001) a synergy of images equates Arabs from Syria to the Sudan with quintessential evil. In hundreds of movies 'evil' Arabs stalk the screen.[5]

The most insidious sort of racial bias is when it permeates between the lines with plausible deniability, so maybe Abraham couldn't see the elephant in the room as to why he was always playing these 'bad guys'. Casual racism can be just as vicious. Manoj Nelliyattu Shyamalan's decision to go by 'M. Night' began in school. 'They'd call me mango or a million things,' he told *Wired* in 2021. 'And so it kind of abbreviated to M eventually.'[6] Then he became a big film director with as many hits as misses; the latter is why a sneering crowd gave themselves permission to turn his surname into a running joke on Reddit threads and in YouTube videos. When his latest movie *Old* was released in 2021, Chris Evangelista, editor-in-chief of *Slash Film*, tweeted:

> With a new M. Night Shyamalan movie on the way, just want to remind folks that writing/saying his last name as 'Shymalamadingdong' is not funny and is, in fact, stupid bullshit you should stop immediately.[7]

---

[5] Shaheen, Jack G., *Reel Bad Arabs: How Hollywood Vilifies a People* (2006), (documentary film).

[6] Shyamalan, M. Night, *Wired* interview (23 July 2021) https://www.youtube.com/watch?v=ltC3VTAwGXM

[7] Evangelista, Chris, Twitter feed (16 June 2021) https://twitter.com/cevangelista413/status/1405241777125212163?s=20&t=vVqtEJLbRAZ8IXJ8fubU6w

To which *Vulture* critic, Bilge Ebiri, replied:

> Also, kinda racist.[8]

Indeed it is, Bilge. Indeed it is.

When I turned eighteen, I legally changed my name. I did not do a *Superbad* and go with a solo moniker inspired by the McDonald's tagline. Or something even more outlandish like Princess Consuela Banana Hammock a la Phoebe Buffay in *Friends*. Nor 'Crap Bag' for that matter. No, via deed poll, I changed my surname to Flint (adding my Dad's surname Cole as a second middle name after Ines) and a weight lifted off my shoulders. With a combined sense of relief and freedom I felt empowered to now get the rest of my life admin in order, passports, bank accounts, etc., to reflect my new legal status and complete my English assimilation. Well, that is apart from the whole looking like I'm not from England thing, as so many people *love* to remind you when they ask the most othering question you can ask a person of colour: 'Where are you really from?'

Nine times out of ten, they are not asking me because of the Yorkshire twang to my accent, and it's always funny how many white people who say they 'don't see colour' have this particular query locked and loaded. If you're reading this and feeling defensive because you've used this phrasing, then don't. I'm sure most of you are not asking it in bad faith, but if you're really that interested in why a person may look different to you, then maybe ask, 'What's your heritage?' instead. Or don't. It's rarely ever that relevant to the conversations I'm having when I happen to be asked by (almost always) strangers on a night out. It's simply not good chat, lads.

My brother changed his surname too, together severing one of the final connections from our father for good. Or so we thought. Mum's decades of public service as a Labour MP has

---

[8] Bilge, Ebiri, Twitter feed (16 June 2021) https://twitter.com/BilgeEbiri/status/1405247690364047360?s=20&t=vVqtEJLbRAZ8IXJ8fubU6w

meant she has a Wikipedia page that has us listed as Hanna Zammel and Karim Zammel ever since my father did a kiss-and-tell on Mum for the *Mail on Sunday* and our privacy became public knowledge, but more about that later.

Yet I'm not stressed out about it. Sure I'd love for someone to do their thing with the backend to accurately name us if we must feature on Mum's page, but nowadays I have less animosity towards Zammel. Don't get me wrong, I'm glad I changed it. Flint is my mother's name and I am proud to share it, but I suppose, as I detach myself from my youthful fears of being Other, there aren't as many prejudices to lay at its feet. It is sad to think that much of that dismissiveness came from places of both external and internal racism. If things had turned out differently with my father, I might be just as proud to wear that name too. There is nothing Other about Zammel to me now, other than it is his. Still, while I won't be reverting to my original birth certificate label, I'm happy to see people in public are doing it for themselves.

For decades her stage name was Thandie Newton, because of an error made during the credits of her first film. The spelling of the British-Zimbabwean actress's real name is Thandiwe, meaning 'beloved' in Zulu and the 'w' is not silent. However, she kept it. Newton didn't want to rock the boat by demanding it back and having to face daily battles of trying to get people to pronounce her name correctly, as one of the only women of colour progressing, slowly, in Hollywood. Then in 2021, she decided no more of that and would only be credited as 'Thandiwe Newton' going forward. 'The thing I'm most grateful for in our business right now is being in the company of others who truly see me. And to not be complicit in the objectification of Black people as "others", which is what happens when you're the only one', she told *Vogue*. 'That's my name. It's always been my name. I'm taking back what's mine.'[9]

---

[9] Evans, Diana, '"I'm Taking Back What's Mine": The Many Lives Of Thandiwe Newton' (4 April 2021) https://www.vogue.co.uk/news/article/thandiwe-newton-interview

Her empowering stand inspired fellow British actress Tanyaradzwa Fear to follow suit after years of going by Tanya. BBC presenter Ben Boulos reclaimed his Sudanese-Egyptian heritage by changing his name back from, ironically, 'Bland'. It wasn't bland anymore.

I've been recently watching the new series of *Picard* and the Borg Queen's appearance reminded me of *Star Trek: First Contact*. In one scene, the antagonist, played by Alice Krige, tells a captured Data (Brent Spiner), 'by assimilating other beings into our collective, we are bringing them closer to perfection.' For more than half of my life, I tried to assimilate closer to the white side of my heritage. I tried to whitewash every part of me to be what our society perceived as English, though what's clear to me now is that the names of ethnic minorities are too often treated as a cultural imperfection. A blot on the Western world. In reality, the flaw is the attitude that tries to enforce its negative biases upon minorities who should be free to express their individual freedom and identities.

My father's surname now only comes with the baggage of abandonment, while my mum's is a symbol of pride for what positive things she's done. I choose hers for that reason, a decision I'm happy to know is no longer entangled with the racial biases of this country.

My name is my power. So is yours. Don't let anybody tell you otherwise.

Chapter 3

'Mom, can I come in bed with you?'

– Obvious Child (2014)

IT WAS ON THE way back from Mum's sixtieth birthday that she offered me a rather unusual Christmas present. We're in the car, Dad driving as usual, when Mum, slightly tipsy from the seven-course meal that came with several glasses of wine, but with utmost sincerity, turns around and asks: 'What if I paid to freeze your eggs for Christmas?' I chuckled. 'Absolutely not!' And thus began squabble #12943803 of our relationship. To be fair, when I was younger, I did imagine that I would become a mother and have two kids by the age Mum had me. Isn't that the conditioning of all little girls? That our purpose in life, our essentialism as women with a uterus, is to secure the biological future of mankind by carrying x-amount of babies through to term. We would shove pillows under our dresses and shirts, cradling the fake bump long before we'd ever been taught about the reality of getting pregnant and childbirth. We were all fed the lies. *Dumbo* (1941) was one of the biggest culprits. It had us believing that a stork would deliver a baby boy or girl in a white sheet as easy as ordering a takeaway. Doesn't look so bad, does it? I'll have one of those and, hopefully, my delivery bird would have a better sense of direction than Mr Stork. Kids' movies make it all look so simple. So painless! Of course, as I got older the reality of motherhood became more apparent and, in the last five years, less appealing. Well, maybe not less appealing. Less urgent? What Mum didn't realise when she offered to freeze my eggs is that she had already given me the best motherhood gift an uncertain daughter could ask for: time.

Mum was twenty-six when she had me. I wasn't planned. Neither was she. My grandma Wendy was just sixteen when she got pregnant by a Scotsman called Robert, in his early twenties, and her parents encouraged her to have Mum rather than give her up for adoption. My great-grandparents ran a pub called the Jolly Blacksmith in Hampton Road, Twickenham – it's a fancy Belgian-themed gastropub now called Brouge – and I guess I have them to thank for that intervention. But, bloody hell, seventeen is really no age to become a mother, especially after a brief encounter with a fella never to be seen again, with the birth taking place in a home for unmarried mothers near Regent's Park. The film *A Taste of Honey* came out in 1961, the year Mum was born. It's a bleak kitchen sink drama, adapted for the screen by Shelagh Delaney from her own play about a working-class schoolgirl facing motherhood and losing her autonomy after a short love affair with a Black sailor. Robert was as white as they come, but whether Wendy's experience with him was as romantic as that between Jo and Jimmie is anyone's guess. 'Women never have young minds,' Delaney wrote. 'They are born three thousand years old.' I wonder if that's how Wendy felt, forced to take on the responsibilities of an adult before she'd even had the time to develop into one herself. She never told Mum much about her father or the night of her conception and I never got the chance to speak to her because she died, aged forty-five, two years after my birth. It's weird to miss someone you don't remember meeting, but not a week goes by that her face doesn't flicker in my mind.

A fortune-teller once said Wendy was watching over me. Lady Lilac, real name Jacqui Cosham, used to be Vogue House's resident psychic and I paid her a visit at her Portland Street flat after hearing about a friend's positive and oddly prophetic experience. So I sent her a text and a few days later I was knocking on her door pleased to find her in head-to-toe lilac. Admittedly, I was somewhat sceptical when the session began. I was in my mid-twenties, knee-deep in singledom, and she'd asked a few questions about my romantic status. The cards told her I was putting barriers up to the relationships. Nothing like stating the bleeding obvious, Jacqui, but do go on. Then she said she felt a presence in the room, a woman close to me who I'd never really known but cared about me deeply. I burst out crying.

Wendy died from liver damage as a consequence of her alcoholism. She wasn't always an alcoholic. In her short life, Wendy went to secretarial school and variously worked as a typist, barmaid and shop assistant while raising three children after the arrival of my auntie and uncle. Mum has fond memories of a woman who was more than the addictive disease that plagued her. But she split from Peter after ten years of marriage, and like plenty of people she turned to booze to numb the feelings of inadequacy and insecurity. The hard drinking started before the divorce when Mum was about twelve. Peter and Wendy managed a pub and, in those days, late-night lock-ins with the regulars was a regular occurrence. It wasn't easy for Mum, who would sometimes be called down to serve drinks behind the bar, and cash up the till at the end of the evening despite her tender age – especially as her adoptive father pretty much ghosted her after the divorce was finalised. Two dads out of the picture is an unpleasant reality for any child and it somewhat explains why Mum never felt the need to keep mine and Karim's father in our lives either.

Mum had the sort of childhood that toughens you up and makes you increasingly self-sufficient, like Rosetta, the eponymous lead of the Dardenne brothers' 1999 cinéma-vérité drama. The sixteen-year-old is trying to pay their bills and keep a roof over their heads without her alcoholic mother resorting to sexual favours for gifts at the trailer park they live in. It's a constant battle to keep her mother sober while trying to find a new job and not resorting to welfare cheques. The adolescent female rage is never far from the surface of Émilie Dequenne's raw performance. I only saw *Rosetta* last year but it was one of the few times I'd seen an alcoholic mother depicted. There have been plenty of alcoholic fathers on screen, probably because there are more roles for men and drinking has historically been considered a more male occupation, while women have been restricted to the domestic sphere. Post-war Britain saw an increase in boozing, especially during the seventies, with more and more ladies infiltrating the male spaces of pubs and clubs as paying customers themselves. But while drunk dads are depicted as much as endearing fuck-ups and tragic heroes – like Frank Gallagher of *Shameless*, Martin of *Another Round* and Travers Robert Goff of *Saving Mr. Banks* – the smaller number of alcoholic mothers are often characterised as something more deviant.

Take the whorish depiction of Rosetta's mother, Helen the 'good time gal' mother of Jo in *A Taste of Honey*, and Mrs Robinson in *The Graduate* who shags the son of her husband's business partner and then cries rape to her daughter after he tries to end their affair. *Days of Wine and Roses* (1962) is one of the most famous films to depict the ravages of alcoholism, but while Jack Lemmon's Joe Clay is the worthy protagonist who overcomes his addiction to look after their child, Lee Remick's Kirsten, his wife who was teetotal before they met, can't stop relapsing and picking up random men at bars. Meg Ryan plays an alcoholic mother, Alice, in *When a Man Loves a Woman* (1994), and counters this pejorative depiction when she recovers and reunites with her husband. In her directorial debut *Bruised* (2020), Halle Berry plays a disgraced, middle-aged MMA fighter who, after becoming a guardian to her estranged young son again, gives up the booze and gets back in the ring to give them a better life. It's an empowering underdog story that shows how deeply-rooted trauma can affect your sense of self, with Berry channelling her own childhood memories of an alcoholic father into the drama. 'They're good people with bad problems,' she said of alcoholics to the *LA Times*. 'They're hurt people [. . .] And that's what I understand about alcoholism and drug addiction and abuse and domestic violence. It's fractured people who are trying to survive, and they just don't have the skills.'[1]

At sixteen, Mum moved into the house of her mother's friend in Twickenham to complete her O levels. Wendy had taken her siblings to Fleetwood in Lancashire where her grandparents had retired so Mum had no other options. A year later, they were back in London, but Wendy's alcoholism worsened and home life got even more fraught and volatile. Mum had to apply for a charitable grant to get financial support to pay for lodgings just so she could complete her A levels away from the domestic disorder. In 1980, she became the first person in her family to enter higher education, choosing to study American literature and history with film studies at the University of East Anglia. It was only after I was accepted to the University of Nottingham to study American Studies and English that I realised how similar our interests really were. Though, when it comes to politics, there's no competition. Mum was a card-carrying Labour party member from the age of seventeen, the Women's Officer of the National Organisation of Labour Students from 1982 to 1984, and variously worked in London local councils and in union roles, at the NUS and GMB, before becoming the first female Labour MP for Don Valley in 1997 – part of the Labour landslide.

She's an impressive woman who showed strength in the face of adversity, both as a child, a teen and as a single mother, to escape a background defined by trauma and secure a promising

---

[1] Olsen, Mark and Ehsanipour, Asal, 'How Halle Berry channeled her childhood trauma in directorial debut, "Bruised"' (21 December 2021) https://www.latimes.com/entertainment-arts/awards/story/2021-12-21/halle-berry-netflix-bruised-envelope-podcast-interview

future in public service. She'd fought hard to get where she was and she kept on fighting to help others. She definitely gave me more privilege than she had thanks to the social mobility her career afforded. We weren't wealthy living in London, but on Mum's MP salary we lived a far more comfortable life after our move to Doncaster. We were living the D:Ream.[2] Things could only get better, right? Yes, mostly, but I'd be lying if I said her professional life didn't come with a personal cost.

It was five days before my tenth birthday when Mum was elected, and for the next eight years she'd spend a significant portion of it away from home. As all MPs have to do, she spent Mondays to Thursdays in London when Parliament was sitting. Even on the weekends, there were always work commitments that kept her busy. It was a big change in our family dynamic. When we lived in London, I would see Mum and Dad every day. One of them would drop us off at school and pick us up from our childminder's house after work. Time stopped there. She'd smack our legs, her sons were mean and her partner always kicked us off the sofa into the backyard so he could watch the races on Channel 4. On good days, our childminder would let us watch *Countdown*, but most of the time we'd have to entertain ourselves with the moratorium of baby toys lying around the concrete garden or play knock-a-door-run on the estate. No sound was more pleasing than hearing her scream, 'Hanna! Karim! Your mum's here!' I would wrap my arms around Mum's waist and not let go until she put me in the car.

Caroline was a very hands-on mum. With Dad, she'd often take us on trips to Gunnersbury Park to ride our bikes, Brentford Leisure Centre to swim and the local cinema to offset the amount of canvassing, marches and political events they signed up to do as active Labour Party members. Come rain or shine, they'd regularly be down Chiswick High Street with their red T-shirts and clipboards with Karim, Nick (when he

---

[2] The actual name of the group who sang 'Things Can Only Get Better', the Labour Party's 1997 theme tune.

wasn't with his mum) and I serving as mascots. I remember one time marching in the rain during an anti-BNP protest, gripping my tiny little brolly in one hand, my Mum's hand in the other, and not quite understanding the significance of my attendance.

Once we moved to Doncaster, the political stuff became exponentially more time-consuming. My brothers and I would still help out every general election and at various campaigning events. Often begrudgingly. We were teenagers, after all. She'd open our own house to host Labour shindigs and fundraisers throughout the years. Her homemade onion bhajis are that of CLP legend. There was always a fair or fete to attend as a local MP, and Mum was the type of person to make time for them all. The homemade cakes were a consolation prize as we waited for her to finish talking to constituents about their multitude of problems. They were mostly lovely people who just needed that bit of help from their local parliamentary representative to cut through red tape and signal-boost their issues. But I've witnessed a fair few over the years acting like Steve Coogan from *In the Loop* who could change the subject from a damaged wall to the Iraq war so quickly I'm surprised Mum didn't get whiplash.

She was fully immersed in her job and it was knackering trying to balance her parliamentary work and being a mother. There's a bit in the movie *Baby Boom*, starring Diane Keaton as a business executive, where her male boss probes her thoughts on motherhood and tells her women can't have it all – despite the popular eighties notion. He says that he, on the other hand, could have it all as a man bringing home the bacon to his wife, keeping house and looking after their children. But that's not having it all, is it? That's just not caring enough to be present for the domestic part of your life. Nancy Meyers would revisit the topic of working mothers in *The Intern*. Anne Hathaway's CEO Jules is desperate to be a good wife to her house-husband and daughter while still fulfilling her work responsibilities, but the conflict puts a strain on her marriage. Dad worked for Mum, managing her constituency office, which allowed him to take care of us kids full time while she was away. It worked for them. But his hours of business sometimes matched hers. A Harvard Business Review study found that 'for *both* mothers and fathers, children were better off when parents were able to be physically available to them.'[3] Even when my parents were physically at home, sometimes it felt they weren't there mentally and for most of my teens I was the only female presence in the house, so I would feel frustrated when Mum would return from London on a Thursday or Friday and be tired, stressed and distracted. I was a typical young girl desperate for the attention of her mum, but I was competing with a job that doesn't really respect the boundaries of family life, and she didn't always have the energy.

I thought the best way to please Mum was to be the golden child at school. *Turning Red*, a film set in 2002 when I was thirteen, just like the main character Meilin, is an acute reflection of that compulsive need to please our mothers and I put pressure on myself to be good at everything – classes, sports, music, drama. But I was also bottling up the feelings of being an outsider at school. Getting teased is part and parcel of adolescence, but when you're dealing with taunts and micro-aggressions because of your accent, your ethnic features, your work ethic, your lack of romantic experience, and even your mum's job, where one minute you're BFFs and the next you're out of the friendship group, sometimes you just want to come home to your mum and talk about your problems. Mine was often 164 miles away focused on the state of the nation.

The fact that Mum also happened to be a beautiful woman only reinforced my own insecurities as an awkward teenager who took a while to grow into my looks and even longer to shake off the ugliness I associated with my ethnicity. Thanks to *American Pie*, boys at school started to call her a MILF and

---

[3] Friedman, Stewart D., 'How Our Careers Affect Our Children' (14 November 2018) https://hbr.org/2018/11/how-our-careers-affect-our-children

make lewd jokes. I shrugged it off in front of them, but I was already comparing myself to my school friends in an unhealthy way. It didn't help my confidence that she was a work of art compared to me. I still cringe when I look at Mum and Dad's wedding photos. She looks like Elizabeth Taylor in her white dress and I'm there looking like a cross between Arthur and D.W. At my eighteenth birthday, I had to deal with my guy friends perving over Mum on the dancefloor. I tried to repress a lot of the emotions sparked by self-loathing over my racial identity, my absent father, the way I looked and how that informed the risks I was taking and the peer pressure I would cave into. There was a conflict inside me that, as much as I wanted to please Mum, look like Mum, and tell her everything, I didn't always feel like she heard me or saw me, and so I couldn't trust her with my misgivings. I thought I'd be judged or shamed. At the time, I had Lindsay Lohan's Anna in *Freaky Friday* to relate to, whose multitasking mother, played by Jamie Lee Curtis, was a bit of a control freak and kept misunderstanding her. Unfortunately, we didn't have a magical fortune cookie to help us arrive at new perspectives on each other – and Chad Michael Murray did not go to my school either – so my teen angst just made me believe she didn't have time to spare to worry about the things that were going on with me.

Don't get me wrong, this wasn't a Miranda Priestly in *The Devil Wears Prada* situation, where she required nannies and ends up divorcing her husband because the demands of her job were too much for him to contend with. Mum did her best to be there as much as she could. She'd take us on holidays, cook us Sunday roasts, let us get a dog, and continued to make movie-watching a family activity. I can remember when she took me down to London to get my year-twelve prom dress. We'd come a long way since the days our wardrobes were mostly filled with car-boot sale, C&A and BHS finds, and she took me to Selfridges to pick an outfit. But the Flints can always sniff out a bargain and we managed to find a Vivienne Westwood Anglomania dress with a massive sale discount. I had a far happier upbringing than a lot of people, but I was raised by an assertive woman who said what she thought and I didn't fall far from the tree. As I found my voice, started to develop my own opinions and sought to have more autonomy for how I wanted to navigate the world as a young woman, a more combative mother-daughter relationship developed.

Greta Gerwig's *Lady Bird* might be the best representation of our dysfunction. Saoirse Ronan's Lady Bird and Laurie Metcalfe's Marion (who reveals her own mother was an alcoholic) love each other unconditionally, but the fissures in their relationship are deepened by frequent slights. I love the opening sequence. Lady Bird and Marion are seen sleeping in bed together then driving in the car, listening to a John Steinbeck audiobook and united in their emotional response to the story. It was like looking in the mirror. Mum and I would frequently snuggle in bed. Even to this day we jump into bed with one another when I go home. We would often have car rides soundtracked by a little carpool karaoke too. A fond memory I think about often is a time we were driving from London to Doncaster and we spent a significant chunk of the journey playing, singing, rewinding, and playing again the B-side cover of Tracy Chapman's 'Baby Can I Hold You' on Boyzone's 'Picture of You' cassette tape. Mum wasn't clear on the lyrics, so we'd laugh, stop and start, picking a verse each before duetting on the chorus. And yet, just as easily as we could bond over songs, we could serve a barb and it would escalate into a slanging match.

I've never jumped out of a moving car like Lady Bird does in that initial scene, but I've frequently had the urge to escape. I ran away once by climbing onto the roof next to my bedroom window, jumping into the back garden and sneaking to my best friend's house on the other side of the village. She came with me to the park and when it got dark, scary and both of us had enough missed calls from our parents, we trundled back to our homes. Mum gave me hell. There was also a dessert incident following a row. I cannot remember what it was about, but Mum threw chocolate cake in my face. We laugh about it now, but at the time, my body, coursing with adolescent hormones, came alive with teen outrage that only closed me off to her even more.

Our inability to communicate properly has caused a lot of unnecessary arguments over the years and neither of us are innocent parties. Teenagers can be selfish dicks and I've been quick to criticise and be cruel to Mum when I didn't get my own way, but after a lot of growing up I can recognise how difficult it was for her. A super-tough first thirty-five years to your life will make you less sympathetic when three teenagers cause a ruckus over dramas that seem somewhat trivial in comparison to the pressures she was under. Being a working mother is bloody hard, especially when you're also the bread-winner in a public-facing position and under immense scrutiny for how you do your job and live your life.

It would take moving away for me to get a better perspective on our relationship and how my unresolved insecurities impacted my sense of self. Finally, I could experience adult life on my own terms, but also the increasing pressures of work in an industry also rife with gender inequality would ultimately help me empathise with the way she navigated the world. It's not all hearts and roses now; there are a lot of things we don't agree on in terms of feminism, relationships, womanhood, politics, the correct way to check cinema times. It's 2022, Mum. You really don't have to print out showtimes to work out a schedule when there's the Notes app, but we are closer today than we've ever been. We call ourselves Little Edie and Big Edie nowadays. My first introduction to this mother and daughter was not through the Maysles brothers' 1975 film *Grey Gardens* but the 'Sandy Passage' episode of the mockumentary series *Documentary Now!* starring Fred Armisen and Bill Hader. They play versions of Jackie O's cousins Edith 'Little Edie' Bouvier Beale and her mother Edith 'Big Edie' Bouvier Beale with hilarious gusto; parodying moments from the original doc which centred on the off-kilter duo's self-inflicted solitude at their dilapidated family estate.

One scene particularly tickled: Hader's Little Vivvy doing a ridiculous dance while waving a little American flag. 'All right, that's enough,' Hader says breathlessly at the end. It really was enough; I was crying with laughter. The next time I saw Mum, I did my own parody. I wrapped a T-shirt around my head, grabbed a stars-and-stripes flag I'd been sent with an *Assassination Nation* press drop, and danced my way into the living room declaring (in my best impression of their very specific New York accent): 'I used to be an amazing dancer!' Mum burst into a fit of giggles. She knew exactly what I was doing. At the time I'd been single for seven years, so we'd often joke about me living out my #spinsterlife with her in our family home, till my last relationship started in 2020. To be fair, she did witness my breakdown after my last boyfriend broke up with me in the final year of university. After a hysterical call to Mum and Dad they picked me up from Nottingham, drove me back to Doncaster and she sat in the backseat with me all the way home, letting me cry until her shirt changed colour. That moment marked a real shift in our relationship.

After years of thinking I couldn't truly rely on Mum with my emotions, she turned up when my heart was broken. Our relationship nowadays has a lot more in common with Donna and her mother in *Obvious Child*. This is my favourite rom-com of the twenty-first century, but it is as much of a reflection of millennial unease with motherhood and the complicated relationships daughters have with their own tough mums who they are constantly seeking approval from. The scene in particular that stands out is when Donna unloads her pregnancy/abortion woes to her mom. 'It was important that this conversation happen face to face and under one duvet,' co-writer-director Gillian Robespierre said. 'But it was a tricky scene to nail because ... there had to be enough tension in their relationship and growth in Jenny's character to finally be able to share her story with her mother.' Donna seeks her mother's support because theirs is an attachment that has weathered many storms. 'Donna doesn't only tell her mom about the abortion because she needs financial aid, she tells her because they're close, and this is by no means the first time Donna's confided in her,' says co-writer Elisabeth Holm. 'As scared as she is of her judgement, she also knows her mom is going to be there for her when it matters most.'[4] Since the age of twenty-one, I've no longer felt afraid of sharing some of my inner thoughts and feelings with Mum even if she might not like what I have to say and I might not like how she responds. Thankfully, I've got a slightly thicker skin than in my teens, so I can take criticism a little bit better [nervous laugh] though she has her moments. Like her ability to zone in on any blemish I might have on my face and say, 'What's that?' The woman could give military aircraft targeting systems a run for their money.

As soon as I discovered a vocation that I was as passionate for as Mum was about politics, I became even more grateful that I was raised to pursue a career and not be held back by men or babies. I've been given the time to invest in myself and my future without the stress of tiny humans to worry about – only those big humans who don't pay my freelance work on time or, you know, internet trolls. I definitely wouldn't begrudge Mum if she told me she would probably not have become a parent so young had she had the chance to do it again. I wouldn't have become a mum at twenty-five. I could barely take care of myself in my twenties let alone be responsible for two small children. As Olivia Colman's Leda says in *The Lost Daughter*, 'Motherhood is a crushing responsibility' and I honestly don't know if I will ever be ready to sacrifice my independence to become one. Maggie Gyllenhaal's 2021 directorial debut, an adaptation of elusive Italian author Elena Ferrante, really felt like a warning, especially in the flashbacks. Jessie Buckley's younger Leda is hot and cold while balancing

---

[4] Buchanan, Kyle, 'The Toughest Scene I Wrote' (17 December 2014) https://www.vulture.com/2014/12/finding-obvious-childs-perfect-fartcry-balance.html

her daughters' care and her academic career ambitions but, ultimately, she abandons them for a few years. Yet, the film doesn't villainise her for that choice. In fact, it highlights the prejudice on women to parent by the fact that Leda's estranged husband immediately takes their daughters to her mother rather than taking care of them himself. I was raised in a household where my dad was the primary caregiver, but how do I guarantee that the father of my potential child will share those values? There are a lot of male feminists in theory who might not be in practice when it comes to child-rearing.

Now I'm in my early thirties, I've long ruminated on my feelings towards pregnancy while people in my social circle are having babies themselves. I still don't feel broody to have my own, the only thing I'm truly broody for is a dog, but I spend a lot of time considering how I'd feel about a child-free life. There aren't too many movies that present that position as a viable option. *Jackie Brown* (1997), *Eat Pray Love* (2010), *Obvious Child* (2014), *Like a Boss* (2020) and *The Worst Person in the* World (2021) are a few instances that have helped to normalise a non-mother-by-choice existence. But mostly there's always extenuating circumstances as to why a woman doesn't have children: the female character is either too young to be thinking about them, an action heroine, a demented, Ms Havisham-type or a mother buffer like Jocelyn in *The Jane Austen Book Club* where she can be child-free because the mothers around her soften the impact. If the female character starts and ends a film child-free, they may just be saddled with one in the sequel. Bridget Jones was finally made a mother for the sake of extending the rom-com franchise in 2016 with *Bridget Jones's Baby*. Or there's *Summerland* where Gemma Arterton's happily child-free lead becomes a de facto parent by the film's end, suggesting any woman could warm to the idea of child-rearing if they were given the right child to rear.

But it's never that simple. There are so many variables affecting a woman's decision to become a mother and it explains why a record number are reaching the age of 30 without having a child.[5] Ambivalence to parenting, fertility issues, economic concerns, career goals and climate-change worries are all influential factors for this decline. The last is one I've been thinking a lot about since watching *First Reformed*. Paul Schrader's 2017 drama film left me in awe. Long inspired by the stylings of French film-maker Robert Bresson, the writer-director would do his own version of a *Diary of a Country Priest* (1951) sort of film with Ethan Hawke as Ernst Toller, an alcoholic Catholic priest whose spiritual worldview is rocked after a meeting with Mary Mensana (Amanda Seyfried), a young pregnant woman, and her radical-environmentalist husband Michael (Philip Ettinger). It's Ernst's first-act conversation with Michael that switched a lightbulb on in my head. Michael wants his wife to have an abortion because he believes that it is immoral to bring a child into a world increasingly ravaged by climate change and will ultimately become inhospitable:

MICHAEL

The world is changing fast. Right in front of us. One third of the natural world has been destroyed in your lifetime. The earth's temperature will be three degrees centigrade higher. Four is the threshold . . . 'severe, widespread, and irreversible impacts'—when scientists use words like that—the National Center of Atmospheric Research, Lawrence Livermore, the Potsdam Institute . . . How can you sanction bringing a girl, for argument's sake let's say my child is a girl, a child full of hope and naive belief into a world . . . when that little girl grows to be a young woman and looks you in the eyes and says, 'You knew all along, didn't you?' What do you say then?

---

[5] Campbell, Denis, 'Record numbers of women reach 30 child-free in England and Wales' (27 January 2022) https://www.theguardian.com/lifeandstyle/2022/jan/27/women-child-free-30-ons

Not to get all Extinction Rebellion here, but the man has a point. In 1950, the global population was estimated at around 2.6 billion. According to the UN, a century on and that figure could rise 'to 9.7 billion in 2050.'[6] At some point, the planet won't be able to bear the burden of human expansion and our children's children will face the apocalyptic consequences. The jury is certainly not out on science, no matter how much Fox News tries to tell us otherwise.

Sure, I can split my rubbish into recycling and general waste, use a moon cup and film festival tote bags for a weekly shop, but how much is that really going to offset the environmental cost of bringing another human into the world? My birthday twin Sir David Attenborough remarked in 2021, 'There is no going back – no matter what we do now, it's too late to avoid climate change.'[7] If the end of times wasn't enough to complicate my maternal instincts then the brutality of pregnancy might just tip the scale. *My Girl* (1991), *Jack & Sarah* (1995), *Whale Rider* (2002), *Jersey Girl* (2004), *Pan's Labyrinth* (2006), all feature maternal deaths that are treated as sad but also somewhat noble. But I ask you, how many cis men have died giving birth to a baby? Zero. How many cis women? Well, of the 2,173,810 women who gave birth in 2017–19, 191 died during or up to six weeks after pregnancy, and 495 during or up to one year after their pregnancy.[8] I know that is a relatively small number, but it's still an insane notion to me that I could

[6] United Nations, 'Peace, dignity and equality on a healthy planet', https://www.un.org/en/global-issues/population

[7] Waterman, Gabrielle, 'Sir David Attenborough tells UN "It is too late to avoid climate change"' (26 February 2021) https://www.climateaction.org/news/sir-david-attenborough-tells-un-it-is-too-late-to-avoid-climate-change

[8] NPEU, 'New report highlights persistent inequalities and continued inequitable care for pregnant women' (11 November 2021) https://www.npeu.ox.ac.uk/news/2188-new-report-highlights-persistent-inequalities-and-continued-inequitable-care-for-pregnant-women#:~:text=Pregnancy%20remains%20very%20safe%20in,one%20year%20after%20their%20pregnancy

potentially die because of childbirth complications. If I was a Black woman, I'd be four times more likely to die in pregnancy than a white woman and twice more likely if I was South Asian.[9] I'm not sure where British-Arab girls fit into that equation, but do I really want to risk it just so I can have my DNA passed on? I mean, it is great DNA, to be sure, but as I submitted my spit to an ethnic heritage testing facility I'm pretty sure a replicant of me will be running around in the future. Forgive a second *Blade Runner* reference but, to quote Roy Batty, 'I want more life.'

I want more life for myself before it might become beholden to another. Before I lose the freedom to go wherever I want, work and spend my money however I want to. I want to be selfish. For too long I've seen the stories of women expected to put the lives of others before their own. It's always felt like a gross injustice. I don't want to have it all. I just want to have my life on my own terms; whether that includes motherhood is yet to be determined, but I'm grateful my own mother provided the time and space for me to feel empowered to make those choices for me and no one else.

9 Summers, Hannah, 'Black women in the UK four times more likely to die in pregnancy or childbirth' (15 January 2021) https://www.theguardian.com/global-development/2021/jan/15/black-women-in-the-uk-four-times-more-likely-to-die-in-pregnancy-or-childbirth

Chapter 4

'Hey, Dad. You wanna have a catch?'

– Field of Dreams (1989)

THERE ARE TWO MEN who made me who I am, but only one of them I call Dad. That guy has been in the picture since I was a baby. Dad was born in Stockton-on-Tees in 1960, to my grandad Colin and grandma Monica, was the second youngest, and only son, out of five siblings, and had a pretty charmed upbringing compared to Mum's. He went to Kingston Polytechnic in 1978 to study quantity surveying because he pissed around during his A levels and it was either that or doing a textile course at Bradford University. The bright lights of London won out. While at uni, he met Mum during those halcyon days of Labour Students and they reconnected as friends and campaign colleagues in the years after. When my first birthday party in 1989 came around, he was invited and brought his son Nick (my now-brother) along too. He also brought his then-girlfriend, the cheek of it, but they split and by the following year he was taking Mum out on their first date to the pictures. They went to see *Field of Dreams*. The film was actually sold out and they only managed to get two tickets because a stranger had been stood up and offered them his. My parents still have the stubs from that fateful night, which are currently framed with an Italian version of the film's poster in our living room. It's partly this backstory as to why

I have such a sentimental attachment to the film, and because I can't get enough of Costner's brand of rugged all-American romanticism. But *Field of Dreams* is also a movie about the complicated relationship fathers have with their children and that's a subgenre that never fails to hit me in the gut.

It's easier to deal with an absent father when you never knew them. Even easier when you have someone subbing in before you can walk – and Dad was Ole Gunnar Solskjaer. Watching Manchester United games together was as an important part of our relationship as watching films, and one of my fondest memories is of us screaming when Norwegian super-sub, along with Teddy Sheringham, came off the bench to score the two injury-time goals needed to beat Bayern Munich in the 1999 UEFA Champions League Final. It was a Wednesday night, Mum was in London and my brothers weren't home, so it was just Dad, our dog Joey and I going mental at the result. My ears faintly ring at the thought. Dad has one of the most intense cheers I've ever heard. Every time I had a basketball match his bellows were a sometimes embarrassing but mostly reas-suring sound. When I was in my final year of university, playing our Varsity game against Nottingham Trent, he took time off work to drive to Nottingham to be there and his defensive cheer of 'go to her!' alerted me to his presence. I'm not going to say we won because he turned up, but I know I played that much harder – and managed to score the baskets that flipped our end quarter fortunes – knowing he was there.

My brother Karim and I never knew the circumstances of our parents' divorce or my father's departure as children, but we were aware that Dad wasn't our biological relation. It's probably why I took Mum for granted because she was genet-ically predisposed to be there for me, to love me and, of course, there's the gendered cultural expectation of mothers being responsible for their children. If women leave, they're selfish, unnatural women, right? Like Leda in *The Lost Daughter* or Joanna in *Kramer vs Kramer*. Meryl Streep had to fight not just against co-star Dustin Hoffman's inflated sense of self, but for her character to be depicted as less of a villain than in the book the film was based on, for walking out on her son and husband Ted. But even with the depth and nuance she brought to a woman not feeling like she was fully formed before becoming a parent, by the movie's end you still come away feeling like Ted's the noble father for sticking around. It's that sort of cultural conditioning that has meant I idolised Dad for choosing to be a father figure to me; inspiring a youthful affection for films that saw a man connect and care for a child that wasn't biologically his.

The 1982 *Annie*, of course, was a favourite as Albert Finney's Daddy Warbucks saved Aileen Quinn's eponymous redhead from a hard-knock life at an orphanage. *Willow* remains iconic for more than just the fact baby Elora gets not one, but two surrogate dads via the titular hero and the rapscallion Madmartigan. I fell in love with Aaron Eckhart in the 2000 biopic *Erin Brockovich* because his George (a character loosely based on a real person) would take care of Erin's kids while she was fighting for justice. Dad was doing that too after giving up his promising career in political PR to work for Mum as her constituency office manager. But it was *A Simple Twist of Fate* that really had a profound effect. A modern-day, American adaptation of George Eliot's novel *Silas Marner*, the 1994 film was written by and starred Steve Martin who was a favourite in our household. We had *Roxanne, Planes, Trains and Automobiles* and *Dead Men Don't Wear Plaid* at home, but he was never more influential to me than when he was playing a dad. Every time I saw the *Father of the Bride* films or *Parenthood*, I would project my own Dad onto George or Gil because I recognised the hands-on, often goofy but endearing approach to parenting from my own life. I remember when we lived in London, Mum was away on a work trip, Dad had to undertake the night-time ritual of braiding my thick hair before bed. This was well before YouTube tutorials and he enlisted my two brothers to hold a section of my hair each so he could thread the thirds into a plait. It was ridiculous and felt like something a Steve Martin character would attempt.

In *A Simple Twist of Fate*, Michael is a lonely cabinetmaker who adopts the orphaned love child of a heroin addict and a politician, after she waddles into his home. He names her Mathilda and grows to love her unconditionally. But their bond is threatened when her blue-blooded biological father and his infertile wife want to claim her back. It's this type of sentimental melodrama that cut me deeply as a child, especially the scene where Michael swoops in strapped to a balloon and saves Mathilda from falling into a quarry. Sigmund Freud once wrote, 'I cannot think of any need in childhood as strong as the need for a father's protection,' and there was definitely a tidal wave of films about hero dads or dad figures during the eighties and nineties that I became accustomed to seeing and, surprisingly, Arnold Schwarzenegger really cornered that market. *Commando*, *Kindergarten Cop*, *T2: Judgment Day*, *Last Action Hero*, *True Lies*, *Jingle All the Way* and *The 6th Day* saw the Austrian actor use everything in his characters' wheelhouse to do right by the children in his care. He really walked so the likes of Liam Neeson in *Taken*, Nicolas Cage in *Kick-Ass* and John Krasinski in *A Quiet Place* could run. In real life, I had a couple of excuses to hero-worship my old man too.

When I was maybe four or five, we went on a caravan holiday to Wales and one day at the beach, I was playing in our blue dinghy, floating in the sea, and not realising the tide was beginning to go out. The next time I looked up, the shore seemed miles away. I panicked. I was too small to paddle back on my own and I'd recently learned about basking sharks. I knew the 30ft monsters were vegetarian but, according to *The Really Wild Show*, they would hold their gaping mouths wide open to collect plankton and I was terrified they'd accidentally swallow me whole. It felt like hours of me shouting for help before I saw a head bobbing up and down in the distance; somebody swimming towards me and soon a wave of relief washed over. Dad had come to the rescue. But even as he pulled us in, I was in tears thinking these bloody sharks were still going to get him and didn't calm down until he touched dry sand. I would experience palpable feelings of anxiety at the idea of losing Dad. In fact, the first panic attack I had was realising that one day he would die. I can remember being in the tiny kitchen of the very first house we lived in, feeling like my stomach was going to drop out at the thought and he said it would be decades before that would happen, to get me over it. Funny thing about that house, my parents only managed to afford it because he stopped an armed bank robbery. Here's hero story number two.

The year is 1994, Mum, Dad, Nick and I are doing some shopping on a busy Saturday in Richmond-on-Thames. We stop by the local Natwest bank to get my brother and I some pocket money – Karim is at his best friend Wilf's for the weekend – so it's just us four, but suddenly we see a man running in towards the bank teller and a kerfuffle commences. The man has got a gun, he's pointing it at a woman's head and shouting. I can't hear, but I'm not too young to work out what he might be wanting from a bank. The next thing I know, Mum is pulling me and Nick out of the bank into a jewellers across the road, then Dad gave chase and managed to tackle the thief to the ground and prevent him from firing it. But security guards at the shop where they had landed thought Dad was the assailant. The robber shook himself free and Dad had to tackle him for a second time; thankfully he had some help from two passers-by, one of which was an off-duty police sergeant. The man – who was using a starter pistol as it turned out – got banged up for ten years and Dad received not only a financial reward from the bank for his efforts but a Sheriff of London bravery award. I didn't even know there was a Sheriff of London! It was incredible; Dad was more George Banks than Bryan Mills. The idea that he thwarted a bank robbery was barmy, but it was another reason to put him on a pedestal.

Whereas Mum did more of the planning, organising and cooking, Dad was more laid back. When we moved to Doncaster and he became our primary caregiver, he reinforced that image by letting us stay up late or getting us a McDonald's after he picked me up from basketball training on a Friday night. We'd eat in the car so as not to make Mum mad! Our bond only strengthened over the years; I was both a son *and* a daughter to him almost. He loved how sporty I was: we'd watch football together at home, and he made sure to drop me off, pick me up, and with Mum was my frequent cheerleader at basketball games across the country for over a decade. But he also liked that I was Daddy's little girl. He still calls me 'Girly', 'Whirly', 'Twirly', or some variation on that nickname and continues to tell me that no boyfriend would ever replace him as the most important man in my life. I believed him. I still do to an extent, because I've put so much weight on the fact that he chose to be my dad.

I used to analyse pictures of us, looking for any potential similarities that could convince people I was biologically his. Mum was white with dark features so maybe people would think I got my ethnic colouring from her side of the family. I think both my parents preferred people to make that assumption. I'd look at the way we smiled, the shape of our faces; my lighter brown hair colour was similar to his when I was younger too. Maybe, just maybe, there was enough white in me to bridge the gap and delete the absent Arab father from the equation. Alas, Dad was and still is a pasty Caucasian, so those youthful assertions were never that convincing. Still, when people referred to him as my 'stepdad' I'd wince. No, he was my real dad and I hated when school friends would argue otherwise. I always wondered why he didn't just adopt me, but apparently my parents didn't want to risk contacting my biological father and bringing him into our lives. At the time, I understood. My father was a stranger and I had Dad, the only dad I needed. The first tattoo I ever got was a dedication to him. I was in Texas doing the SXSW festival in 2012 and had recently finished watching the entirety of the American football series *Friday Night Lights*. I visited the True Blue tattoo parlour in Austin where young quarterback Jason Street gets himself inked.

I picked the Joni Mitchell lyric from 'My Old Man', off the album *Blue*, 'We don't need no piece of paper' and had it committed to my skin in a font as close to her handwriting as possible. The song is supposedly about Graham Nash, a romantic tune, but the sentiment of it, that she didn't need a legal document from 'the city hall keeping them tied and true' represented mine and Dad's relationship.

We didn't need an adoption certificate to say he was my dad. He simply was. And Joni was one of the many musicians he introduced me to. Bruce Springsteen, Joe Jackson, Patti Scialfa, Tracy Chapman: these were the artists who soundtracked my childhood, who Dad would play on every car journey and we'd sing along to. Like Nick Offerman and Kiersey Clemons' father and daughter in *Hearts Beat Loud*, music connected us and I still love these singers to this day, but I wonder: did I make such an effort to like them – not that it takes that much effort, really – so he would love me more? In *The Unbearable Weight of Massive Talent*, the meta-Nicolas Cage movie where he plays a version of himself, there's a scene where his daughter explains feeling like she had to appreciate the same movies as her dad or he wouldn't want to see her. Now Dad never sat me down to watch *The Cabinet of Dr. Caligari*, but I associate so much of my cultural tastes with his influence rather than Mum's. I was always anxious to please and make him proud that he raised me in his image.

Of course, we weren't always best mates. Sometimes Dad was like Jekyll and Hyde and if there was an argument between Mum and I, he'd take her side. The traitor! But as much as Mum taught me I didn't need to rush into having children or settling down, my relationship with Dad confirmed that having biological children wasn't necessary to becoming a parent. He might not have adopted me, but maybe I could adopt a child and pass on the sort of non-biological love I received. There are certainly enough children in the world without parents and adoption would also assuage that pesky climate-change guilt and mortality fears of birthing a child. But there's one major thing I'd do differently if I were to parent a child of colour who wasn't my own: I'd raise them to embrace their ethnic heritage rather than pretend it didn't exist.

For most of my childhood and adolescence, neither of my parents talked about my biological father or Tunisian background. Why would they? Mum had provided a replacement father figure and because of the circumstances of the divorce, Dad needn't concern himself with another man who was 1,681 miles away. Together, they had provided a stable, two-parent home to raise us children, but while my brother Nick still had a close relationship with his mother, Karim and I had no such connection to our biological father's side of the family or culture. We had a small number of pictures from his and Mum's wedding day and Karim's birth. There are next to no images of me with him because of how swiftly their separation occurred and the only clothing remnants left from Mum's Tunisian life – she lived there for a time with Karim – were packed away in the fancy dress box. We volunteered the kaftan dress for the Nativity play in primary school because they were so fitting to the Middle Eastern bible story, but at the time I had no idea of the cultural significance. I rarely ever inquired about my father, and my parents never offered much beyond throwaway comments. When Grandma Monica visited, she'd go to Church and I liked to go with her and sing the hymns. I was also fearful of death and wanted to make a good impression on whoever might have been waiting upstairs, but because I was not Catholic I was not allowed to eat the bread or wine, just cross an arm over my chest and get blessed like a little heathen. I asked Mum about my religious status and she said neither Karim nor I were baptised because she was Christian, my father was Muslim, and they wanted us to decide for ourselves. When I did think about my father, guilt would weigh upon me. It felt like a betrayal of both Mum and Dad, especially. I was also becoming aware of images of Muslim and MENA men who looked similar to my father, as people to be scared of, making me less inclined to pursue a dialogue with my parents on the subject.

Raiders of the Lost Ark used Tunisia as a substitute for Egypt in a sequence laced with Arab stereotypes, including snake-charming music, veiled women and an aggressive Egyptian bringing a knife to a gunfight against white American hero Indiana Jones. Producer George Lucas has since admitted regret for playing this scene for laughs,[1] but he and Steven Spielberg repeated problematic Arab imagery in *Indiana Jones and the Last Crusade* via the introduction of a Nazi-sympathising Sheikh while also continuing the Hollywood practice of whitewashing Arab characters by bringing back John Rhys-Davies to play Egyptian ally Sallah. Even the Egyptian Christians in this film, who are trying to protect the Holy Grail, are presented as fanatics while the white knight guarding the legendary artefact at the end is presented as a saint-like warden. *True Lies* and *Executive Decision* perpetuated the Palestinian terrorist stereotype within the action movie genre; where Arnold Schwarzenegger and Kurt Russell, respectively, must thwart the fanatical threat from blood-thirsty Arabs who will stop at nothing to take Western lives. *Aladdin*, and *The Return of Jafar* even more so, established Arab men with foreign accents as grotesque villains in comparison to the Americanised romantic leads as well as the Genie and Sultan.

I used to have this recurring dream. There was an alleyway that connected our flat in Chiswick village to Gunnersbury Park station, that went under the Chiswick Flyover and was scary to walk down at night. I would have nightmares about a man trying to snatch me away from Mum there. She didn't have that dream, but she had this fear too and it's why we never visited Tunisia. Mum was scared that once we got there, our father might find out and government officials would refuse our return home. This might sound like an outlandish concept, but my father's father was Hechmi Zammel, Tunisia's Attorney General of the Republic under President Habib Bourguiba, so Mum's fear wasn't without merit. There was also a very famous case

---

[1] Handy, Bruce, 'Cinema: The Force Is Back' (10 February 1997) http://content.time.com/time/subscriber/article/0,33009,985896-5,00.html

in recent cultural memory of an American mother and her mixed child who claimed they were violently forced to remain in their father's country of origin during the mid-eighties. Betty Mahmoody detailed her account in the memoir *Not Without My Daughter*, which was subsequently turned into the 1991 film starring Sally Field as Betty and non-Iranian actor Alfred Molina as Sayyed Bozorg Mahmoody, her Iranian husband, who switched from loving, agnostic family man in the US to Islamic domestic abuser in Tehran after tricking them into visiting his relatives. The film dramatises her and daughter Mahtob's eighteen-month captivity, several years after the 1979 Iranian Revolution, under the iron fist of her husband and Islamic orthodox family members, before escaping back to Michigan. When the Iranian characters speak in Farsi, there are no subtitles which cements the Otherness of this foreign land considered at the time an enemy of the US which was allied with Iraq. Sayyed beats his wife and child frequently, voraciously. She is forced to wear a chador (a religious veil) from the moment she arrives and her perspective provides a 'primitive' perception of Iran, its people and customs. In 2002, the documentary *Without My Daughter* served as a rebuttal by offering Sayyed's side of the story, but the damage to Muslim, Persian and MENA representation had already been done. As noted by Sally-Ann Totman:

> Although the factual basis of this book and film is widely disputed, many people believe that everything that is portrayed is not just possible but true and likely to occur to any Western woman who is 'unfortunate' to marry a Muslim . . . *Not Without My Daughter* does not treat Muslim characters impartially. It is vitriolic and spiteful, and if such a movie were to be made in America about any other ethnic group, it would be denounced as racist and prejudiced.[2]

---

[2] Totman, Sally, *How Hollywood Projects Foreign Policy.*

Vulture's culture editor Gazelle Emami reflected on *Not Without My Daughter*'s legacy twenty-five years after its release. 'It endured as a troubling albatross for Iranians that, often, was presented as evidence of the barbarity of Iranian men,' she writes. 'I'd best describe it as Iranian culture through the looking glass, distorted and stripped of all its warmth.'[3] The daughter in question, Mahtob Mahmoody, has since reinforced her mother's account in her own memoir *My Name Is Mahtob*, but acknowledges the by-product of presenting their unique story to the world when Islam and the Middle East continue to be maligned and vilified on screen. 'It's really unfortunate my Dad's behaviour and his decisions reflected so poorly on his culture and his country and even his religion,' she said. 'I am not a Muslim, but certainly not all Muslims behave the way my Dad did, and not all Iranians behave the way my Dad did.'[4]

So what to make of my own father in the face of all these negative cultural stereotypes of MENA men I was absorbing. For two decades he was nothing more than a handsome face in a photo album collecting dust. A surname that prevented me from full British assimilation. But then in 2007 the *Mail on Sunday*[5] found him and my world was rocked. It was February, I was coming home to Doncaster from Nottingham for the weekend when I got a phone call from Dad telling me Jim, my school friend Shelley's dad, was going to pick me up and take me to their house. Apparently, there was a journalist hanging out in front of our home because of a story that was being published the following day. I was confused but followed orders. It wasn't

[3] Emami, Gazelle, 'The *Not Without My Daughter* Problem' (11 January 2016) https://www.vulture.com/2016/01/not-without-my-daughter-problem.html

[4] Reynolds, Jason, 'Mahtob Mahmoody shares her life beyond "Not Without My Daughter"' (4 February 2016) https://tnchristiannews.wordpress.com/2016/02/04/mahtob-mahmoody-shares-her-life-beyond-not-without-my-daughter/

[5] Perthen, Amanda, 'Minister for Fitness's "secret" Tunisian husband' (18 February 2007) https://www.pressreader.com/uk/the-mail-on-sunday/20070218/282093452273077

the first time Mum's job as an MP had frustrated our private life. At one point, we had a panic alarm installed by police because of threats she was receiving. But this time, the press attention concerned my brother and me too. When I eventually got home a few hours later I found Mum lying on her bed and she looked stressed and pale. She explained to me what was happening: two journalists had connected with my father in Tunisia and persuaded him to take part in a kiss-and-tell interview that would reveal details about their relationship.

At the *Mail*'s request, Saief had fired off some messages to Mum's work email address asking her to get in touch. A short time later, a stringer for the paper knocked on the door of our Doncaster home asking Mum, 'Why are you denying your ex-husband's requests to see his children?' I asked what the story would say, but she was vague and in defence mode. When the article landed online I read it several times and finally demanded the story from Mum. I didn't get all of it, but this is what I've since learned over the years.

Saief was four years Mum's senior, 'a stock market dealer at a leading Tunis bank' who lived a middle-class life with armed guards because of his father's high-profile job. From my own internet sleuthing I discovered he was the lead judge on a major case in 1987 concerning Islamic fundamentalists who were charged with 'trying to overthrow the secular, pro-Western regime of President Habib Bourguiba and install an Iranian-style Islamic republic'.[6] That same year, Mum used her maternity leave to move to Tunisia but, according to Saief, my grandfather was supposedly furious at their relationship and demanded they wed so my brother wouldn't be a 'bastard'. Mum married Saief in London, August 1987, but they returned to Tunis to plan how they would ultimately settle in the UK. She found it lonely living in his parents' home where she had no real role and didn't speak the language.

---

[6] Serrill, Michael S., 'Tunisia Punishing the Pious' (12 October 1987) http://content.time.com/time/subscriber/article/0,33009,965739,00.html

When Mum fell pregnant with me, his aggression began. She hoped it would get better once they were on British soil. Mum says it got worse. She returned to England with Karim before I was born and Saief followed not long after, having got his spousal visa confirmed so was able to be present at my birth where he wasn't at my brother's. But the job prospects he expected through his Tunisian banking connections didn't materialise. All he could secure were cleaning jobs and later a teller position at a bureau de change which, given his stock-broker credentials, smells a bit like *This Is England '88*. He felt demeaned by the work and they struggled both financially and romantically as a couple. Now he felt like an outsider. He falsely implied to the *Mail* that Mum's relationship with Phil Woolas – a family friend back then – was inappropriate, but he and his wife Tracy were an uncle and auntie to us growing up so the accusation reeks of an angry man, feeling isolated, and looking for external things to blame for the breakdown of their marriage.

In August 1988 my father was arrested for breaching the peace, then again in September 1988, and this time charged because of the aggressive incidents towards Mum. She separated from him the same month, changed the locks and eventually moved us into a new rented apartment in the same area. He says he was homeless and sleeping rough. There was a short period where his behaviour improved and he had contact with me and Karim, but in February 1989 there was an assault leading to a further breach of the peace charge. I asked what he did, but Mum didn't want to think about it and I didn't want to retraumatise her, so I let it go. When I speak to Karim he says he has a vague memory of our father assaulting her in our Chiswick flat. My father started turning up at her work at the NUS and our childminder's. Mum was worried he would abduct us. She applied for a restraining order and during this time the authorities became aware his visa was no longer valid because of the split. After he was arrested for turning up at our childminder's, he was sent to Haslar Detention Centre for illegal immigrants, near Gosport, Hampshire and subsequently deported back to Tunisia in 1990 as an overstayer, the same year their divorce was finalised with Mum retaining sole custody uncontested.

He remarried and had a son, the *Mail* story said. Did he ever get in touch again, I asked? Mum and Dad said no, just a letter from a male relative once which they ignored. They decided together to draw a line in the sand, not really thinking about the long-term effect that might have on two mixed kids who would experience othering throughout their lives and might want to have a connection to their father's heritage.

I was shell-shocked at the time, but looking back it is some-what bemusing to find the *Mail on Sunday* being sympathetic to an Arab Muslim. The right-wing paper is one of the worst offenders for Islamophobia news coverage,[7] but I guess getting one over a Labour politician was worth tempering that hate for one story. And yet, it managed to inspire in me even greater prejudice towards my own Arab heritage. I was so angry that this man would choose to speak to journalists rather than trying to contact us directly. He had twenty years to write, and since 1997 Mum was a public figure with contact details readily available online. Why not reach out that way? I was so angry that this man hurt her enough to warrant a restraining order and not attempt to maintain contact because of his aggression. Had the movies been right all along about the violence of Arab men? I was mortified to have any genetic connection to him at a time when anxiety of my ethnic identity had renewed.

My university housemates, Neena and Jenny, are South Asian and the more they would tell me about the blending of their cultural background with their British lives, how much it informed their family attitudes, tastes and comforts, the more I realised that my ethnicity is the only thing I have to

---

[7] Waterson, Jim, 'Most UK news coverage of Muslims is negative, major study finds' (9 July 2019) https://www.theguardian.com/news/2019/jul/09/most-uk-news-coverage-of-muslims-is-negative-major-study-finds

show for my Tunisian heritage. Doing American studies and English introduced me to diverse thinkers and writers from across history and as I learned about the concepts of the Melting Pot and Orientalism, I started to increasingly feel like a fraud. I felt like a coconut, a Malteser, or whatever nickname is given to ethnic minorities who have assimilated into white culture. My brothers used to tease me by saying I was adopted after being found behind a dumpster. I used to worry that was true. I felt like one of those children from Africa or Asia who are adopted by white parents. They bring them home to the UK and raise them as though they are white rather than Black or brown babies who will have to navigate this world very differently to their parents.

For many their connection to their heritage is severed the minute they arrive in the UK and mine was severed the moment my father was sent back to Tunisia. And now with this newspaper article filling some of the blanks of my mixed family history, I began to resent Mum and Dad for keeping me in the dark for so long, for never trying to foster pride in mine and Karim's Tunisian background. Because what I was slowly realising was that my father's behaviour, while awful, is not an innately Arab trait. I've seen just as many movies positioning white men as domestic abusers, but as an ethnic group they get considerably more opportunities for positive representation to offset the stereotype compared to Black and Brown folk and MENA people especially. No one's watching *This Boy's Life* starring Robert De Niro as an abusive husband and stepdad to Ellen Barkin and Leonardo DiCaprio and thinking all white men are violent beasts! Recent stats show one in four women experience domestic violence[8] before the age of 50, which seems more indicative of a male tendency to take out their dissatisfaction on their partners. That's not to say domestic violence is not prevalent in the Arab world, it is and

---

[8] (https://www.theguardian.com/society/2022/feb/16/one-in-four-women-experience-domestic-abuse-before-50-study)

too many countries continue to inhibit the rights of the female populace due to archaic notions of morality. But gender-based violence is a virus that continues to plague every country on Earth, even in the Western world, and the more I learned about the cultural richness and progressive history of Tunisia, especially after the Arab Spring, I realised my brother and I no longer needed to demonise our heritage just because our father mistreated our mother. Even Mahtob Mahmoody got to a point of forgiveness with her dad and pride in her heritage:

> In Iran, during the war when people had nothing, everybody still had dinner parties. You would invite people over for dinner and you would never, ever enter their house without taking a bouquet of flowers. Being respectful. We need to talk about that in society. We hear horrible things about the Middle East. There is danger there. But at the same time, these other things are true too.

From 2010 I made slow but sure steps to embrace my Tunisian heritage through film, food and literature, but again, what to do about my father? In the years since, I've been variously contacted by him, his wife and their son on social media. My knee-jerk reaction has been to block every attempt, especially when they would comment publicly on posts. I recently discovered my father had set up a Twitter account and was following various film critic peers of mine. It felt humiliating because he had tweeted dramatically about getting in touch with me. Could you just not, Saief? It's one thing to accept the background you've long suppressed, another to unpack the conflicted feelings toward a father you know did bad things to your mother and failed to be there for you during the most important time of your life. He was like Darth Vader to me; a parental figure who caused harm to his wife, was estranged from his two children and behaved badly enough to warrant a scream of 'NOO!' from Luke in *The Empire Strikes Back* at the revelation of their paternal connection. At least Vader redeems himself in *Return of the Jedi* by sacrificing himself to beat the Emperor and protect Luke. What had my own father done to mend things? Fuck all.

In *Field of Dreams*, Kevin Costner's Ray Kinsella builds a baseball diamond behind his farm and gets the chance to reconcile with his dead father after years of regret over their fraught relationship. But Ray's not reuniting with the over-bearing dad he once knew, but a younger version who hasn't been beaten down by life's disappointments just yet. Céline Sciamma would use this sort of magical realism with *Petite Maman*, except the mother-daughter bond would be explored as eight-year-olds to beautiful, naturalistic effect. Both films stirred up uncomfortable parental truths and I've found myself more frequently losing sleep over what it would be like if I chose to meet my father.

During lockdown, I came across the movie *Bezness as Usual*, a 2016 documentary made by Dutch-Tunisian film-maker Alex Pitstra with weird parallels to my own life. Not only does he share the same birth name as my brother – Alexander is his middle name, also similar to my brother's Iskander – but he was a product of a holiday romance that ended badly between his European mother Anneke and the Tunisian father Mohsen she met decades earlier. Shot over ten years, Pitstra pieces together his cross-cultural heritage and family history as he attempts to get to know the father who left when he was a child long before. He also establishes a sibling bond with his half-sister Jasmin whose mother similarly endured a short rela-tionship with Mohsen who seemed to take part in a practice in the region of poor young Muslim men seducing vacationing white women in the 1970s. I genuinely believe my parents were in love and it wasn't some sort of scam on my father's part – back then he was financially more sound than Mum – but the film articulates so many of the anxieties I have about potentially opening a channel of communication with my father. Once the toothpaste is out of the tube you can't put it back in and I feel as apprehensive about going to Tunisia and meeting him as

Jasmin felt about meeting Mohsen because she believes any relationship would be transactional. Mohsen does ask his film-maker son for financial support a lot. Would my father expect that from me? Would his family? Would they want to come to visit? How much of a relationship would I want if I reached out? And would it only open me up to more pain and disappointment? Sometimes I honestly wished he was dead. Harsh, I know, but it would make it so much easier to reach out to his side of the family and learn the things I wanted to know without having to deal with the messy emotions that plague my mind at the thought of him. But in 2020, I tested the waters and they were choppy.

For years, I'd received random video links from him to my professional journalist page via Facebook Messenger, with the caption 'un pense' so I decided to finally respond. It was after watching *Bezness as Usual* and I had *un pense* it could lead to some closure. In the best-case scenario, he would detail exactly what happened over the last thirty years that prevented his ability to remain in touch with his children. Worst case he would get defensive and try to manipulate me into thinking he was the victim. Alas, I was confronted with the latter, though a positive was that I did manage to find out there was no problematic medical history on his side to worry about which offered some comfort. Still, it was disappointing to be faced with a man who refused to offer any straight answers, who would one minute call me 'little lady' and ask to meet in Sousse and beg to hear the sound of my voice, but the next minute, go ALL CAPS mad, arguing 'YOU ARE JOURNALIST DO YOUR JOB' when I asked for a straight answer. I don't know what to tell you, Saief. This was me doing my job, going to the primary source and you're refusing to offer any explanation. I cut my losses and left him on read because all this interaction really did was confirm to me that I've had thirty-four years without him in my life and I'm doing pretty well in spite of it.

I have great parents who acknowledged and apologised for the mistakes they made in raising Karim and me, but are now supporting me in my journey to fill in those gaps in my Tunisian identity. I certainly don't need another father figure right now, and I'm not ready to forgive him either. The chip on my shoulder is lodged in pretty deep, but I do sometimes wonder, slightly hope maybe, that I could get to an enlightened state of being and feel comfortable meeting the man who helped give me life. Could I see Anakin Skywalker behind the Darth Vader mask? Deep down I know I'd like to understand who he is, what history he has passed on to me from my ancestors and get to know the family I've spent so many years without, but it's still too complicated, too wrought, too anxiety-inducing a situation for me to open the door to again. 'Hey, Dad,' Ray says to his young catcher father in the final moments of *Field of Dreams*. 'You wanna have a catch?' It's a touching, earnest moment of the acceptance of a parent for who he was rather than what his son had wanted him to be. Maybe one day I'll have a catch up with my father. In the meantime, I'll always have Dad.

Part Two

Coming of Age

Chapter 5

'I'm a ball player.'

– Love & Basketball (2000)

I WAS ALWAYS A sporty kid. Sport and games played a big part in our family culture. Tennis, football, cricket, frisbee, swimming – for as long as I can remember, Mum and Dad kept us active at local parks and leisure centres and it nurtured a competitive streak. School made it even more pronounced. On my first day of year one in primary school, the teachers split us, new students, into four colour-coordinated groups, a bit like the Sorting Hat in *Harry Potter*, to foster friendly rivalry when it came to the annual sporting events. If you have an older sibling you could choose to go in their group, but ever the independent spirit, I joined the Blue team over Karim's Red and the gauntlet in our sibling rivalry had been thrown for the remainder of our time together at Strand on the Green. From the swimming gala at Brentford leisure centre to sports day on the rec behind the junior school, these were my favourite days in the calendar year. In 1998, on my last birthday in London, before we moved to Doncaster, my parents organised my own special sports day at the Brunel University Campus opposite our house and we spent the entire day playing every ball game possible. I slept very well that night. Even as an asthma sufferer from birth, I didn't care if I was left breathless and in need of a few puffs of my inhaler to continue this sporting life. There was truly no greater feeling than the exhilaration of athletic competition and it would come to define the next fifteen years of my life.

There wasn't a girls' sports team that I wasn't on: football, netball, rounders, hockey, badminton, and track and field where shotput and 800m were my events. I would spend nearly every lunchtime, and after school, training or playing matches with my classmates or against other schools. There was a ballet phase when I was younger. I loved the elegance of it and begged my parents for pink pumps, a leotard and a tutu and for a few months I couldn't get enough. I starred in a local ballet company production of *Snow White and the Seven Dwarfs*, as a very cute yet insignificant mouse, but when practice moved to Saturday evenings, well, it began eating into my television schedule and I wasn't having that. *Black Swan*-in-the-making, I was not; I didn't love ballet enough to miss *Baywatch* and *The New Adventures of Superman* each week and I still think my mum was a bit miffed about that choice to quit. The whims of kids can prove expensive for parents trying to support hobbies and she was left with a load of ballet gear no longer fit for my sporting purpose. Still, that didn't stop either her or my dad from later investing in my basketball future.

As sports go, basketball, in my humble opinion, is the coolest. An American import, not much time was dedicated to it in P.E. classes over the usual British pastimes but when *Space Jam* came out I had to play. I hadn't really heard of Michael Jordan; we were more of a football household and any television coverage of the NBA used to play out well past my bedtime. But Jordan became something of a hero of mine after watching that 1996 film. The opening sequence gave me a crash course on why he was and still is considered the Greatest Of All Time. Dunk after dunk after dunk, he flew through the air with the greatest of ease. Coming in hard with a block. Whoomp, there he was. I was in awe. Fortuitously, Dad was working for a political lobbying firm that took him to New York on business and he went to a local sports shop to bring me back a Jordan's

23 Chicago Bulls shirt after I'd begged for one over the phone. I still have it, I still wear it, and I love that I've got an iconic piece of sporting history in my wardrobe. But Jordan wasn't the only player who inspired me to seek out basketball to play. Lola Bunny might fall victim to the weird sexualisation of female animated characters, but she is depicted as the best player of all the Looney Tunes. She runs rings around her pretty much all-male comrades, and that was all the incentive I needed to give the game a go myself. A few years later, my hoop dreams would materialise.

During one week of year seven, our P.E. teacher was invited to enter a team into an interschool tournament and I was scouted by Sue, the coach of the Doncaster Panthers women's basketball club, who happened to be a teacher at a rival school. Now let's be clear, I was not great or skilful but I was a hustler, baby(!), and she saw my raw potential underneath all the fouls. The following week my dad took me to my first ever training session with the under-14 squad. We actually went to the wrong school. Hall Cross has two separate campuses and we went to the upper instead of the lower school first, which made us about twenty minutes late. In that time I managed to psyche myself out. I was the only person from my school that was invited to train, I was going to be an outsider again and my little anxious brain was overthinking the awkwardness of arriving after everyone else had already been introduced. But my dad wasn't going to let me quit before I started and I'm thankful that he didn't.

Learning how to play this game is one of the greatest joys of my life. From lay-ups to free throws, reverse hook shots to, admittedly, the occasional three-pointer, there is no better sound than the swoosh when the ball passes through the net. There's no better taste than the sweat dripping from your forehead after sprinting from one end line to the other after catching a rebound and going on the attack. There's no better feeling than when your defensive stance and quick feet cause your opponent to smack into your chest and your team steals the ball because of the hours upon hours of training you've invested into learning the technical skills required to excel. My life soon began to revolve around the game calendar. We'd train two to three times a week and play home and away league fixtures nearly every Saturday and Sunday as well as one-off tournaments with teams in the surrounding region. As my playing abilities improved, I fostered a newfound confidence and I put that down to two female coaches, Des and Sue, who didn't sugar-coat what was expected of me as a player or as a team member. They demanded excellence and I wanted to give them that every time I stepped onto the court. My reward for listening and actioning their instruction was going from a benchwarmer to starting five. By the age of fifteen, I was playing for Doncaster Panthers' under-16, under-18, and senior women WBBL national league squads and selected to play for England too. I was so dedicated to this sport that I once played a game with a sprained wrist which, after my second visit to the hospital, turned out to be fractured and required a pot. No pain, no gain, right? I powered through broken bones and torn ligaments just so I could get my minutes playing the game I adored.

This was sport unlike I'd ever experienced before. Schools cater to the mixed abilities of everyone in the class and most of the time my P.E. teachers weren't really there to push you further than getting a passing grade, nor did they have the necessary training to teach you the ins and outs of a game like basketball either. The top five most popular sports in the UK are football, tennis, rugby, cricket and badminton and they were reflected in our UK curriculum, along with athletics, rounders, hockey and the gendered netball thrown in as an extracurricular activity for girls. Despite that first year-seven tournament, a girls' basketball team wasn't maintained so I transferred my ball skills to netball, as goal attack, until I requested in year ten to play on the boys' basketball team because they were getting local fixtures. My coach made me captain. I felt like Julie Connor in the TV series *Hang Time*, except, my male teammates were nowhere near the skill level of hers, and I was better than them by a country mile, but it was one of the first times I've ever really felt respect from the boys in my year. Their insecurities about a girl being better than them didn't translate well on the court when their lacking skill is on display, so rather than trying to undermine me, they would defer. Ego, for me, has no place on the court when it requires a collective effort to win and my female coaches instilled this in me. Yet, the more seasons I played and the more dedicated I became, the more emotional investment I had in our success and *Love & Basketball* really reflected that competitive mindset.

It was the first time I ever really saw myself represented on screen. The feature film-making debut of Gina Prince-Bythewood, a former elite high-school player herself, it tells the story in four quarters (just like a basketball game), from 1988 to 1998, and follows the changing relationship of two young ballers Monica and Quincy in their pursuit of athletic success. It was the first film since *Woman Basketball Player No. 5*, a 1957 Chinese film inspired by professional player Yang Jie, to centre a female basketball player, and Monica was my kind of girl. She cared so much about the sport that she put her mind, body and soul into every game she played. One of the best scenes in the film is when Prince-Bythewood takes us into Monica (Sanaa Lathan)'s perspective on the court during her high-school championship final. Lathan's internal stream of consciousness is heard as the camera shoots the game play from her point of view. When Monica makes a mistake, she's back in shot and we see the defeat on her face as she makes her fifth (and final) foul. Unbridled emotion spill over as she hits the bench and, watching, I empathised deeply. I'd been there. I'd had the exact same experience of being fouled out and blaming myself for a loss. If only I had been that much quicker, got that shot in, not fumbled the ball. This scene is one of the best at showcasing the physical and psychological impact on players dealing with the pressures of high-stakes sporting competition authentically with an actor who can actually play. I loved the movie *She's the Man*, but it was very clear

71

that Amanda Bynes was no football player, although it does offer a progressive view of womanhood unconstrained by gender stereotypes, just like *Love & Basketball*. Monica is beautiful and both mentally and physically strong, with her Black skin and athletic build putting her at odds with the typical skinny and white romantic leads of the era. She was a strong female character in the best sense; a woman who wants love and whose vulnerability is just as powerful a part of who she is as her ambition to become a professional basketball player. Like Ice Box in *Little Giants* and Jess in *Bend It Like Beckham*, Monica shows that femininity is not defined by the clothes you wear or the sport you play.

But she represents one of the only female ballers I've seen. Either at the cinema or from the shelves of Blockbuster, I'd consume every basketball movie I could. *White Men Can't Jump*, *Teen Wolf*, *O*, *Hoosiers*, *He Got Game*, *Like Mike*, *Coach Carter*, *Glory Road*, *High School Musical*, *Semi-Pro*, *Just Wright*, but apart from *The Winning Season*, all of them centred on male teams or players. I shouldn't be surprised given how little attention female sports get compared to male sports, which Prince-Bythewood reflects in her film. While at college, Monica's team plays in a small sports hall while Quincy's team gets a massive arena. He is also able to drop out and join the NBA draft whereas Monica has to go to Europe to play professionally because the WNBA hadn't been formed yet. The women's league was actually created during the film-making process so Prince-Bythewood was able to realise Monica's ball playing dream with her ending at the LA Sparks. But over twenty years later, there's still so much work to be done to stop the women's game being treated like an afterthought. Just last year, it took a viral TikTok post by University of Oregon player Sedona Prince from the 2021 NCAA women's tournament in the US to trigger a gender equity review into the college basketball event. She compared the women's weight room (one tower of dumbbells) to the men's (a fully stocked area of weights and machines taking over an entire court) and five months later, the Kaplan report, named after the civil rights lawyer Roberta A. Kaplan who conducted the investigation, found the NCAA had failed in practically every respect to foster equality and equity:

> While it is true that some progress has been made, all too often, the proposed reforms that came out of these efforts ended up doing no more than sitting on a shelf. With respect to women's basketball, the NCAA has not lived up to its stated commitment to 'diversity, inclusion and gender equity among its student-athletes, coaches and administrators [. . .] The NCAA's broadcast agreements, corporate sponsorship contracts, distribution of revenue, organizational structure, and culture all prioritize Division I men's basketball over everything else in ways that create, normalize, and perpetuate gender inequities.[1]

I played my last ever basketball game at university, but my career ended on a high. I'd captained Nottingham to Division 1 league victory which got us promoted to the Premiership, we'd beaten our local rivals Nottingham Trent in the varsity tournament and were crowned Team of the Year by our Athletics Union. That was a very messy night at the AU Ball. I'm pretty sure I was drinking booze from the trophy. But you might also be wondering, 'Hanna, if you loved the game so much, why did you stop?' Well, there were a few factors in that decision. I'd already pulled back on my commitment to the sport, before going to uni, when I realised my love for playing with the Doncaster Panthers had been diminished by team politics. I adored my coaches, and credit them for pushing me to become an assertive person on and off the court. They created a real belief in teamwork too as well as supporting other women, but I guess some of my teammates' mums didn't

---

[1] Hecker, Kaplan & Fink, 'NCAA External Gender Equity Review' (2 August 2021) https://kaplanhecker.app.box.com/s/6fpd51gxk9ki78f8vbhqcqh0 b0o95oxq

get the memo. A certain three became rather passive aggressive towards me after I was selected to play for England over their daughters who were a year or two younger. It made training and games so unpleasant when their influence caused their daughters to become cold towards me.

Joining the Panthers made me feel like I belonged for the first time since moving up North, but I was back to feeling like an outsider again. On one of the rare occasions that Mum took me to and picked me up from training, I watched her, through tearful eyes, give these three particular mothers an earful. I'd told her and Dad about my treatment and she'd witnessed it herself, even getting the cold shoulder from them too, but even after she had words the damage had already been done. Then there was the inescapable fact that I wasn't going to go professional. I was a great player, but not as good as my older Panthers' teammates and Des's daughters Helen and Sarah, or some of the players in my England squad. I was not a starting five for the national team, unlike the brilliant Lauren Thomas-Johnson who went on to play college ball for Marquette, professionally in Europe and the UK as well as major international tournaments with GB basketball. And given how much of my life I had already dedicated to the game, I chose not to seek out membership to the local women's team, Nottingham Wildcats, but to play solely for my university so I could have more time to enjoy my undergraduate studies. Without the additional pressures of national league games and training, my love for basketball solidified, but so did my passionate interest in becoming a journalist. When I started working in the field, the routine of my job, including overnights, did not give me the flexibility required to keep playing.

So I chose to focus on my journalistic career, leaving me small, sporadic moments of joy shooting hoops down the park in the years since. But all the skills I picked up from over a decade of playing remained intact. I truly believe that young women can gain so much from playing sports, but they need to be inspired by seeing women playing at the highest level both in real life and in fiction. Sky Sports now offers WNBA coverage in European prime-time spots, while ball movies like *Uncle Drew* and *Space Jam: A New Legacy* featured WNBA players, like Lisa Leslie and Diana Taurasi though, admittedly, they were in smaller supporting roles. *Love & Basketball* was the last film to truly reflect the experience of a professional women's basketball player but *I, Tonya, Irudhi Suttru, Ride Like a Girl, Bruised, Fighting with My Family* are a few of the more recent films that have managed to spotlight the varied female sporting experience in ice-skating, boxing, MMA and wrestling. Documentary is also providing a wider space for female athletes to be acknowledged as well as usurp gendered expectations. The Netflix series *Cheer* presents the real athleticism that goes into becoming a cheerleader and the gender-neutral nature of who makes up a successful team. Mayye Zayed's *Lift Like a Girl* is a coming-of-age story examining the struggles of a young, Egyptian girl training to become a weight-lifting champion despite her derelict surrounding. Short film *The Queen of Basketball* just won an Oscar for its depiction of Lusia Harris, a former college ball player who became head coach of Delta State University women's team, her alma mater, and being drafted by and declining an opportunity to try out for New Orleans Jazz – the only woman in history to be drafted by a men's team. Watching her story, her achievements, in the face of both sexist and racial discrimination, is a staunch reminder of how few female athletes get the recognition they deserve.

Basketball gave me far more than I ever gave it and I'm grateful for every second. Even the suicide drills. But would I have fallen in love with the sport had I not seen a girl excel at it? Love it or hate it, *Space Jam* served up a female animated bunny baller holding her own and that was all the inspiration my younger self needed. Especially when watching women play onscreen outside of my own tournaments was not an option. Now young women have the Sue Birds of the world to look up to as well as the few cinematic athletes pushing the boundaries of female representation by depicting women who can be angry, messy, confident, domineering, loving, intelligent, funny, emotional and vulnerable all at the same time. That's the sort of strong female character I vibe with. That's the type of strong female character I am. That's the type of strong female character young girls need to grow up seeing.

Chapter 6

'What a hunk.'

– Little Giants (1994)

THE FIRST REAL-LIFE crush I ever had was on a boy called Aidan. We went to primary school together at Strand on the Green in West London. He was tall – well, tall for someone in my year-four class – had blonde hair and was by far the prettiest boy of all the boys, but with that sort of jockish confidence that would come to define the male romantic leads in high-school movies that I would soon become accustomed to. There was a game we used to play called kiss chase, which in the cold light of 2022 might not have been the most appropriate playground activity for a bunch of eight- to nine-year-olds, but it was the nineties and we didn't know any better. The basic premise is that whoever was 'it' had to kiss another person and if a boy who was 'it' targeted you, they liked you. One fateful summer's day, Aidan picked me. I was elated. The game was afoot and I nervously laughed, while trying to evade capture, but not really wanting to evade capture, as the girls ran around shrieking and the boys cheered. Aidan caught up to me, gave me a kiss on the cheek. My skin burned, I feigned nonchalance, but the blush gave me away before we went back to class. The next time we played kiss chase, he chased another girl.

Is that why they call it a 'crush' – because it mostly ends in crushing disappointment? It was just a silly game to him. It *was* a silly game. But to me, for one day, I felt seen. I felt pretty. I had all the feelings of Becky 'Ice Box' O'Shea in *Little Giants*, one of the most formative films of my childhood. Not just because she is a sporty girl like I was, still am, but because of the confusion and anxiety she experiences crushing on a boy for the first time – relatably capturing the innocence of developing these desires that initially feel so foreign. What are you meant to do with them? It's messy, obsessive and stressful, and it doesn't help that certain people around her are trying to dictate how girls are meant to navigate the world. There's a bit where Becky is manipulated into quitting American football, and her squad, to become a cheerleader because she's told her crush Junior, played by Devon Sawa, wouldn't be interested in a teammate. She's made to believe that boys are only interested in girls if they adhere to an archaic notion of femininity and sacrifices her nonconformist identity in the process. That she claims it back at the end and leads her team to victory is an empowering moment and shows you shouldn't change who you are for the sake of a boy.

Having said that, I can understand why Becky might have initially done so for Devon Sawa. What a babe! The young actor would later inspire heart eyes across the globe as the titular friendly ghost in *Casper*, but as quarterback Junior, the combination of his blonde curtains, crystal-blue eyes and winning personality was enough to cause my heart to flutter. Movie star crushes were definitely a safer bet than IRL ones. The characters they play exist in a fantasy realm where it's far easier to imagine your own romantic storyline without real-life variables threatening to burst that bubble.

I had plenty growing up and most revolved around cute white boys because Hollywood rarely saw men of colour as romantic love interests. I had an Elijah Wood phase. I mean, who didn't have an Elijah Wood phase? From 1994, he starred in *North*, *The War* and after *Flipper* was released many more young people than me were hooked. As Sandy in the 1996 summertime caper, he had those big round eyes that you could dive into, floppy hair with a slight curl you wanted to run your hands through, and just the right level of teen angst and dolphin affection to melt the heart of this particular subscriber to the RSPCA's *Animal Action* magazine. When Mum picked me up after seeing *Flipper* for the first time I raved so much she asked the cinema workers if we could have one of the film posters when it had ended its theatrical run. They obliged and in a few weeks, we took home a six-foot poster. Unfortunately, it spent the rest of its life in the attic because it was just too big to go up on my bedroom wall. In hindsight we probably should have asked for a smaller one, but my Elijah crush remained intact through to *Lord of the Rings*.

However, my eyes did begin to wander.

The great thing about movie star crushes is that there's simply no limit to how many you can have. You can enjoy several imaginary polyamorous relationships and never have to worry about hurting another crush's feelings. Or maybe they know, and wanting to get involved is part of your fantasy. It's your imagination, so anything goes! And for me, I was adding to my crush list: Heath Ledger in *10 Things I Hate About You*, Jesse Bradford in *Bring It On*, Channing Tatum in *Step Up*, Freddie Prinze Jr. in *She's All That*, Paul Walker in *The Fast & the Furious*, Jonathan Rhys Meyers in *Bend It Like Beckham*. Meyers was an utter dreamboat: the accent, the jawline, the trackies, the way he comforts Jess after receiving racist abuse during a football game. I too had been called the P-word a few times during my teens. I can remember one such occurrence happening in year nine at the end of the school day. I'm heading towards the bus stop with a girl who is taking my route. Some of the lads are gathered at the bike shed and are roughhousing with each other. We stop and laugh when one of them trips and falls. 'You can shut up,' he says to her, then looks at me: 'You too, P***.' I walk off, but you can never really shake the hurt of a racial slur, especially when, like Jess, it doesn't even match. But that's the point, we all look the same to racists and using a one-slur-fits-all dehumanises us even further. What I would have given to have some pretty white boy comforting me after that, accepting me. In an article written by Jennifer Freed, PhD and Melissa Lowenstein MEd, they say crushes can be seen 'saviour-like' and can have you fantasising 'that having this person in your life might solve all your problems.'[1] *Bend It Like Beckham* provided that person and a romantic scenario that I was pining for.

Of course, not all crushes are healthy. In *The Crush*, Alicia Silverstone's feature debut, she plays a fourteen-year-old developing into womanhood, which her dad is pretty skeezy about, and begins crushing hard on the writer renting the guesthouse on their family estate. In an interview with *Fangoria*, Silverstone – who was sixteen at the time – describes her obsessive alter-ego:

> She's a very complex girl but I think there's a side of [Adrian] in every single person . . . I don't believe that [Adrian] does anything to hurt anybody intentionally; it's just that she's so passionate about Nick, or anything she believes in. As far as she is concerned, she's in this huge romance with her boyfriend, and they're gonna get married eventually, and all this, you know, nice stuff. But it gets kind of distracted. People keep getting in her way, and she has to eliminate them![2]

With you there, Alicia. *The Crush* exaggerates the all-consuming feelings of attraction a teen can experience at a time because of adolescent hormones. Writer-director Alan Shapiro based the story on his own experience with the daughter of a family he was renting a guesthouse from in Beverly Hills while a struggling writer in 1989, but not only did he embellish the

---

[1] Goop, 'Viva la Vulva', https://goop.com/gb-en/wellness/relationships/the-upside-of-a-crush-even-if-youre-in-a-committed-relationship/

[2] Newton, Steve, 'Horror in Vancouver: 16-year-old Alicia Silverstone talks The Crush' (7 March 2014) https://www.straight.com/blogra/17751/horror-vancouver-16-year-old-alicia-silverstone-talks-crush

story to psychotic levels, he also used the girl's name too. After the film's release, her parents sued him and Warner Bros for libel and part of the out-of-court settlement was that Silverstone's character's name had to be changed in all marketing and dubbed over with 'Adrian' in future releases.

Clueless, meanwhile, explores teen crushes with less hostility. Cher's initial infatuation with Christian proves futile; he's gay so her calculated attempts to make him fall in love with her were never going to work. After he's outed, Cher feels stupid for not recognising the 'signs', but accepts who he is in a nice conclusion to that unrequited romantic storyline. When the friction in her relationship with Josh, her dad's ex-wife's son, heats up into a full-blown crush we see how even the most confident beauty can become a well of insecurity when the butterflies start fluttering. It's almost reassuring to see how awkward she is around Josh after her Rodeo Drive epiphany; not knowing how to hold her body in his presence, being hyper-aware of their closeness as they help her father's legal case. When Josh eventually kisses Cher on the staircase, my entire body unclenched and relaxed along with hers. Swoon.

I loved seeing crushes ending in happily-ever-afters. *He's Just Not That Into You*, *Angus, Thongs and Perfect Snogging*, and *Easy A* earned repeat viewing because the young women in question – Gigi (Ginnifer Goodwin), Georgia (Georgia Groome) and Olive (Emma Stone) weren't positioned as bomb-shells like Cher. They were the types of characters who would normally be written as the best friend, or would have to go through a makeover in order to get the guy, but actually didn't have to change their appearance or personality in order for a crush to requite their affections.

Nowadays I'm more appreciative of films that present crushes that don't exactly work out, or at least, where the woman crushing isn't utterly crazed. Here's looking at you, *My Best Friend's Wedding*. Sometimes you're forced to remove the rose-tinted glasses and you don't let the disappointment be a reflection on yourself. In secondary school, I had a crush on a guy two years above me. My best friend liked him too. She was blonde, skinny, and most of the boys I fancied actually fancied her first, so I didn't expect anything to come from it. I just let the romance play out in my mind, coyly smiling whenever he was in the vicinity, imagining what it would be like if he scooped me up and claimed me as his. Well, my dream came true during my first year of sixth form. I'd grown out of my awkward phase and he took notice. It helped that my friend began going out with his best friend over the summer and we all hung out together. When it came to the start of the school year, he'd rock up in his Cinquecento during lunchtime. I'd eagerly jump into his ride with pride – look at me with my hot older guy! – and we'd go for a spin listening to the dulcet tones of Mr Tupac Shakur. It was all very sweet and he was quite a shy guy too, so we didn't immediately kiss on our first car date, just chatting and me pretending I knew all the songs he was talking about. Then it happened. The moment I'd fallen asleep many a night thinking about: he leans in, I do too, our lips meet, his lips open, my lips open, and then he practically swallows my face. It was like he dislocated his jaw just get that much coverage and room for his tongue to coat me in saliva. It was the end of the affair.

Bursting the crush bubble can really give you a new perspective. In *The Edge of Seventeen*, Nadine's infatuation with an older student ends after she realises he was only interested in having sex because of a lewd text she accidentally sent to him. A sext does not equal consent, Nick! Corey, in *Empire Records*, has her crush on eighties pop star Rex Manning extinguished after the romantic expectation of losing her virginity to her teen idol, in the record store's backroom, is ruined by his entitled behaviour. While initially hurt and humiliated by Rex's response to her romantic proposition, which she takes out on her workmates Gina and A.J. (he has a crush on Corey too), she gets over it. Say no more, mon amour, indeed.

I don't think I've ever crushed as hard on movie stars as I did during those adolescent years; hormones flaring, pangs of sexual desire becoming more prominent as I absorbed as many rom-coms, teen comedies and YA adaptations as humanly possible. Robert Pattinson and Edward Cullen may well have been the last proper crushes I ever had. I was introduced to two through an *Empire* magazine interview on *Twilight* and was sucked in by the fact the film was centred on one of my main passions in life: hot vampires. After watching the film at Vue Leicester Square, I immediately bought the first book so I could relive the romance in literary detail. I'd practically inhale the rest of the book series, reading and re-reading for dear life, and was a day-one attendee for all the subsequent sequels. I still maintain that the final battle scene in *Breaking Dawn Part Two* is one of the greatest plot twist moments in cinematic history. Impatient to see more of Pattinson, in between *Twilight* releases, I'd watch films from his back catalogue because if there is one undeniable positive to come from having a movie star crush it's being introduced to films you may not have normally gone for. It happened when I was crushing on Leonardo DiCaprio and it sure as hell happened during my Robert Pattinson phase, though I wouldn't rank *How to Be* and *Little Ashes* that highly.

My *Twilight* obsession was so great that my housemate gifted me an Edward Cullen doll for my twenty-first birthday and I'm pretty sure it's still collecting dust at my parents' house. But in the years since, the passion for fictional and real man has dwindled: Edward because, as much as the idea of being the centre of his universe plays on my more idealised romantic desires, he is a controlling stalker with old-fashioned ideas about sex that I no longer subscribe to; Robert, because I've graduated from that overwhelming obsession with hot actors, especially as I now do a job that puts me in the same room with lots of them and it would be kind of unprofessional if I was a quivering mess. Funnily enough, it wouldn't be through work that I'd meet Robert for the first time. A couple of years ago, I was my best friend's plus-one for a New Year's house party and he was there with his girlfriend Suki Waterhouse.

I'd just seen both their latest films – *Assassination Nation* and *High Life* – at Toronto Film Festival and waited till I was a bit tipsier to drum up the confidence to share my love for both. They were quite lovely and we spent the rest of the night having a good chinwag – yes, I did tell Robert I had an Edward Cullen doll; and no, he didn't call security, he found it rather amusing. They say never meet your heroes, but maybe it's OK to meet your former actor crushes.

Now I no longer crush, I simply lust. From Dev Patel in *The Green Knight* to Jonathan Majors in *Da 5 Bloods* and, OK, Jake Gyllenhaal in basically everything. There was a running joke between my ex-boyfriend and I that Jake is my hall pass. To my ex's credit, he fully accepted that scenario. He even sent me interviews and social media mentions of the actor I might approve of. These messages usually came days after I'd already seen the coverage, the casual social media user that he is; but, you know, it was the thought that counts.

Chapter 7

'The PC term is "Hymenally Challenged"'

– Clueless (1995)

THE FIRST TIME I saw someone lose their virginity in a movie was in *The Lion King*. Technically, it wasn't someone, it was a pair of lions, but it still counts. It was the first movie I can remember seeing on the big screen. The year was 1994, I was six years old, and my parents had taken my brothers and me to Waterman's cinema in Brentford to catch it. Little did they know what smut they were introducing their children to. After nearly being traumatised by the stampede, when the second-act romantic interlude came around, I was fully invested. It may arguably be the sexiest scene in Disney history (let alone Disney animation) and the studio's only, well, maybe not explicit, but implicit sex scene to boot. The reunited Simba and Nala, now young adults, run after each other in a sequence soundtracked by Elton John's iconic tune 'Can You Feel the Love Tonight?' Yes, Elton. Yes, I could. As their playful gallivanting causes them to fall into a vertical embrace, Simba on top and Nala underneath, her 'I want to bang you' look in her eyes says it all. That and the lick on his cheek that serves as a non-verbal invitation to get it on. Simba's eyebrow-raise of acknowledgement before it cuts to what I surmise is a post-coital embrace certainly confirms things for me. That and the cub they present at the end – just have to wonder if Timon and Pumbaa were watching . . . I bet they were, the dirty little voyeurs!

Virginity is one of the most milked themes in cinema, especially when it comes to female representation. Where films about boys popping their cherry are frequently depicted as 'yeah, bro!' rites of passage – a la *Porky's*, *Almost Famous*, *American Pie*, *The Girl Next Door* – for girls it's more often presented as a harbinger of doom. *Kids*, written by Harmony Korine and directed by Larry Clark, might be the bleakest depiction of teen sex of the twentieth century. It opens with Leo Fitzpatrick's Telly statutory-raping a twelve-year-old before telling his friend he only wants to sleep with virgins. The kicker is he has HIV and spends the rest of the day pursuing his next target as Chloe Sevigny's Jennie discovers he gave it to her her first time. 'There are these innocent girls having sex with the worldly boys and it reproduced all of these stereotypes that [weren't] in any way transgressive or critical in a way as to intervene on the status quo and that was really sad,' says feminist scholar bell hooks, before pointing out the gross presentation of rape in the final act:

> The message of that is, if you go to the bad party, nice girl, you can be raped and violently abused with people all around you and they are not going to care about your well-being. While the little white boy's raping her, he's saying all these tender sweet things. And since we know that she's knocked out, she's not really awake, you don't hear her voice at all, so you hear no protesting voice. If you close your eyes and listen to what's taking place, you would have no idea that a violent rape was taking place. Because it's all couched in seductive language. These to me were so much of the conservative strategies underlying the transgressive surface of the film.[1]

---

[1] Hooks, Bell, 'Cultural Criticism & Transformation' (1997) https://www.mediaed.org/transcripts/Bell-Hooks-Transcript.pdf

John Carpenter didn't intend to perpetuate conservative ideas about virginity with *Halloween*, but by having the virginal Laurie Strode (Jamie Lee Curtis) survive until the end of his 1978 slasher film – while her sexually active friends are picked off by Michael Myers – he might have done just that and defined the 'Final Girl' trope in the process. 'The sadomasochistic teen horror films kill off the sexually active 'bad' girls, allowing only the non-sexual 'good' girl to survive,' says film scholar Linda Williams.[2] This is why film nerd Randy Meeks outlines the virginity rule in *Scream*, though director Wes Craven subverted that narrative by having his final girl Sidney Prescott survive, despite her having sex with her boyfriend/killer Billy. Other horror-makers have likewise flipped the non-virgins-must-die trope as with *Cherry Falls*, the Brittany Murphy-led film where virgins are targeted by a serial killer, and in *Buffy the Vampire Slayer*.

It pains me to reference Joss Whedon given the allegations about his conduct on the set of this show, its spin-off series *Angel*, *Justice League* and others, but the season one storyline that saw our eponymous heroine lose her virginity to tortured vampire Angel, only for him to turn into soulless monster Angelus once the deed was done, spoke to the countless young women who have similarly been discarded by a guy after having sex for the first time. I was around eleven when this narrative played out across episodes 'Surprise' (written by Marti Noxon) and 'Innocence' (written by Whedon), and my heart broke with Buffy's. I might not have been hyper aware of the ins and outs of sex just yet, but I shipped the two and his total dismissal of her at her most vulnerable was upsetting to watch. I did cheer up when she kicked him in the balls – fuck him up, Buffy! She reclaimed some power and I got my first significant insight into what losing one's virginity could be like. Without

---

[2] Williams, Linda, 'Film Bodies: Gender, Genre, and Excess' (1991) *Film Quarterly*, https://online.ucpress.edu/fq/article-abstract/44/4/2/39822/Film-Bodies-Gender-Genre-and-Excess?redirectedFrom=fulltext

the vampires, of course, sadly. It was around this time that I was experiencing a sexual awakening of sorts.

I probably watched Ridley Scott's *Legend* once or twice a year in my youth between the ages of five and ten. It was during my early teens, however, that a sexual curiosity was sparked. The 1985 film has everything: fairies, unicorns, a young Tom Cruise, goblins, glitter, a forest elf, a Lord of Darkness, bubbles, an impromptu dance number. Scott enlisted the help of author and screenwriter William Hjortsberg to pen *Legend of Darkness* (that was the working title at the time) in the five weeks before he began shooting *Blade Runner* in 1981. The director wanted to create an original mythological story that had all the charms of a Brothers Grimm fairy tale, but with a cinematic purpose. And we all know the sexual element in the classic fairy tales. Angela Carter proved that with her 1979 short fiction collection *The Bloody Chamber* which extracted the themes of sexuality and violence from those stories. *Beauty and the Beast* and *Snow White* were sources of inspiration for Carter, as was *Bluebeard* for the titular story that centred on a virginal heroine being corrupted by a debauched marquis. That theme, of losing one's sexual innocence, is more than obvious through the characterisation of Princess Lili (Mia Sara) and Darkness (Tim Curry).

Lili, our virginal heroine dressed in white, is constantly doing things she shouldn't; whether it's running off with the forest boy Jack (Cruise) or attempting to touch one of the sacred unicorns. It's because she gives into temptation and distracts the stallion, that the goblins are able to injure the creature and see off the source of his magical power: its horn. If that isn't some major phallic imagery for you I don't know what is, but it's at the moment of the unicorn's castration, as it were, that Lili's womanhood is also put on pause. As the world descends into a wintry tundra, she throws her crescent moon ring into a pond declaring that she will marry the person who retrieves it. Anyone who has ever owned a mooncup knows the clear celestial connection between women's menstrual cycles and the big space rock, though as a child I was none the wiser. These elements of sexual imagery went straight over my head and it wasn't until the film journeyed further to Darkness's domain did it start to awaken my senses.

Darkness, our marquis, is the epitome of brutish masculinity, who I, weirdly, found more alluring than Jack. Maybe it's because he's a bad boy and who could be badder than a red-blooded devil lookalike with washboard abs and a sexy baritone voice? Ever the fairy-tale villain, Darkness tries to lure the virginal maid into his dark world with sly tricks. After she and the female unicorn are captured, he bamboozles Lili by creating an illusion that she is dancing with a masked woman, in a glittering black dress. As the waltz gets more passionate, more feverishly seductive, Lili's defences begin to slip and soon she becomes the woman in black. Forget *She's All That* and *Never Been Kissed*, Lili's goth makeover is one of the most iconic on celluloid and I just wanted to be as sensuous and captivating as she was.

Black Lili is the picture of sexual liberation, despite the film implying her association with Darkness is something she should fight against. I was confused, just like my odd attraction to the Satanic villain rather than Cruise's handsome hero. Both consciously and subconsciously, I was absorbing a lot of knowledge about gender roles, feminism, sex and so forth that maybe my pre-teen self welcomed the idea of sexual liberation and empowerment that Black Lili stood for, but really it was the dark and light side that presented a more realistic heroine for the time. Instead of allowing herself to totally succumb to her baser instincts, she tricks Darkness into thinking she would kill the last unicorn when she actually lets the mare escape. By setting that magical female creature free she was set free and proved that the best version of herself was one that was both dark and light, innocent but also full of desire.

* * *

The first person I ever kissed was a girl called Emily. She was in my year-five class and her aunt, or maybe it was her grandmother, lived on the same housing estate as my childminder. Sometimes Emily would go there after school and we'd play together. One day we decided to practise how to kiss, so hid behind her aunt's, or maybe it was her grandmother's armchair, and gave each other pecks on the lips, holding them for one, two, three seconds before releasing. It was all sweet and innocent; nothing like the 2000 MTV Movies Award-winning kiss between Sarah Michelle Gellar and Selma Blair in *Cruel Intentions* and we'd have a little giggle about it after, then went back to our perfume project. We used to pick the lavender plants outside and put the blooms in water. That's how fragrance works, right?

It would be several years before I'd have my first romantic kiss. I can remember the almost-kisses rather vividly. One was during a game of spin the bottle, but I was deemed too ugly to pucker up for when it landed on me. A few years later, I was in what I considered a dramatic love triangle between two best mates in the year above. I liked Danny but his mate Brendan had said he liked me first and had given me a ripped copy of *Nellyville* so, I guess, that was his down payment on my affections even though they were unrequited. One late afternoon, Danny walked me halfway home and the romantic tension was palpable, but bros before hoes and all that. We kept glancing at each other's lips and our hug farewell was lingering. As I walked the rest of the way home, I looked back. I still wonder if he looked back at me too.

I was fifteen when I kissed a boy I liked for the first time. This was quite late for a girl at my school. Several of my friends had already parted ways with their hymen at fourteen and I was the one dragging my feet over it. Also my parents were strict and I had basketball training several nights a week including Fridays. While my friends were down the park getting to know the lads outside the confines of school and uniforms, I was in my kit doing suicide drills down the sports hall. 'Frigid' was one of the labels I received. You've got to love the male ability to shame you for either not putting out or putting out at all, but that's what they've been taught; a patriarchal contradiction that both wants to sexualise and then admonish us if we act on those sexual impulses. *Easy A* is a great example of that double standard; when Olive (Emma Stone) doesn't correct her friend's assumption that she lost her virginity and the lie is spread around school, she leans into the slut-shaming by taking a cue from the book they're studying and wearing *The Scarlet Letter*'s famous 'A' variously over her skimpy new wardrobe. Things escalate when she makes deals with a few male social outcasts to let them boast they had sex with her. While it has a positive effect on these guys' reputations, there is an increasingly negative impact on Olive's even as she tries to reclaim her sexual narrative and autonomy in the face of moral righteousness. *Easy A* makes a good faith attempt at tackling the Madonna-Whore dichotomy that continues to plague the female existence but, like the hymenally-challenged Cher in *Clueless* and Samantha Baker in *Sixteen Candles*, Olive's virginity remains intact by the end of the movie.

It came out six years after I would lose mine, but I had already been introduced to a slew of new female characters that weren't being shamed for it. The year 1999 offered some of the best. The complex sexual politics of *Cruel Intentions* lived up to its title, but by the movie's end Reese Witherspoon and Selma Blair's formerly chaste, now sexually-empowered, Annette and Cecile live to tell the tale. In *10 Things I Hate About You*, Kat embodies a riot grrrl feminist gusto when constantly confronted by her father's controlling, sexist attitude towards his daughters' bodies and the misogyny of an ex who dumped her after they had sex. The experience reinforced her sense of self and, when Kat shares her truth with her sister Bianca, their bond strengthens. Bucking the heteronormative trend was *But, I'm a Cheerleader!* which ripped apart the homophobia of conservative America and the immorality of gay conversion therapy in truly camp fashion. It featured a scene showing Natasha

Lyonne's Megan losing her virginity to Clea DuVall's Graham with sensual flair and that they got a happily-ever-together was a critical moment for lesbian representation.

In 2000, Gina Prince-Bythewood's *Love & Basketball* would arrive and it introduced to me a woman of colour's experience of sex outside of the white default. The writer-director delivered a truly tender love-making sequence between lead Monica (Sanaa Lathan) and her neighbour Quincy (Omar Epps) where the romantic tension in their relationship mellowed to allow them to nervously act on their desire to have sex with each other. 'I wanted this to be real for both of them,' Prince-Bythewood told me in 2020:

> The three of us talked a lot about what each of them would be feeling, you know, Monica being naked in front of someone for the first time. Quincy is a guy who has obviously slept with a lot of women, but knew that it was her first time and being respectful and mindful of that. Those things were important and the things that they brought by looking at each other and her looking down and reacting, his little smile. What makes a great sex scene or love thing is that there's a story to it. There's a beginning, middle and end. It's not just to accurately simulate effects, but it has to go deeper than that. And the condom was a really big deal. I know, there's an argument sometimes, how it takes the 'sexiness out of the scene,' to bring a condom up but these are two people in high school. It's something his father and mother have imparted on him constantly but it's also such a protective thing that he cares enough about her to do that. I hope that that scene itself imparts on other young men how to be in that first time.[3]

To my secondary school's credit, they did provide a few sex education assemblies that offered the clinical detail of sex as

---

[3] Personal interview with Gina Prince-Bythewood, 2020.

well as a parcel of condoms and leaflets to take home in the year-nine instalment. The Netflix series *Sex Education* is earnest and expansive in its sex ed delivery, but most films I've come across only treat these scenes as a joke. *Mean Girls*, *Never Been Kissed* and *Lady Bird* all play them for laughs, but I adore the way Diablo Cody wrote her scene in *Juno*, describing the titular teen's virginity status while calling out the language used:

JUNO

I hate it when adults use the term 'sexually active,' ... What does that even mean? Can I deactivate someday, or is this a permanent state of being? I guess Bleeker went live that night we did it. I guess he hadn't done it before, and that's why he got that look on his face.

Mark[4] was a virgin like me. He was in my GCSE P.E. class and that's where my feelings for him started to emerge. The other boys used to tease me for being a girl good at sport, but Mark wasn't like them. Eurgh, can you hear me? 'He was not like the other boys!' Anyway, one Friday night when basketball training was cancelled, I joined my friends across the road at the park and, soon enough, Mark and I went to a secluded area in the high grass to make out. With an overwhelming need to please and be seen as desirable I gave him a handjob. It was quite stressful, actually, because I was paranoid someone would interrupt for a joke, but luckily with teen boys you can guarantee their speed and soon enough I was wiping his semen off my hand on the ground next to me. We soon were officially going out and after about three months I said we should have sex. At that point I wasn't really thinking about my pleasure. I had no idea what should stimulate my arousal as the few times he'd fingered me didn't produce much of a reaction, just a dry ache, but I just wanted to get it over with because most

---

[4] Not his real name.

of my friends had and I was approaching the legal age to do it. Once I turned sixteen, I made the arrangements. My parents were away so my grandma Monica was looking after us and I invited Mark over. While she was busy with ironing in the downstairs backroom, Mark and I were getting naked under my covers for the first time. It was still daylight outside, but I had my curtains drawn, my door closed and a condom at the ready. We kissed a bit, he cupped my boobs and soon he was erect. Then there was the awkward two-minute pause while he put the condom on and so I lay back and anxiously waited. I'm not sure what the optimum point of wetness is required, but as I'm also keeping my ears peeled in case I can hear my grandma shuffling up the stairs, my focus is split. I have a very creaky bed that we got in the bargain basement of Ikea so we can't get at it too hard either. Not that I'd want Mark to. Once sheaved and on top, we manoeuvre into position and that's when the pain hits. It felt very uncomfortable, I did not enjoy myself, but the deed was done and now it could only get better, right? Well, not with Mark. It would be several years before I'd experience intercourse of mutually orgasmic pleasure, but I'm not regretful that it happened the way it did because it was what I wanted.

It's why I loved seeing the matter-of-fact approach Aubrey Plaza's Brandy takes in Maggie Carey's *The To Do List* nine years later. Instead of waiting for some guy to pick her, the young feminist goes on a mission to experience all the different avenues of sexual pleasure for herself and for the most part her girlfriends are supportive. She even has a sex-positive mother willing to have The Talk™ in a calm and empathetic way. Mum didn't know that when she was giving me The Talk™ I'd already had sex. She'd found my monthly contraceptive pack – mothers are notoriously nosy and mine is no exception – so sat me down on the sofa and said: 'Hanna, you don't always have to have penetrative sex. He can do cunnilingus and you can do fellatio.' I might have died, but I think using the Latin phrases that I didn't quite understand dulled the cringe-inducing impact. Still I nodded, rolled my eyes a bit and excused myself as soon as possible.

Brandy, like me, didn't climax during her first tryst – though it's not for want of trying. She stipulates two conditions pre-coital: condoms and for her to be on top to increase her chance of having an orgasm by forty per cent. That strong assertiveness in the bedroom is exactly the feminist attitude women should be taught rather than being submissive to the whims of their male sexual partner.

There is nothing inherently lost when you have safe, consensual sex for the first time. I would say you gain something: a better understanding of your body, your needs, your likes, dislikes, and experience to put into the next time. Whether that's in a few minutes or a few years even, the first time you have sex doesn't have to define who you are. Unless you are Lizzie in *Prozac Nation* and become campus-famous by throwing herself a party to commemorate the event to the disdain of the guy she popped her cherry with. 'He told me afterwards that in terms of absolute value, sex and drugs were equally meaningless to him,' she says in voiceover. 'Just two different ways to have fun. Which is all well and good until a girl tries out the same approach.'

Nothing like taking control of your sexual narrative in spite of male ego. Of course, I'm saying this from a privileged position in a country with more progressive values than others. There are still places in the world where pre-marital sex is punishable by law and women often face the harshest punishments. I was reminded of this after reading Leïla Slimani's book, *Sex and Lies*, a collection of stories from Moroccan women detailing their experiences under repressive laws that stigmatise their sexual identities. 'Virginity is an obsession in Morocco and throughout the Arab world,' she wrote.

Whether you're liberal or not, religious or not, it's impossible to escape this obsession. According to the family code, before she is married a woman is meant to provide a 'certificate of unmarried status'. Of course, the man's virginity, which is impossible to prove and which isn't in demand anyway, bothers nobody. [. . .] During my discussions with women, many of them described girls who were no longer virgins as 'broken', 'spoiled' or 'ruined' by men, and said that this had to be managed as a terrible 'scar'. Idealised and mythologised, virginity has become a coercive instrument intended to keep women at home and to justify their surveillance at all times.[5]

Moroccan film-makers like Fatima Jebli Ouazzani explored the subject in 1997 with her documentary *In Her Father's House*, while Narjiss Nejjar's 2011 drama *The Rif Lover* is a deep indictment of the same patriarchal culture that sees feminine desires as impure. It seems we are at a stage where virginity in film is enjoying a cultural reappraisal because of female film-makers presenting a much-needed new perspective on the topic. So the sooner we stop framing virginity as a fragile state of being that women need to protect, in every country, the better the world will be for it. As Slimani says, 'sexual rights are human rights'[6] and it's not and should never be up to women to pass a Purity Test in order to gain access to them.

---

[5] Slimani, Leïla, *Sex and Lies*.
[6] Ibid.

Chapter 8

'I'd built up such an illusion about him. I thought he was so perfect'

– *The Shop Around the Corner* (1940)

THE FIRST BOYFRIEND I ever had lasted for forty-five minutes. I was twelve and the relationship was peer-pressured into existence after school one day while we were waiting for the bus home. We'd danced together at a friend's birthday disco on a Saturday – my all-white Tammy outfit, featuring a blue dragon print top and three-quarter-length cargo trousers, was clearly a hit – so by Monday my classmates had decided we had to be together. Those were the rules. I can still remember the chanting and shouts as the poor lad asked me out in the bus queue. I said 'yes' just so the noise would stop. We held each other's hands on the ride home. His were sweaty. Mine were too. When we got off at the stop at the top of my road, I pulled him aside and let him down gently. I'm just not ready for a boyfriend yet, I said. He said, OK, and we parted ways. By the next week he'd told everyone that I was ugly and frigid. My next boyfriend couldn't say the same. I'd given him my first blow job and my virginity, but if I'm being honest, my undying love wasn't part of the deal.

I've had a considerable amount of time to work out who exactly my first love was; some might even argue that I've spent too much time overthinking the subject. Over a decade being out of love will do that to a girl. Still, in my opinion, there's a big difference between someone you might crush on, another you might adore and the feeling of being in love with a person for the first time. Emphasis on the 'in'. Falling-in-love stories were the films that I repeatedly viewed in my teens and that's probably because cinema had long conditioned me to associate female-led films with the romance genre. If it wasn't the melo-dramatic nature of the early 'woman's film' genre it was Disney Princess movies or 'chick flicks' that grew out of the eighties, nineties and noughties. From *The King and I* and *The Sound of Music* to *Pretty Woman*, *Pretty in Pink*, *Pride and Prejudice*, every Jennifer Lopez rom-com, my romantic expectations were influenced by female leads whose main objective was to find love with a man and enjoy a happily-ever-after. That was the ultimate endgame, and sure, while an increasing amount of these so-called chick flicks posited there was more to life than falling in love – get a job, girl! – there was still an underlying romantic essentialism wrapped up in the subplots of each female character's story. As critic Molly Haskell describes the genre: 'I'm emancipated but it's OK to long for romance, to get hung up on a guy, to obsess about mothers or children.'[1] Well, I've already obsessed enough about my mother and shared my unease about children in this book, so let's focus on the being hung-up on guys bit.

Boyfriends number two and number three, who I briefly dated between the ages of fifteen and sixteen, had my sincere affection and though we might have freely bandied those notorious three words around, it wasn't until boyfriend number four that I really meant 'I love you.' Pete[2] was four years older than me and in my brother Nick's year at school. They weren't friends and I was not on his radar. Like Amy in *Little Women*,

---

[1] Haskell, Molly, 'Why chick flicks have greater emotional integrity than men's movies' (28 March 2003) https://www.theguardian.com/film/2003/mar/28/artsfeatures

[2] Not his real name.

it would take a few years of womanly development for the older boys I fancied to take notice of me. That, plus contact lenses and GHD straighteners, so maybe I was more like Mia Thermopolis from *The Princess Diaries*. During my first year in sixth form, I was on a night out, on Donny town down Silver Street, sneaking in with my underage friends at Trilogy nightclub where mine and Pete's paths collided. There he was with his spiky bleached blonde hair, sharp nose and these enviably long eyelashes, wearing the air of arrogance of a man who hasn't realised he peaked in high school just yet. As the R&B playlist pumped through the speakers, he eyed me up and after brief chats in between me digging up the dance floor, I'd given him my number. I felt like Sam in *Sixteen Candles* getting the attention of Jake Ryan. Better yet, I was Sabrina in Billy Wilder's 1954 romp, who'd finally caught the eye of David after two years away in Paris transformed her from a child into a chic woman. OK, it was the early noughties and there was nothing chic about my wardrobe, but it was thrilling to have one of the most popular, fancied guys from my school taking notice of me, wanting my number and soon texting me regularly. I felt bad about breaking up with boyfriend number three, but what could I do? My heart had been stolen; although the guilt only lasted for a few weeks as my ex chose the day of my seventeenth birthday party to tell me I should be put in a cage and sent back to Tunisia. So, you know, so long, farewell, auf wiedersehen, good night!

Pete was all I wanted and, after some casual dating where the butterflies fluttered recklessly in my body, we were soon official. I felt validated for the first time; I still had my beauty hang-ups, still saw myself as the brown nerd who was grateful that anyone would fancy me in the first place, but being with him made me feel attractive and popular by association. That's what cinema had told me was an acceptable way to fall in love and we should aspire to date the biggest names on campus. *Angus, Thongs and Perfect Snogging* saw Georgia come to the conclusion that she 'didn't need a nose job or blonde hair 'cause my sex-god boyfriend likes me just the way I am.' It might have its sexist moments, and a somewhat uncomfortable age gap between fourteen-year-old Georgia and her sixteen-year-old rocker paramour Robbie, but Gurinder Chadha's 2008 teen comedy had a lot better self-love messaging than *Never Been Kissed* and *She's All That*, two 1999 high-school rom-coms with more of a problematic influence. Drew Barrymore's Josie gets to relive her school days as an undercover journalist, but this time around gets both the most popular guy in school and her even more gorgeous English teacher to fall for her. And sure, *She's All That* doesn't start off romantically between art nerd Laney Boggs and smart jock Zack Siler, but the more they pretend to date the sooner they fall for each other. That is after Rachael Leigh Cook's lead, like Barrymore's, undergoes a makeover to appear more acceptable to their male love interest which gives them conventional beauty and popularity points to boot. Not that Laney was ever unhot!

My favourite musical of all time, *Grease*, was guilty of this too. Sandy curls her hair, plasters herself with make-up, squeezes herself into disco pants and starts smoking in the name of love for Danny and social approval. Meanwhile, he's dramatically ripping off the Letterman cardi he wore for Sandy before he's even finished the first verse of 'You're the One That I Want'. It's obvious who compromised the most for these relationships and so much emphasis in these types of movies were about getting the hot popular guy to fall in love with you. It's that sort of cultural conditioning that made me put so much stock in superficial by-products of my own relationship. There was social clout from being Pete's girl; our small Doncaster social circle comprised of current students and recent graduates from local secondary schools and sixth forms, and I was treated with far more respect than I had been. I was no longer the background extra, but now it felt like I was in the ensemble, better yet, the romantic lead and so much of my self-worth was based on the fact that I was Pete's. But in loving him for so long I nearly lost myself altogether.

We rarely see what happens to couples after the happily-ever-after. Sandy and Danny ride off into the horizon in a flying car. In *The Shop Around the Corner*, we aren't privy to what happens when rivals-turned-lovers Klara Novak and Alfred Kralik enjoy that final first kiss. We assume these relationships are going to turn out well because the cinematic journey they went on left us feeling all gooey inside and hopeful for their future. The latter 1940 romantic comedy, starring Margaret Sullavan and Jimmy Stewart, sums up this sort of fantasy-building perfectly in the closing scene. After Kralik convinces Novak her mysterious pen pal is an unemployed older gentleman, broken by the supposed revelation, she says: 'I'd built up such an illusion about him. I thought he was so perfect.' Of course, the illusion wasn't too far from the real thing as Kralik is the real pen pal, after all, but I do wonder, after the credits rolled, if Novak would ever have had an honest conversation with him about his game-playing. Still, what I love about this line is how it captures the fact that when we fall in love, especially during our adolescent first-love phase, we often create this idealised version of our paramour that is so overwhelming that we often ignore the potential faults in the relationship.

I know I did with Pete. When we first started dating, it was so exciting to be picked up by a mature guy, in his own car, who had a full-time job but could whisk me away from my house or sixth form, and take me out with his friends. If I wasn't with him, I'd text him. If his days off were when I had classes, I'd skip them. My entire life began to revolve around his schedule and even when I saw the hoisting of red flags, I made excuses for them. We'd often spend afternoons together watching cricket, even though I hated cricket, but that was what Pete wanted to do so we'd sit in his parents' living room, where he still lived, and I'd have to sporadically hear him deliver racial slurs towards Asian players, like Monty Panesar, when they made a mistake. I'd wince and ask him to please stop using the P-word, it's racist, but his mother told me he can't be a racist because he goes out with me. When it came to racism I've experienced, I'd been told to ignore it, rather than confront it, so I pushed the icky feeling down and reminded myself that Pete loved me and he'd never call me such a name and maybe his mum was right. Maybe someone can use racist slurs and not be racist. I'd built up such an illusion about him. I thought he was so perfect.

During our first three months of dating, I went from a straight-A student in year eleven to getting Bs, Cs, and Ds at AS level because I was not dedicating enough time to work and revision in favour of seeing him. I was like Jade in *Endless Love*, whose obsessive love for David has a detrimental effect on her grades. Pete wasn't fussed about my education; after GCSEs he got a job at a local supermarket and I think he would have preferred it if I had not got my act together. Of course, my parents did care. They were on my case to improve and thankfully I pulled myself back to earn the two As I needed for university. But it was clear they didn't approve of my relationship and, by 'clear', I mean they told me on several occasions that this was obviously not going to last longer than university. Deep down I knew they were probably right, but I guess love and teen rebellion were fuelling my decision to keep things going. A real 'fuck you, Mum and Dad!' that ultimately harmed me more than them. I was a wilful seventeen-year-old dating a twenty-one-year-old, so I thought I was an adult and could handle it. When it came to applying to universities, I picked campuses within driving distance from Doncaster so Pete could come visit or I could come home every weekend. I told my parents it was so I could keep my Sunday gig at House of Fraser as added income, but I could obviously have found a job in Nottingham. But I loved him, he loved me, and we couldn't bear to be without each other for long periods, you see. It spoke to every romantic bone in my body. I'd built up such an illusion about him. I thought he was so perfect.

My parents took me to Cuba on holiday mid-relationship and it was a time when you had to ring your mobile provider to let them know you were going to another continent or your phone number would get blocked. Roaming charges were immense so I wasn't planning on using my pink Motorola Razr that much anyway, and told Pete this, but he wanted me to keep it active. I forgot to make the call though and because of a lack of internet on our first two days in Havana, I was out of touch. I shared my concern with my parents, that Pete might be worried, which confused them. But on maybe the third day my phone switched on and I had voicemails and messages from him. I eventually found a way to access my email and there was a message from him, asking me to check in with him to make sure I was OK. I felt so guilty for not keeping in touch, so I decided to call him and through tears he told me he had contacted my mobile provider several times to persuade them to switch on my phone for travelling to reach me. I never really pushed to find out what he told them – so they would breach privacy laws in order to give him control over my account – but I was young, in love, and thought it was a powerful romantic gesture, despite the massive phone bill. I'd built up such an illusion about him. I thought he was so perfect.

Pete's jealousy was a slow burner. I thought it was normal boyfriend behaviour to be cold to my guy mates, offer to pick me up from girls' nights out earlier than I had planned to end the night, and check my messages. When I went to university, the heat only intensified. He'd check my phone for boys' numbers and get upset if there were any because why would I need their contact info? He refused to socialise with my new housemates or classmates if he came up to Nottingham – we'd spend most of the time in my dorm room – and if I wanted to go out like a normal Fresher, he'd demand that I send him several messages during the night, telling him that I loved and missed him. I could see the weird look on my friends' faces when I tried to convince them this was normal! His phone would be switched off, but he'd want to read the messages in the morning to reassure himself, of course. But if they weren't to his satisfaction, I'd get an angry message or the cold shoulder.

Before, his love felt like a hug, now it just felt oppressive, like it was choking the life out of me and, even though I knew that my mental health was suffering for it, I couldn't split up with him. He had control over me and because I was still the little brown nerd inside, I worried that no one would ever love me like the hot popular guy did. I welcomed conversations about marriage and babies. In a theoretical sense I wanted all that stuff at the age of eighteen, but the more distance university forced upon us, the more space I had to realise I didn't want to build that life with him. When he was gone and I was alone in Nottingham, I could finally breathe and recognise just how noxious our relationship had become, might always have been. For close to eighteen months I'd excused his overbearing behaviour, excused his racism, his developing gambling habit, and yes, excused the fact that he was a Tory, but no more. The illusion was broken. He was no longer perfect.

It wasn't a clean break. I ended things over the phone and though he turned up to try and work things out I was clear it was over. University was a welcome distraction to the conflicted feelings I had. Relationship patterns are hard to shake off, but I finally came into my own amongst my peers who began to question where the hell I had been during the first term. Playing basketball, doing lectures and living under Pete's thumb, lads! I used to be a ghost that haunted my freshers' halls, but now I was the life of the party. I was finding my feet and discovering more about myself as an individual than I ever had before. It was tough coming home for the Easter and summer holiday after our break-up. It's a lot easier when your ex is out of sight and out of mind, but Doncaster is such a small town and I found myself consumed by the resurfaced emotions. We'd all go to the same tragic bars, reunite with the same circle of friends, which meant I'd see Pete and old feelings of love would flood back, threatening the walls I had built to protect myself from reconciliation. The muscle memory of our love story had me repeating the steps while the logical side of my brain tried to plant them in the ground. A few times I faltered, and I'm ashamed of how needy and jealous I was when confronted with him and new girls. Pride is a hard pill to swallow when so much of your self-worth is wrapped up in another person's affection for you. That and the sad realisation that for the rest of your life you have to accept that your first love was not true, it was toxic. Mia Hansen-Løve's *Goodbye, First Love* articulates this painstakingly well, shown through her semi-autobiographical lead Camille, from a young teen to an architecture student, whose early head-over-heels affection for an older student leaves a heartbreaking scar on her soul. I caught glimmers of my younger self in Camille's intense love for Sullivan. But even while nursing a shattered heart, she was building herself into a stronger person through her new architectural ambitions. *Goodbye, First Love* is a perfect example of a woman's film, a chick flick, a female-led story, whatever you want to call it, that shows there is strength, nuance and worth in presenting the multifaceted emotions that young women experience without judgement. That first love often makes a deep psychological impact on who we are and how we carry ourselves in the world.

Watching *Eternal Sunshine of the Spotless Mind* made me wish the mind-altering technology was a real thing. That I could just erase all memory of Pete rather than having to overthink and overanalyse our failed relationship or why I allowed myself to be diminished and controlled in such a way. I wanted to simply move on so in lieu of Lacuna, inc., I embraced random hook-ups. Then I fell in love again and, well, I didn't learn my lesson.

I was dumped by my university boyfriend in January 2009 after a year together and had to spend the rest of my final term bumping into him in nightclubs and witnessing him either getting off with or chirpsing on other girls. Well, you know what they say: anything he can do, I can do better, and I was doing a lot of lads during the end-of-year 'gold rush' to bang as many people you fancied before graduation. I racked up a fair few notches on my bedpost with lads from the football team and other such corners of the student body, putting on a carefree mask of indifference. But broken hearts aren't easily fixed by a rebound or six and it would take me several years to recognise that being dumped was the best thing that ever happened to me. I had planned my future around him. I thought we'd get married, have kids, the whole shebang. He was on a four-year physics course and I was thinking of completing a master's in English just so I could stay with him in Nottingham another year. I convinced myself it was the right choice for me, for us, but like Helen in *Sliding Doors* I was forced onto a diverging path.

Before multiverses became the go-to sci-fi trope it is today, this British rom-com starring Gwyneth Paltrow offered a rather simple concept of witnessing how the life of a woman would play out had she caught or missed a train, with these realities unfolding concurrently. In one timeline, Helen, after getting fired from her PR job, catches the train and finds her parasitic boyfriend in bed with his mistress. She dumps him and goes on to find professional success and a guy who respects her. In the alternative timeline, the sliding doors of the Tube train close in Helen's face, causing her to miss the romantic betrayal and remain stuck in the rut of her life longer than necessary. The cruelty of the film is killing off the empowered version of Helen, but writer-director Peter Howitt doesn't leave us without hope, as the alternative Helen eventually breaks free from arbitrary expectations concerning her career and relationship in order to live a more fulfilling, independent life. '*Sliding Doors* just became the new way of saying "what if?"' he explained to me in 2019. 'It's focused the sort of romantic collective mind on specific major events that people feel have had a distinct effect on their path going forward.'[3] Would I be in the position I am right now had my relationship survived eleven years ago? I really don't think so. I think I would have played a supporting role to my ex's leading man and never

[3] Flint, Hanna, 'Sliding Doors is turning 21 and is still as relevant as ever – here's why' (2019) https://www.stylist.co.uk/life/sliding-doors-rerelease-gwyneth-paltrow-peter-howitt-interview-exclusive/264965

have achieved the sense of self, sense of purpose and love for myself that I have in this moment. But I hope, like Helen, I would eventually get to that point. *Sliding Doors* hints at a romantic future through an end meet-cute between the surviving Helen and her timeline's version of the man her other self fell in love with. The same happens in *Under the Tuscan Sun*, where Diane Lane's divorcee gets reacquainted with a writer she once edited and a mutual attraction forms. Yet both are still single as the credits roll.

As someone who was single between 2009 and 2020, I relished watching films that allow women to remain romantically independent. I love the way that Agnès Varda allows her titular heroine in *Cleo from 5 to 7* to explore her cosmopolitan city while in a fluctuating state of morbid anxiety, yet never tying herself down to any man she comes across. In *Someone Great*, Jenny still chooses her journalism career and the security a staff job will provide despite the fact her boyfriend of nine years breaks up with her because of the long-distance relationship it will create. She's depressed, heartbroken, and an evening hearing songs connected to memories of their relationship puts her even more on edge. A drunken dream sequence finale imagines him asking for her back, but she wakes up to find her friends and accepts that it is over and she can move on. *Roman Holiday* is a joy because Audrey Hepburn's brief affair with Gregory Peck's reporter goes no further than the day it took place. *Before Sunrise* similarly sees its romantic leads spend a short amount of time together after meeting in random circumstances. 'Listen, if somebody gave me the choice right now, of to never see you again or to marry you, alright, I would marry you, alright,' Ethan Hawke's Jesse says at one point to Julie Delpy's Celine. 'And maybe that's a lot of romantic bullshit, but people have gotten married for a lot less.' Yet Richard Linklater's meandering love story, co-written by Kim Krizan, has them departing at a train station with the promise to meet again in six months. As we learn in the sequel, *Before Sunset*, their reunion takes place nine years later where they are both unsatisfied by their current circumstances. Delpy and Hawke share the writing credit this time and its clear they bring much of their own experiences of life, love, work and relationships to fill out their characters with a maturer perspective that only makes the conversations of Celine and Jesse ever more intriguing to hear. It ends with another promise, though there is no need for it to be explicitly expressed because we are watching it be kept. As Jesse takes in Celine dancing to Nina Simone, the choice to stay and watch rather than catch his flight is a renewed promise of themselves to each other. That they've come to each other now, only makes their union more beautiful and less whimsical than giving *Before Sunrise* a cliched happily-ever-after.

These films are still outliers. From classic Disney movies to teen romps to rom-coms and sappy dramas, female-led narratives have upheld a romantic standard for women to end up in heterosexual relationships. *No Strings Attached* and *Friends with Benefits* are both films based on the idea of women enjoying sexual freedom, yet both see their wings clipped by the end in order to appease conventional romantic narrative expectations. Even when a film might show a woman going on a journey of self-discovery as a single woman, she's likely to end up with a guy. In *Eat, Pray, Love* it's there right in the title how her story will end. What I like about Julia Roberts's Liz is that she divorces her husband because she's sick of financing his every professional whim and she also makes a case for a child-free life; though not every woman is in the economic position to take a year off work to find herself. I had worked and saved enough to go interrailing with three school friends around Europe for a month in the summer after I got dumped, but the only thing that I discovered was I really, truly, hate beer. After dispensing with another futile relationship, Liz heads to Italy and breaks free from the shackles of diet culture to eat what the hell she wants with director Ryan Murphy making a proper meal out of everything she consumes. Who needs sex and romance when you can eat? 'I'm in love,' she says. 'I'm having a relationship with my pizza.' She gains a bit of weight, not too much, of course, because heaven forbid fatness be an attractive, romantic position for a female lead in Hollywood.

By the film's end she's thinner and shacked up in Bali with Javier Bardem's Felipe. 'Hunger and desire are expressed, only to be tempered by an individual choice to remain slender or seek fulfilment in heterosexual coupling,' assert Janani Subramanian and Jorie Lagerwey. 'Hunger for food, for sex, for a public life, even for self-love must be achieved in "balance," and the excess [. . .] is tested out and rejected in favour of moderation that is in line with dominant norms of white middle-class femininity.'[4] They're right, though I did appreciate the line in the film where Liz asks a friend, concerned about calories, if a man had ever kicked her out of bed because of a 'muffin top'. That quote has been seared on my brain ever since because, certainly from my sexual exploits of over a decade, that has never been the case. The line was reassuring during my first few years back in London, in the infancy of my journalism career, where I had developed bulimia and gained three stone in a very short amount of time. It would take several years to revert back to my previous size, non-disordered eating patterns and give my body love including the rolls, bulges and dimples it comes with. Self-acceptance can be really hard when you feel like a stranger in a body you've manufactured in an unhealthy way and so casual sex was a way to make me feel desired when looking in a mirror did not.

Hook-ups, during my early twenties, used to serve as a distraction from the anxious, negative thoughts that were plaguing my mind about my disordered eating, body and the realities of millennial working life where even though I was working to the bone to cover my bills, I didn't have a full-time job and was

---

[4] Subramanian, Janani, and Jorie Lagerwey, 'Food, Sex, Love, and Bodies in *Eat Pray Love and Black Swan*' (2013) *Studies in Popular Culture*, https://www.jstor.org/stable/23610149

highly aware that it was unlikely I'd get on the property ladder without my parents' help. It's still unlikely. Hook-ups weren't empowering acts, but does every female action have to be so? Can't they just be human? Going out and taking part in a few one-night stands temporarily sated my anxiety and depression, even if they didn't always make me climax. 'Many different biological factors, social, and psychological factors come together to make women twice as likely to be depressed as men,' says Dr Susan Nolen-Hoeksema. 'Overthinking is one of those factors.'[5] More recent scientific research has found that you can experience happiness from sex even if you didn't enjoy it because of the way it can distract from excessive worrying,[6] and that's certainly a glass-is-half-full way of depicting the unsat-isfying sex I was mostly having during this period. I was more interested in focusing on the guy's pleasure because I was grateful that they thought I was attractive enough to take me to bed. Yet after an increasing amount of solo exploration of my own body, erotic cinema, and online porn, I became more decisive in what I wanted to get out of casual sex and Samantha Jones was, as with a lot of women, a big inspiration for that sort of sexual agency.

I was too young to watch *Sex and the City* when it first aired but I'd got access to the boxset and watched these four women's escapades with abject delight. Seeing the rollcall of sexual partners Samantha would go through each episode proved to be the most influential of them all. When people asked, 'which *Sex and the City* character are you?' I used to say Carrie or a Miranda, but by my mid-twenties I was 100% a Samantha. The PR guru exhibited exactly the confident, blunt and defiant mindset that I was trying to build in my

[5] Nolen-Hoeksema, Susan, *Women Who Think Too Much: How to Break Free of Overthinking and Reclaim Your Life*.

[6] Killingsworth, Matthew A. and Daniel T. Gilbert, 'A Wandering Mind Is an Unhappy Mind' (12 November 2010) http://www.sciencemag.org/content/330/6006/932.abstract

own head. Her ambitious outlook taught me that looking for a man was a distraction from achieving the career I wanted yet I could still have all the sexual fun without having to manage my schedule around their movements. That I could make demands in the bedroom and kick them out after. I remember this one time I was on a date and on the bus back to mine I said to the guy he would have to leave after we banged because I had work the next day and wouldn't sleep well if he stayed over. I thought about all the times I'd heard about guys kicking girls out after sex without warning and I thought this was a far more transparent way to give the guy the choice to say no, but he agreed. So we got to mine and did the deed and when I asked him to leave he was shocked. 'I didn't think you meant it,' he said. I was like, er, yeah dude I was very clear, but he kicked up a fuss, said it was too late to get home – it was only one am. I told him he could sleep on the sofa and I went to bed. The next morning he was rather embarrassed as I shuffled him out and carried on with my life.

Samantha worked hard, played hard, fucked hard and I was following suit. My friendship group was made up of models, photographers, DJs and actors, people far hotter, slimmer, cooler than I was, but I felt more attractive in their company. We'd hit The Box nightclub during the week, brush shoulders with young hot celebrity things and rave at Bussey Building over the weekend. We'd go to fashion week and launch events, then hit the hotel after parties. I might leave with a guy and get home at either 6am or 6pm the next day depending on how late we chased the night. Samantha was a self-described 'trysexual', and I tried a few things out myself. I had my first threesome with two male models because there was nothing more ego-boosting to me than bedding and these two were pretty boys of summer. But reality crashed into the fantasy I had imagined of enjoying the ultimate pleasure. When we got back to one of their flats it looked like the bedroom of a teenager who shoved food under their bed. Needs must and we started kissing, touching and sucking, but one of them got performance anxiety and it was all a bit *Inbetweeners*, so I decided to cut my losses and call it quits. My second threesome happened a few years later with an actor and an older woman after I met them at The Box. I'd had a drunken kiss with a couple of girls in the past, mainly because they were pretty and had come on to me, but I never felt aroused to pursue something further sexually. This night, I had my #WWSD hat firmly on. I'd hooked up with this guy before and we were all consenting adults, but by the time we got to his place and started having sex I realised going down on a woman, or having a woman go down on me, was leaving me cold. Even more so when the guy removed himself to his chair so he could watch. I've never felt so male-gazed-upon, and so detangled myself, made my excuses, booked an Uber and headed off.

Having authority over your sex life is always healthy. Tiffany Haddish's full-bodied commitment to her character's sexual needs in *Girls Trip* is delivered with unwavering confidence and blunt comedic force. The entire cast get to have explicit discussions about their sexual appetites and act on their baser impulses too and it serves as a celebration of Black women, older Black women to boot, engaging their desires without judgement or the racial overtones that have often seen them abused on screen. 'Black female sexuality has always been such a loaded concept,' writes Zeba Blay. 'Where white women have had more room in pop culture to challenge the very real constraints placed on their bodies by society, Black women have languished at the intersection of race and gender and sexuality, weighed down by a storied history in which their sexuality has either been exploited or flat-out denied.'[7] In *Appropriate Behaviour*, Desiree Akhavan offers a self-aware

---

[7] Blay, Zeba, '"Girls Trip" Celebrates The Unapologetic Sexuality Of Black Women' (25 July 2017) https://www.huffingtonpost.co.uk/entry/girls-trip-celebrates-the-unapologetic-sexuality-of-black-women_n_59774f-2fe4b0e201d5783743

reflection of millennial sexual politics through a Persian-American lens. Shirin is not exoticised as Middle Eastern women have historically been through Orientalist stereotypes, but Akhavan touches on her Exotic Other status in some interactions to hilarious effect. That doesn't mean she is not sexually adventurous, but she's also a dryly funny, somewhat rudderless Brooklynite anxious about failing her successful immigrant parents because of her lack of career focus and closeted bisexuality which leads to her girlfriend dumping her. 'Who we are sexually is so telling of who we are and where we are in our lives, and what we think of ourselves, and our bodies, and intimacy,' Akhavan said of writing the script.[8] This is presented so clearly and thoughtfully through Shirin. She goes out on the lash, on the pull, and even finds herself in a threesome situation which has the awkward, unsexy vibes of my own, but being single forces Shirin to confront herself and her past relationship to realise new personal truths she was never going to discover while cuffed. As a queer woman, there's an authenticity and understanding that Akhavan offers in the film which she continues in the East London-set, messy sexual exploration of love, romance and desires through *The Bisexual*. This time, her character Leila has ended her long-term relationship with a woman to seek lustful encounters with men because she's yet to tap into that side of her sexuality. A string of meaningless and meaningful, intense, funny, awful, uncomfortable sexual liaisons follow as Leila confronts and contends with the multiple identities she's juggling as a bisexual, Iranian-American living in the UK.

Television has certainly become a fruitful place for complicated single women to work out their kinks while not having to be completely likeable all the time or end up in a relationship by the end of the episode. *Fleabag*, *I May Destroy You*,

---

8 Hans, Simran, 'Desiree talks comedy, her web series and the success of Appropriate Behaviour' (6 April 2016) https://network.bfi.org.uk/news-and-features/on-first-features/appropriate-behaviour-desiree-akhavan

Girls, *We are Lady Parts*, *Broad City*, and *Pure* capture a wider range of millennial female experience that has moved the conversation on from groundbreaking shows like *Sex and the City*. For all its other sins, when it came to its lack of intersectional representation and pube shaming, Samantha was never demonised for having that sort of sex-positive, single, party-girl outlook. She wasn't a perfect woman; she made mistakes, had personality flaws and was anxious of growing old when she still felt so young, but that's what made her so relatable even if she was a wealthy, conventionally attractive white woman. Drinking, dancing and fucking gave me pleasure and was a welcome respite to life's stresses and my darker thoughts. It was why I couldn't put Emma Jane Unsworth's *Animals* down when I got it because she articulated so much of my feelings and experiences of millennial hedonism, sexual revelry and the torturous hangovers in frank detail. When she adapted it to the screen, director Sophie Hyde carried through all of that intoxicated debris, with Holliday Grainger and Alia Shawkat delivering deep and believable performances as co-dependent BFFs Laura and Tyler. The complexity of female friendship is presented through their relationship; it's passionate, loving, dark, wild, toxic, debauched and tested when struggling writer Laura settles for a guy in the hopes of putting her life into clearer focus. And that his dedication to his craft might rub off on her too. While Amy Schumer's *Trainwreck* disappointingly sees her character symbolically giving up her party-girl ways for a guy, by literally giving a cardboard box full of booze away, Unsworth offers Laura a more satisfying, independent alternative. She doesn't quit booze, just drinks more modestly, and after cutting ties with both Jim and Tyler moves out on her own. It's like when Samantha breaks up with Smith in the *Sex and the City* movie and tells him, 'I love you but I love me more.' Laura's not forty-nine, but the relationship she too needs to work on is the one with herself and it is important for women to be able to do that for themselves, even if it means cutting out friends as well as lovers.

By the time I hit thirty, I couldn't wait to assert a new way of living for myself. I was done with my twenties. They'd been a wild, eventful ride, but I was ready for my flirty and thriving phase to really kick in. So like Laura, I cut back on my partying each week, cut ties with friendships that were sapping energy and renewed my focus on my writing future. I was still having fun, adventurous sex with a variety of men, including a few rather handsome conquests I'll be telling my friends' grandkids about (who knows if I'll be having my own). Sex is never more casual than with a celebrity and I felt no motivation to tie any of these hot actors down, but the confidence these no-strings sessions gave me pushed me towards a place where I felt good about myself, what I wanted from life and was ready for a partner who would love me for me no matter how blunt, opinionated, self-sufficient or sexually active I had been. I remember a friend's boyfriend suggested the reason I was still single was that I was sleeping with men on the first date. I told him if that's the reason why a guy wouldn't want to be with me then I'm glad I didn't waste my time by holding back and finding out what a sexist he was later. There's far too much good TV and movies to keep you company than settle for a relationship with a person who doesn't embrace every part of who you are. That and the more important point is that it may distract you from the life you could be building for yourself on your own terms rather than someone else's.

It took me years to rebuild my sense of self and I promised I would never again allow love to let me lose sight of who I was. In 2020, I confidently welcomed the sensation, but the difference between this, my third love, and my first love is that it doesn't feel quite so intoxicating. It was a steady feeling that caught me by surprise when he turned up at my front door on my thirty-second birthday in a gift-box costume. After two years, I chose to end the relationship. I love him but I love me more and knew the problems we developed were not making either of us happy. Maybe we'll find our way back to each other. I'm under no illusion that people can't change. Nobody is perfect.

The pain and passion of love has taught me to be a bit more cynical and stop looking for a rom-com standard. Sure, I still love to escape into this fantasy world. I felt like I was about to spontaneously combust into a ball of glitter and butterflies after watching *Marry Me*. On paper, Jennifer Lopez and Owen Wilson look like a bizarre pairing. But with their rom-com credentials, personal romantic melancholy, her meta pop-star narrative and his normcore wardrobe, was exactly the right concoction to please my idealised romantic sensibilities. It took me back to the days I repeatedly watched *13 Going on 30* and imagined my own movie romance and a journalism career to look forward to. But as the adult Jennifer Garner, with her thirteen-year-old neighbours, sings along to Pat Benatar's 'Love Is a Battlefield', I, a veteran soldier, now find solace in the first love films that put the messy reality front and centre of the story. I'm not talking about tragic stories akin to Baz Luhrmann's *Romeo + Juliet*, *A Walk to Remember*,[9] or *Moulin Rouge*, where love ends when one or both of them die. I'm talking about the films that show that love can be beautiful but doesn't always work out the way we imagine.

Like Crazy, for example, captures so much of the weightlessness of first love and the burden. Drake Doremus's 2011 feature starring Felicity Jones and the late Anton Yelchin achieves one of the most searing statements of first love committed to screen. So much of this is down to the actors. Their subtle performances were almost entirely improvised and the film had me rooting for this relationship to survive long-distance. My heart swells and aches and swells and aches again, every time I watch this film because it reminds me that love is never the only thing that matters.

---

[9] Mandy Moore is a forever angel and the ballad she sings 'Only Hope' is a bop that I listened to on repeat for most of 2002.

To quote the inimitable Cher, 'I adore dessert, I love men. I think men are the coolest, but you don't really need them to live.' What you do need is to find contentment with yourself, who you are and how you want to navigate this life. My single twenties gave me more than enough time to work that out, my poor vagina might say too much time, but I wish every person could experience something similar. A man doesn't maketh the woman. Woman maketh the woman and giving yourself some extended alone time might just help you work out who she could be. First love taught me there is poetry in the falling. There is an adrenaline rush of possibility in discovering an unknown person as you catapult into the romantic abyss, but once you hit the ground, reality will always set in. Being single taught me I needed to love myself first.

Part Three

Adult Material

Chapter 9

'I read somewhere that their periods attract bears'

– Anchorman (2004)

THE FIRST TIME I got my period was during basketball training. I was in year eight, I'd nipped to the loo for a quick wee, but when I pulled my bottoms down there was a reddish stain there too and I was caught off guard. I knew it was coming – us girls suffered through a rather awkward sex education assembly on the topic – but I was totally unprepared for this shock of red and had to improvise a few layers of cheap toilet tissue to line my pants until the end of practice. It was a weekday, so Mum was in London and Dad picked me up. During the car ride home I shyly mentioned what had happened. He was pretty chill about it, the modern man that he is, and once we got back to the house he showed me to the bathroom cabinet where Mum's private collection resided. The super tampons were a bit intimidating, so I went for the sanitary pads instead and from then on Mum and Dad would include some teen-friendly versions of period products on the monthly Big Shop until it was my responsibility to buy them myself.

I don't think any girl gets comfortable with their periods. Sure, nowadays, there are apps to keep track of our menstrual cycle and an abundance of new environmentally-friendly products to protect our underwear, but the frequent irregularity of our crimson flow, and often mood-affecting, body-aching side effects that come with it each month, is a bloody ball ache. Vada in *My Girl* (1991) was right. 'It's not fair,' she says to Shelly after coming on for the first time. 'Nothing happens to boys.' It's exactly because men don't get periods that girls, women and people with uteruses can't seem to escape the taboo treatment of this very natural, normal human occurrence either. Cinema has played a part in this stigma.

Coming-of-age stories are a good place to start and there's been several that show young girls and women horrified by the sight of blood between their legs. At eleven years old, Vada (Anna Chlumsky) has yet to have the period talk. Her mother died in childbirth in textbook children's film fashion, and her mortician father Harry (Dan Aykroyd) has managed to avoid any sort of puberty subject with his daughter thus far. So when her first period blood starts flowing, the death-obsessed hypochondriac screams, 'I'm haemorrhaging!' It's an interesting choice that the young girl understands the meaning of that medical condition, but not the female anatomy. Luckily, Jamie Lee Curtis's trusty cosmetologist Shelly is on hand to calm her down and explain about the birds and the, er, bees (RIP Thomas J.). It's a nicely handled scene that shows how menstruation can positively bond women, but it reinforces the gendered responsibility of the conversation, letting her dad off the hook. Men should be just as capable as women to handle puberty conversations, especially in circumstances where a female presence might not be available at home. My dad managed alright! But even with a female presence, the conversation might prove lacking.

Both Brian De Palma's *Carrie* (1976) and Kimberley Peirce's 2013 remake, based on the Stephen King novel of the same name, see the eponymous heroine cry out in distress at the sight of blood in the school shower. It's a scene made all the more harrowing by the mockery of her classmates throwing sanitary products at her. 'Plug it up,' the girls chant. Had Carrie's religious fanatic of a mother Margaret explained what would happen, the young girl might not have been so traumatised. But Margaret believes menstruation represents the Curse of

Eve, God's punishment of pain when it comes to anything related to child-rearing, so I'm not sure a pre-emptive period chat would have alleviated her daughter's fears. Still, despite the Bible's claims that menstrual fluid is impure (Leviticus 15:9), it also says that blood is a creature's life force (Leviticus 17:14) so in Carrie it becomes a symbol for female evolution from girlhood into womanhood, and with the iconic pig blood prom scene, human into superhuman when her telekinetic powers truly manifest on Maine. Sorry to that town.

Like Carrie, but with far more self-awareness, the sisters at the heart of horror film *Ginger Snaps* (2000), from director John Fawcett and screenwriter Karen Walton, face the onset of puberty via the curse of lycanthropy. Sixteen-year-old Ginger and her younger sibling Brigitte have wanted to avoid any form of womanly transformation to rebel from societal norms. We find out later that this attitude is wrapped up in social anxiety and insecurity, but before they get to that realisation, Ginger is bitten by a werewolf just as her menstruation begins. Maybe Brick Tamland in *Anchorman* was right. Maybe our periods *do* attract bears and other beasts because they can 'smell the menstruation'; it's certainly implied in the film. What is more explicit is the connection between a woman's monthly and a werewolf's lunar change because of the side effects: increased body hair, sexual desire and mood swings. Horror is one of the most political genres of film and the body politics at the centre of *Ginger Snaps* showcased the messy, erratic and complicated reality of what it can be like for some young women experiencing their periods for the first time and feeling like they are losing their autonomy, especially at a later age than others. As Walton said in an interview with *Bloody Disgusting*:

I wanted their problems to be what my problems were back then, which is like, 'Wow, it's really stressful when you finally got your period to figure out what the hell you were supposed to do with this whole thing.' We didn't have a great system. Just the anxiety of like, oh god, my friend had hers and I don't, so now she is literally growing in more ways than one ... The more I could ramp the feminine experience, the better, right down to your period, right down to whether you were shaving your legs yet or not, and why not, right down to the very fiber of your being, what people did to distinguish themselves, what kept them together in their little war against being teenage girls, and then what would pull them apart.[1]

Where *Ginger Snaps* somewhat severs the sisterly bond through menstruation, *The Tale of Two Sisters*, reinforces it. This 2003 horror depicts psychological and supernatural warfare between several female presences in a house where the threat of both womanhood and motherhood is presented in vivid red. Director Jee-woon Kim floods the screen with bloody imagery, figuratively through house interiors and the costumes, and literally in a frightening scene where the female protagonist Su-mi, witnesses blood trickling down the leg of the ghostly presence above her. In another scene, the titular sisters wake to find they both came on in what Lauren Rosewarne describes in her book, *Periods in Popular Culture*, 'menstrual synchrony':

The menstrual synchrony narrative is perhaps the strongest example of on-screen menstrual bonding, presenting women not merely united by menstruation, but by the experience of bleeding simultaneously.[2]

Menstrual bonding has come in handy over the years, especially when I was in the middle of class during secondary school. I can remember a few occasions when mild panic set in because

[1] Tenreyro, Tatiana, 'A Different Kind of Monster Movie: Writer Karen Walton Reflects on "Ginger Snaps" 20 Years Later' (25 September 2020) https://bloody-disgusting.com/interviews/3633638/different-kind-monster-movie-writer-karen-walton-reflects-ginger-snaps-20-years-later/

[2] Rosewarne, Lauren, *Periods in Pop Culture: Menstruation in Film and Television*.

of a growing sensation of wetness in my pants. Am I menstruating, or was it just my vagina naturally cleaning itself? The wait to find out could be excruciating. I'd sit there, legs crossed, hoping I could stop the flow of any potential blood before I could sprint to the nearest girls' toilet across campus. In the meantime, I'd discreetly look through my school bag to see if I'd had the good sense to plant an emergency sanitary towel in there for such a moment, then mentally admonish myself because, oh shit, I hadn't. Congratulations, Hanna. You've played yourself again! So I'd scout the class for friendlies who might be able to help a girl out, but I'd be sitting next to a boy and have to be extra careful so he wouldn't discover my shame. I'd look intently at my female classmate next to me until the heat of my stare turned her head in my direction. I'd mouth two syllables at her: 'TAM-PON'. She'd nod. Relief would flood my body. She'd scootch her bag across to me and I'd reach in, grabbing the long, yellow applicator tampon and shoving it up the sleeve of my school jumper like it's a shank I'm hiding from the prison guard. Except this wouldn't spill blood, it would soak it up. I'd smile at her, she'd smile back. A small, silent victory for female solidarity had been won, but the period shame would take a long time to shake off.

God forbid you menstruate and your male peers become aware of it. In *Superbad*, Jonah Hill's Seth says he's going to 'fucking throw up' after discovering that the drunk girl he had happily let grind on him had 'perioded on his fucking leg'. Star and co-writer Seth Rogen tweeted in 2017, that the scene was inspired by a real-life event, 'The period blood on the leg scene in Superbad actually happened to my friend at a high school dance and we discovered it after the dance,'[3] and the responses from men were a chorus of disgust. The scene normalised how men are allowed to be grossed out when confronted by it.

---

[3] Rogen, Seth, Twitter feed (18 August 2017) https://twitter.com/Sethrogen/status/898369963836231682

Amy Schumer's *Trainwreck* would reiterate that socially accepted male position as she tries to talk herself out of committing to the man she's dating:

AMY

What if I, like, forget to flush the toilet? And there's, like, a tampon in there and not like a cute, like, ooh, it's the last day, like a real tampon. I'm talking like a crime scene tampon, like, the Red Wedding, *Game of Thrones*, like a Quentin Tarantino *Django*, like, a real motherfucker of a tampon.

Well, first of all, maybe as a magazine writer you shouldn't be falling in love with the person you're meant to be doing a profile on. Second of all, why are you flushing your tampons down the toilet, Amy? That's just poor sanitary etiquette. Thirdly, as much as she articulates the fears of many women being seen as undesirable because of their periods, it doesn't do much to push back against the stigma.

There have been outliers to this trend. When I first watched *Clueless* in my youth, the period euphemism went straight over my head, but in years of repeat viewing, I've come to appreciate Amy Heckerling's smart and sassy way of dealing with it in a school environment. In a classroom scene, Mr Hall is reading out the tardy list and when he arrives at Cher's number she questions the count and defends her lateness on one of them. 'I was surfing the crimson wave, I had to haul ass to the ladies,' she confidently tells her teacher, which he acknowledges in a positive way by not punishing her for it. 'I assume you're referring to women's troubles so I will let that one slide.'

It's such a simple back and forth yet it manages to destigmatise menstruation from both a male and female point of view. Similarly, I loved how the tampon storyline plays out in *She's the Man*. This is a film I watched repeatedly during my teens, especially in my first year of university with my roommates Neena and Jenny. It was our comfort movie for those days during Freshers when we were nursing hangovers, so you can imagine the wear and tear on that DVD. We couldn't get enough of Amanda Bynes's comic performance, Channing Tatum's abs or screenwriters Karen McCullah Lutz and Kirsten Smith's brilliantly modern take on a Shakespeare classic that exposed a lot of the archaic ideas about gender that are still prevalent today. But to the point; when Duke and his pals first discover Viola-as-Sebastian's tampons they ridicule him and the 'I get bad nose bleeds' excuse she/he uses to cover her/his back. Later, Duke is found using one to block a nosebleed caused by a fight with Viola's ex. He can't quite bring himself to say the word, the wimp, but it shows that a) actually tampons *are* a good fix for nosebleeds and I don't know why this isn't mainstream now; and b) men are often far less fragile about their masculinity as individuals than they are in groups.

In *20th Century Women* (2016), Mike Mills depicts how internalised misogyny can affect women of different generations in the period discussion, even when the women are all pretty right on. Greta Gerwig's Abbie is vocal about the discomfort of being on her period at a dinner party which Dorothea (Annette Bening) takes umbrage: 'Abbie, ok you're menstruating, do you really have to say it?' Yes, is the answer, so Abbie turns to Dorothea's son Jamie with some real talk:

ABBIE

You want to have an adult relationship with a woman you need to be comfortable with a woman having her period. Say menstruation like there's nothing wrong with it – menstruation.

Not that men should get a pat on the back for showing the nuanced reality for many people assigned female at birth but, *20th Century Women* is a great example of how male film-makers can be allies in presenting female stories and characters that break stereotypes and taboos. I will, however, give Mills two pats on the back for having the dreamy Billy Crudup deliver this line:

WILLIAM

Sex during menstruation can be very pleasurable for a woman, even provide relief from cramps. Jamie, I also want to say, never have sex with just the vagina, have sex with the whole woman.

That's one for the wank bank! I have actually lost count of how many times I've turned down sex because I was on my period. To be fair, a lot of the time it's simply because I've not been in the mood, I feel bloated and the last thing I want is some man's dick or digit fannying around down there. I also happen to be one of those unfortunate people who can endure a cystitis flare-up when I'm menstruating and sex only makes it more likely to occur. However, when I first started having intercourse, I thought it was just as gross a concept as my sexual partners did. There was always a look when you'd inform the guy, boyfriend or not, about your menstrual status. They'd either cringe and pull back, as though it was contagious, like utter tools, or smile and request a blowie or handjob instead. It pains me to say, I'd often concede to this sexual alternative. The people-pleaser in me, who still didn't quite understand why boys might be attracted to me and ingrained with a sense that male pleasure should come first, felt guilty that I was on my period and wanted to make it up to them somehow. Eurgh. I shouldn't be mad at myself, but it's so frustrating to think of a time when I would acquiesce to this sort of demand rather than demanding more for my sexual self.

Thankfully, the more personal exploration of sex and desire I undertook, the more confident I would feel about my body and in my ability to vocalise my preferences. Part of that was enjoying time with male partners who were far more evolved when it came to the period discussion. Well, there was one

Italian guy who seemed so sure that blood coming from my vagina during sex was me coming on my period, it took me literally shouting, 'It's not period blood, your penis has ripped my vagina!' for him to shut his flipping mouth. Long story short, I was in Australia, he was a one-night stand and while I was on top and clearly not wet enough his dick managed to cut my vaginal lining during one particularly energetic thrust. There was a pop. I thought I'd snapped his penis at first, but after using the selfie function on my phone to assess the situation I confirmed my vag was the victim and would take several days to heal. Making love is truly a battlefield sometimes, but cinema in the last ten years shows there aren't always casualties in the pursuit for feminist representation of period sex.

In Andrea Arnold's *American Honey*, Sasha Lane's character removes her tampon before having sex and the guy doesn't make a song or dance about it. In *Saint Frances*, Bridget (played by the film's writer Kelly O'Sullivan) wakes up after a night of passion to find blood on her and her male sexual partner's face. That situation happened to me once; I hadn't realised I'd come on during the night, while I was receiving oral sex, and I woke up the next morning to find a little redness around his face. It was far less of an abstract painting than that in *Saint Frances*, but my guy, similarly, didn't mind. He washed his face and wanted to go another round. Morning wood, eh?

There's been many a bloodied towel thrown into my laundry basket in my time and it was a joy to see that sheet-saving tactic in Michaela Coel's TV series *I May Destroy You*. Not least because so far, most of the period representation I'd seen on screen has been through a white lens. *Turning Red*, recently bucked the trend in Disney animation by explicitly mentioning period products, and showing them too, in an Asian-led story, but for older audiences, watching Coel's protagonist Arabella have sex, after a towel is laid down, her tampon removed and blood clot eagerly examined by her lover Biagio (Marouane Zotti), was jaw-dropping. Sex can be messy, no more so than when you're on your period, and that the show didn't treat it like a gory nightmare has everything to do with a ground-breaking creator willing to push the bar of what is socially and culturally expected on screen.

And as we're talking about TV, it would be remiss of me to not shout out *Broad City* and its fantastic final season episodes that truly reclaimed period humour from men. In 'Getting There', episode nine, Ilana plays on male discomfort around menstruation by donning jeans crotch-stained with period blood to smuggle weed through airport security. Nothing like reclaiming *Superbad*'s period stain narrative, ladies! The next episode, 'Jews on a Plane', sees Abbi unexpectedly hit day one of her period and she and Ilana go on a mission to find suitable protection, but end up with a DIY tampon made with a hand towel and pitta bread.

It was at Tony's Pita in 2021, that I found myself, once again, in a similar situation. On the Tube to Swiss Cottage my Mense Sense tingled and I knew another eggy comrade had begun its bloody descent. Unfortunately, I was wearing grey knickers and a cream knitted dress so I knew a stain would steadily be developing, but luckily my coat was long enough to protect my backside from exposure. I arrived at the small Greek joint, said a quick hello to my then boyfriend and asked the waiter where the loos were. I nearly tripped down the steep stairs in my hurry to assess the damage and once I got into the toilet/storage room and locked the door, I stripped down to my bra and used toilet tissues with industrial hand soap to try and rub the stains out. I did an acceptable job, and after rubbing remnants of tissue paper from the dress and throwing a few sheets in knickers to hold me over, I returned upstairs and told my boyf what happened before my gyros arrived. Maybe in a few years I'll be as confident to rock a period stain as Ilana, but not keeping my shame in is growth, right?

Beyond Western culture, in countries where menstruation is maligned more than most, there are bold steps being taken to both expose the dangers faced by women in oppressive patriarchal societies as well as normalise the experience in others. In the Afghanistan drama, *Osama*, the onset of its lead's period exposes her secret identity and forces her into a marriage without her consent. In Nadine Labaki's *Capernaum*, young Zain has to help his eleven-year-old sister Sahar hide the evidence of her first period so their parents don't sell her off to a local man once they realise she can conceive. Absent are the privileges we have in 'more progressive' countries. Egyptian film *Withered Green* bucked conservative ideals by showing a sanitary towel as part of its lead's menstrual storyline. That historically Islamic law has been against women praying or entering a mosque while 'unclean', it was an especially revolutionary image. Other films across the world highlight the problems that can arise with such silencing expectations on communities, like *Pad Man*. You've got to chuckle that a film 'dubbed the world's first feature film on menstruation' centres on a fella, but Arunachalam Muruganantham, did in fact invent low-cost sanitary pads – because he found out his wife was using old rags as the imported products were too expensive – and distributed them in the Indian subcontinent. Period poverty is an issue that continues to plague the world and it's important that cinema plays a part in reflecting how difficult it can be for people to get access to products.

These recent cinematic gestures, great and small, speak authentically and honestly, but there's always room for improvement. We still must expand our understanding of how periods are experienced by people beyond the cis, straight female experience. Simone de Beauvoir said 'the basic trait of woman: she is the Other'[4], in relation to man as the dominant Subject. Our menstrual experience is part of that othering. But thinker Judith Butler notes De Beauvoir also says that 'one is not born, but rather becomes, a woman,' which they interpret as 'it is our genders which we become, and not our bodies.'[5] Kimberley

---

[4] Beauvoir, Simone de. The Second Sex. United Kingdom, Vintage, 2011
[5] Butler, Judith, 'Sex and Gender in Simone de Beauvoir's Second Sex' (1986) *Yale French Studies,* https://www.jstor.org/stable/2930225?origin=crossref

Peirce's *Boys Don't Cry* presents this dichotomy in a scene where its trans male protagonist, Brandon (Hilary Swank) wakes up in despair to find he has come on his period – betrayed by his body and the sheer exertion of trying to get the period stain out of his jeans. This film came out in 1999, and there hasn't been a great deal of films that have continued this conversation. In 2015's *3 Generations*,[6] Elle Fanning's Ray reacts with 'Thank god' when a doctor tells him his transition will see a drop in his menstrual cycle.

The menstrual cycle can be experienced by those who do and do not identify as women. Period sex can be enjoyed, or endured, in relationships beyond heteronormative romance, beyond white romance, beyond able-bodied romance too. The more we show those diverse experiences, the more compassion we might have for those whose lives differ from our own. It can also show how much we have in common too.

---

[6] *3 Generations* trailer, https://www.youtube.com/watch?v=maUZLJaHhcg

Chapter 10

'I can't even remember to shave my legs.'

– *The Other Woman* (2014)

I WAS GETTING A Groupon facial one day in 2018 when the beauty therapist said, while working on the pores on my chin, 'You need to wax here.'

'Oh really,' I replied, brows furrowed and thinking back to the last time I looked in the mirror and wondering how I might have missed a soul patch developing below my lip.

'Yeah, we do waxing here,' she added bluntly.

Cool, cool, cool, cool. I had twenty minutes left of the procedure and the pan flutes on shuffle were no longer mellowing me out. I kept thinking about the hairs on my chinny chin chin. Were they that noticeable? I know I've got a couple of black hairs that keep me on my toes, but the rest is the brown peach fuzz that's common among women of colour like me. Unless it's more obvious than I realised? Should I have been waxing my face as well as Nairing my upper lip all these years? Did I look like Granny S. Preston in *Bill & Ted's Bogus Journey*, leaning into young Bill for a kiss with gross hairs sprouting from her face?

Suddenly, I was filled with the anxiety and humiliation of my eleven-year-old self after a boy in my class had said I had a moustache. The minute I got home from school, I pulled out one of Dad's Bic razors and shaved off the barely-there hair above my lip, cutting myself in the process and creating another unattractive thing to deal with. Why, Lord, why!!! My fair-featured girlfriends didn't have to worry about this sort of juvenile prejudice. It was the first time I ever felt shame over the natural state of my body hair and, of course, it would be a boy to point it out. For isn't the weaponising of our body hair a patriarchal tool to uphold the tight parameters of femininity? 'Visible body hair on women served as tangible evidence of a surfeit of manliness,' notes Rebecca M. Herzig in her book *Plucked: A History of Hair Removal*, where she asserts that girls and women were expected to exhibit fuzz-free faces and body parts at the turn of the twentieth century:

> Social psychologists, in particular, have found that women who resist shaving their legs are evaluated as 'dirty' or 'gross' and that hairy women are rated as less 'sexually attractive, intelligent, sociable, happy and positive' than visibly hairless women [. . .] The overall effect of the norm, social scientists suggest, is to produce feelings of inadequacy and vulnerability, the sense that women's bodies are problematic 'the way they naturally are.'[1]

I was born with lighter features. My eyebrows, lashes and hair were a caramel colour and the latter had a wave to it more than a curl. Gradually, as I got older and puberty hormones announced themselves, they increased the production of melanin in my body to turn my eyebrows and lashes black and my hair dark brown. My barnet became thicker and curlier too which made styling it a nightmare. Before GHDs arrived, I'd get a blow-dry from a hairdresser and try to make it last as long as possible because I wouldn't be able to recreate the sleek, straightness at home. After I purchased a pair, I'd straighten the ethnic out as often as possible because all my white friends wore it poker straight. After all, it was *the* hair trend of the

---

[1] Herzig, Rebecca M., *Plucked: A History of Hair Removal.*

noughties. It was not really the time or place for natural, untamed curls if movies like *The Princess Diaries* were anything to go by. The dorky female character Mia Thermopolis is mocked by her peers for many things but most obviously her locks. 'What a frizzball,' says one mean classmate, 'look at her hair.' When it's time to get her royal makeover, Mia's head is victim to the most dramatic transformation. I say Mia's, because it wasn't Anne Hathaway's hair, but a wig the cast and crew behind the scenes apparently called 'The Beast', while her unruly eyebrows – nicknamed 'Frida' and 'Kahlo' in reference to the famous, unibrowed German-Mexican artist – took an hour to apply. The scene makes a big deal about the beauty overhaul. Mia is plucked and blow-dried to beyond an inch of her life to achieve a more aspirational Northern European aesthetic that ultimately suggests natural curls and thick eyebrows equates to ugliness. Any young girl watching this with similar hair to pre-makeover Mia no doubt felt as insecure as I did, but when women with African or MENA heritage are more likely to have this sort of appearance, or as they say in Latin America 'pelo malo', the film manages to racially stigmatise us too.

When my underarm and pubic hair began to grow it came out coarse and obnoxiously black, as did the hair on my legs, while the downy fuzz on my face and top of my back became more prominent. I was embarrassed by it. As a teen, I'd shave my armpits, legs and vagina the minute a shadow developed and stole Mum's Nair to deal with my upper lip and cheeks. The post-red blotches be damned! Hair removal habits have long been passed on from female generation to generation, especially since the early 1900s, but according to a 2014 study, on average, white women exhibited less hair than any other race and Asian women had the most, after analysing photos of 2,895 women's faces.[2] It's fitting that my university friend Neena

---

[2] Javorsky, Emilia, 'Race, Rather than Skin Pigmentation, Predicts Facial Hair Growth in Women' (May 2014) *Journal of Clinical and Aesthetic Dermatology*, https://www.ncbi.nlm.nih.gov/pmc/articles/PMC4025516/

introduced me to the practice of threading and when I moved to East London to complete my MA, I saw the beauty treatment offered at every Asian- or Arab-run salon I walked by.

Hair removal has a long history in ancient civilisations across the Mediterranean and the hairless expectation is not limited to the West as other cultures adhere to white beauty standards stemming from colonialism or because of religious doctrine – certain branches of Islam require followers of all gender to keep a clean ship downstairs and under their arms. Threading in Arabic is known as 'khite' and 'fatlah' in Egyptian, and works by using cotton thread to remove vellus and sometimes terminal hair by the root. I'd go a few times to sort out my eyebrows and upper lip, but my pain threshold was too low for that sort of consistent epilation. So for most of my twenties, I resorted to DIY hair removal treatments involving wax, cream and razors that were far cheaper and more private than going to a salon. Everywhere I looked, from magazine articles to TV ads, the message was clear: visible body hair was unacceptable, here's how to fix it. As an avid film fan, I was getting that message from Hollywood too.

At the turn of the twentieth century, right when cinema was establishing itself, women's clothing became less prohibitive and revealed more of their bodies. A big hygiene movement had expanded to perpetuate the myth that body hair was unsanitary and uncivilised, stemming from Darwin's evolutionary theory that suggested excess hair was a sign of 'primitive' ancestry.[3] By keeping themselves tidy, clean and shaven compared to the unruly hair of Black and brown people, white supremacy in the West and across the colonies could prevail. Gillette was part of that problematic myth-making when it released its first razor targeting women – a thinly-veiled attempt to double their profits – that promised, in various magazine advertisements, female customers 'need not be embarrassed' about unsightly body hair when wearing sleeveless garments

---

[3] Herzig, Rebecca M., *Plucked: A History of Hair Removal.*

and later shorter dresses because their Milady Décolleté would keep offending areas 'white and smooth'.[4]

While the women in Georges Meilies films, like 1902's iconic Voyage dans Le Lune, displayed their underarm hair, you could count on Old Hollywood starlets, under strict orders by studios to look the feminine ideal, to lean into that beauty standard. Before the talkies, Joan Crawford was a silent film star and in the 1927 horror film *The Unknown*, her polished pits and legs show no sign of fuzz. I can remember watching on the telly, Esther Williams's movies of the Golden Age, like *Bathing Beauty* and *Million Dollar Mermaid*, where she spent much of the movie in swimwear with nary a hair on show or out of place. Pablo Picasso did a portrait of the star and amusingly painted brown underarm and pubic hair back in place, but to be fair, as a former swimming champion, going hairless was par for the course. Even today, swimmers believe it makes them more streamline in the pool, but other Hollywood actresses in skimpy outfits and bikinis were treating their bodies just the same. In the fifties, Dorothy Dandrige in *Tarzan's Peril*, Jane Russell in *The French Line* and Sandra Dee in *Gidget* appeared hairless while emergency measures were taken during the making of *Singin' in the Rain* when ballerina Cyd Charisse's pubic hair could be seen through her silky costume during the Crazy Veil sequence. Once the problem was fixed, costume designer Walter Plunkett is said to have proclaimed, 'Don't worry, fellas, we've got Cyd Charisse's crotch licked!' [5]

Celebrity facialist Kate Somerville told the *New York Times* that both Marilyn Monroe and Elizabeth Taylor would shave their faces,[6] and if films like *How to Marry a Millionaire* and

[4] Komar, Marlen, 'The Sneaky History Of Why Women Started Shaving' (14 December 2016) https://www.bustle.com/articles/196747-the-sneaky-manipulative-history-of-why-women-started-shaving

[5] Freer, Ian, 'EMPIRE ESSAY: Singin' In The Rain Review' (26 January 2006) https://www.empireonline.com/movies/reviews/empire-essay-singin-rain-review/

[6] Newman, Andrew Adam, 'Sometimes, Even Women Need a Smoothly Shaved Face' (9 June 2015) https://www.nytimes.com/2015/06/11/fashion/sometimes-even-women-need-a-smoothly-shaved-face.html

Suddenly Last Summer are anything to go by, they shaved the
rest of their body hair too. Sophia Loren was an outlier. She
was frequently pictured at glamorous events with her underarm
hair confidently on display, as well as in Alessandro Blasetti's
Too Bad She's Bad, but maybe that's because of her Italian
background. European cinema was certainly not as squeamish
about women's hairy bits as the US. Luis Buñuel's *Un Chien
Andalou*, Ingmar Bergman's *Summer with Monika* and Pier
Paolo Pasolini's *Mamma Rosa* had no qualms showing female
characters with fuzzy pits; and further East, film-makers like
Tetsuji Takechi were capturing women in all their natural glory
as with *Daydream* and *Black Snow*. It would take Italian film-
maker Michelangelo Antonioni and MGM to introduce
American film audiences to pubic hair on screen, albeit briefly
in a long shot, in 1966 upon the release of the London-set
thriller *Blowup*. Even though it contravened censorship rules
instituted thirty years earlier by William Hays via the Motion
Picture Production Code, the morality police weren't being
quite as stringent about depictions of nudity and sex thanks
to more liberal, sexually progressive politics permeating US
society in the sixties. Its box-office and critical success led to
the Hays Code being abolished in 1968 and the establishment
of the Motion Picture Association of America (MPAA) rating
system, which inspired a new wave of film-makers to present
the naked form through erotic dramas, softcore comedies and
hardcore porn.

At first, pubic hair was all the rage. Paul Verhoeven's *Turkish
Delight*, Liliana Cavani's *The Night Porter*, and Ken Russell's
The Devils delivered full-frontal, full-bushed exploits. However,
the notorious 1972 film *Deep Throat*, written and directed by
Gerard Damiano, sees Linda Lovelace shave her vagina in a
symbolic image for the new standard of female body hair in
the coming decades and indicative of how male directors have
long dictated the terms of sexual engagement. Into the eighties
and nineties, porn mags and films increasingly featured women
who were hairless: a culture that influenced fashion to create

skimpier underwear styles that required more pruning in order to achieve clean lines and keep up appearances. There's a scene in Martin Scorsese's *The Wolf of Wall Street* which speaks to this vibe shift perfectly:

JORDAN BELFORT

It's crazy out there, some of these girls you should see them. Oh my god. They're fucking, the things they're doing now, Pops. I mean, it's on a whole other level.

MAX BELFORT

Really?

JORDAN BELFORT

And they're all shaved too.

MAX BELFORT

Get out of here.

JORDAN BELFORT

All shaven.

MAX BELFORT

Are you kidding me?

JORDAN BELFORT

Yeah, no bush.

MAX BELFORT

Bald?

JORDAN BELFORT

Bald as a child down there.

MAX BELFORT

No bush?

JORDAN BELFORT

I know! All of a sudden, one week, nobody had anything down there.

MAX BELFORT

It's the new world.

JORDAN BELFORT

They're bald, bald from the eyebrows down.

MAX BELFORT

Wow.

JORDAN BELFORT

Nothing, not a stitch, it's like . . . lasers.

MAX BELFORT

I was born too early.

JORDAN BELFORT

I've never been a fan of the bush to be honest.

MAX BELFORT

Really. I don't mind it.

This back and forth shows just how male taste plays into women's bodily aesthetics which I experienced when I became sexually active in the late noughties. I believed hair removal was a necessity to be desirable. On several occasions, ex-boyfriends or guys in general made jokes or flinched at the touch, or sight, of stubble on my legs and underarms. One ex would only go down on me if my labia was hair-free and I used to think, yeah, fair enough. It is pretty gross. No grosser than having to pull a pube out of your teeth because you've given your hairy partner a blowjob, though.

French-Algerian film-maker Karin Albou highlights the oppressiveness of waxing in her 2008 film *The Wedding Song*, set in Tunisia during World War II, where a Jewish girl Myriam is required to wax her genitals at the behest of the fiancé she is being forced to marry. The scene that follows is painful to watch; her Muslim friend Nour holds her face while another woman mechanically applies the hot wax to her pubic hair, pulls and Myriam flinches in response. It is the most intimate, honest portrayal of waxing and at no point does it ever feel sexual. 'Albou articulates her critique of such a humiliating and painful practice by fixing the camera silently on Myriam's genitals which are framed in an unsettling extreme close-up,' writes academic Dr. Marzia M. Caporale. 'The spectator's gaze is made to identify with Myriam's as she powerlessly observes the tortuous ritual and experiences the pain of the waxing procedure.'[7]

Julia Ducournau added a waxing scene in her coming-of-age horror *Raw*. 'I really wanted to take the female body outside of its niche and to make it universal,' she told *GQ*. 'You don't need to have had a bikini wax in your life to understand that this is torture.'[8] Neither moment is played for laughs but offers this sort of hair removal with a patriarchal undercurrent. In the US and the UK, you're more likely to see these moments played for laughs. *Bridget Jones's Diary* and *Miss Congeniality* show the pain, but the latter film is so on-brand for the cultural fear of female body hair that, like most shaving ads, there is literally no hair on Sandra Bullock's skin in the first place. Not a comedy but *The Twilight Saga – Breaking Dawn Part 1* similarly shows Bella shaving already hairless legs before her wedding night and it's seen as far more sensual. The very idea that a man might be confronted with unsmooth legs is repulsive, so don't even think about getting naked without sorting them

---

[7] Caporale, Marzia M., 'The Semiotics of Change: Re-writing the Female Body in Contemporary Tunisian Cinema' (2014) *Dalhousie French Studies*, https://www.jstor.org/stable/43487467

[8] Kim, Kristen Yoonsoo, 'The Woman Behind *Raw*, the Horror Movie So Scary It Makes Audiences Pass Out' (12 March 2017) https://www.gq.com/story/raw-julia-ducournau

out first. I watched *One Fine Day* so much as a kid that it subconsciously influenced the way I presented myself to men. The George Clooney and Michelle Pfeiffer rom-com from 1996, about two single parents falling in love over one (not especially) fine day, ends with a scene where Pfeiffer's Melanie excuses herself to the bathroom as things are about to get sexy with Clooney's Jack. 'Let me first freshen up, so I'll feel a little more like a woman and less like a dead mommy,' she tells him before proceeding to brush her teeth, shave her legs and returns to find him asleep. Congratulations, Melanie. You could have fucked Jack, but you're now going to have to wait!

If you don't shave, you've let yourself go and your husband will cheat on you, is what Leslie Mann's Kate believes when she meets his mistress in Nick Cassavetes's *The Other Woman*:

KATE

You have the perfect place and you are the perfect girl and you can probably take off your clothes right now and have no flab and not need a wax or anything and just be ready to go.

CARLY

My situation's pretty situated at all times. It's true.

KATE

And see I am not situated, I can't even remember to shave my legs. I need at least a week of prep minimum.

CARLY

Doesn't Mark see you naked all the time?

KATE

No!

CARLY

Is it like a 70s situation?

KATE

It's like now I'm totally serious, it's not [pause]

CARLY

No man likes that. I'm not saying that you have to be bald or anything like that. I'm just talking about, like, a fig leaf. That's all they want. They just need to have a pretty little patch of happiness.

The Other Woman, written by Melissa Stack, might have pegged itself as a shining example of female solidarity but all this scene does is explicitly reinforce patriarchal gender norms about body hair. That's because the vast majority of female characters that we've watched on screen for the past 100 years have been presented free of excessive body hair, even when the circumstances make zero sense for that aesthetic. Take any apocalyptic or dystopian screen offering like *Lost*, *Mad Max: Fury Road*, and *Divergent*, and ask where do the women find the time? Why would they even bother when their lives are in constant peril? *Wonder Woman* might be the most glaring example of unnecessary hair removal. This is a feminist superhero raised in a matriarchal society without men or gendered beauty expectations, but still, she, and every single one of those Amazonians, is, well, bald from the eyebrows down. Is it a warrior thing? Does it make Diana more streamlined when she's nailing a dude with a punch or a tackle? Or is it simply that hairlessness is so entangled with societal constructs of femininity that to depict strong female characters in any other way would make them look too masculine and reduce their sex appeal? I'm leaning towards the latter.

In *Some Like It Hot* and *Tootsie* there are shaving references and scenes in which male characters, disguising themselves as women, attempt to look more feminine by removing hair and signalling the reduction of their masculinity. But in Beeban Kidron's *To Wong Foo, Thanks for Everything! Julie Newmar*, starring John Leguizamo, Wesley Snipes and Patrick Swayze,

143

these shaving scenes, and shaved bodies, are far more poignant and speak to the pressure on transwomen to adhere to traditional markers of femininity for acceptance. 'There were straight men pretending to be women to get out of trouble or into trouble but this was not that,' Leguizamo said about the history of cis straight actors dressing up as women compared to his 1995 film. 'I was trying to make Chi-Chi a real-life trans character and Patty and Wesley were trying to be real drag queens.'[9] Body hair has historically been used by misogynists, sexists and anti-feminists to demean women, so it's a shame now we are seeing more trans-exclusionary feminists using the same kind of narrative to shame transwomen too.

Body hair in mainstream cinema has a long history of being used as a punchline, like in *Scary Movie* where Bobby has to get a bush trimmer out to tackle Cindy's lady shrubbery, and *Without a Paddle* with the various hairy legs quips made about two hippie girls. In *Revenge of the Nerds*, the line 'We've got bush!' and 'Hair pie!' are now funny T-shirt slogans despite the fact it refers to these male students illegally watching their female peers without their consent. Body hair has also been used as a trope to code women as ugly, as with the dark moustache given to Roseanne Barr's Ruth in *She-Devil* and the unibrow sported by Missi Pyle's Fran Stalinovskovichdavidovitchsky in *Dodgeball*. Female film-makers like Jane Campion, Catherine Breillat and Maren Ade have served to normalise pubic and armpit hair in their respective films *Holy Smoke*, *Anatomy of Hell* and *Toni Erdmann*. Dare I say it, they've managed to make it look aspirational on the big screen too. Mostly, though, period films are where female body hair is at. Film-makers just love to add artistic, historical authenticity to proceedings, though there are still limits to how hairy women can be. In Julie Taymor's *Frida*, Salma

---

[9] Kacala, Alexander, 'How Hollywood heartthrobs and Steven Spielberg helped make a drag queen cult classic' (3 September 2020) https://www.today.com/popculture/how-steven-spielberg-made-film-wong-foo-cult-classic-t190808

Hayek plays the eponymous artist and while she does sport her famous unibrow with pride and shows light underarm hair in one bath scene, her upper lip hair is only depicted at the very end when she's on the verge of death. Kahlo famously accentuated her facial hair in self-portraits; it was a clear part of her identity, both as a female explorer of androgyny and indigenous Mexican. She took ownership of her natural body hair in her art, but the film fails to reflect that reality to the fullest, sanitising what little is shown and ultimately associating upper-lip hair with middle age and declining health. We may have disgraced producer Harvey Weinstein to blame as his company Miramax distributed the film and Hayek has spoken about the toxic gaze through which he wanted the story to be told:

> Halfway through shooting, Harvey turned up on set and complained about Frida's 'unibrow.' He insisted that I eliminate the limp and berated my performance. Then he asked everyone in the room to step out except for me. He told me that the only thing I had going for me was my sex appeal and that there was none of that in this movie.[10]

Elsewhere, Kate Winslet rocked a bush in *The Reader* and grew her underarm in *Ammonite* while Penélope Cruz sported armpit hair in *Captain Corelli's Mandolin*. It shows just how taboo armpit hair continued to be in English-language film that certain critics made note of Cruz's in their reviews despite the fact she has played characters with similar growth in Spanish films like *Brujas*. While filming the 1880s Paris-set drama *Bel Ami*, Christina Ricci made an appearance on *The Graham Norton Show* and revealed her anguish at having to grow her underarm hair out. 'It's not cute,' she told the presenter and fellow guests Ricky Gervais and Stephen

---

[10] Hayek, Salma, 'Harvey Weinstein Is My Monster Too' (13 December 2017) https://www.nytimes.com/interactive/2017/12/13/opinion/contributors / salma-hayek-harvey-weinstein.html?

Merchant.[11] All three men make jokes about braiding it and show disdain for the idea of not shaving, which is rather uncomfortable to watch nowadays, though Gervais makes a valid point as to why producers hadn't also required her to grow her leg hair out. A few years later, Thandiwe Newton visited the BBC talk show and was far less embarrassed about showing off her 'full 70s bush' for her role in *Westworld*. She'd been asked if she required a merkin – a pubic wig – to complete her sex scenes like Amy Landecker did for a naked sunbathing scene in the sixties-set *A Serious Man*. Sometimes they are used in contemporary films to protect an actor's modesty as with Jake Gyllenhaal and Anne Hathaway in *Love and Other Drugs* or in some cases CGI has been used. For *Fifty Shades of Grey*, cinematographer Seamus McGarvey revealed that not only did Dakota Johnson, who played inexperienced student-turned-sexual-submissive Anastasia Steele, have 'a kind of a patch that went over her pubic area', but also pubic hair was added 'in postproduction', in order to cover her privates.[12] I support the representation of pubic hair even if it is a wig or computer effects; it all contributes to the normalisation of natural beauty even if trimmed and tidy still appears to be the most pervasive setting. We still have a long way to go to accepting hairy legs and upper-lip hair onscreen without negative connotations.

At this point, it's hard to disentangle the patriarchal influence over hair, especially when ethnicity comes into play. Recently, I had a very engaging conversation about this and 'The Beauty Myth' with a beautician while she waxed hair from my asshole. The internalised racism women of colour from Arab, African

[11] Ricci, Christina, interview on *The Graham Norton Show* (21 January 2017) https://www.youtube.com/watch?time_continue=167&v=_wnEwtCk3Ng &feature=emb_title&ab_channel=BBC

[12] Ryzik, Melena, 'Shooting Film and TV Sex Scenes: What Really Goes On' (26 February 2015) https://www.nytimes.com/2015/03/01/movies/shooting-film-and-tv-sex-scenes-what-really-goes-on.html?_r=0

and Asian backgrounds have had to contend with because of the veracity of their body hair is a hard thing to shake off. It's all good throwing your razors away when you're a white woman like Miley Cyrus with light, fine hair that looks cute on Instagram, but for, say, a Desi girl with a thick black shadow over their forearms going au naturel is not as simple. Still, even as I've grown to become more accepting of my body and its features, I do wonder how much landscaping has to do with my personal taste or deeply ingrained cultural expectations. If I shave my legs or wax my bikini line,[13] am I doing it because I like the way it looks or am I doing it because society prefers it that way? If I blow-dry my hair straight, am I conforming to a white standard? It's a conundrum that female-identifying persons of all backgrounds face and will continue to face on a daily, weekly, or monthly basis depending on how committed they are to hair maintenance. Maybe if cinema didn't continue to treat body hair as such novelty, the rest of the world would care less about it too.

Now, in my thirties, I don't feel as anxious to streamline myself. I haven't plucked my eyebrows since 2015 and I've fully embraced the wildness of my head of hair by discovering beauty products that embolden my curls rather than flatten them. Hot tip for curly girls: there's a slew of Black beauty products out there that are designed with textured follicles in mind, so why not give the Frizz Ease a break and try Cantu Beauty, for example, instead. When it comes to everything else, well, I play things by ear and only bother when circumstances might require a little pruning. I'm certainly not going back to my youthful days of religious maintenance. I don't have the time, the energy, and am still too cheap to spend all that money! I have too many commitments to worry about how hairy I am

---

[13] My top tip if you're getting it done at a salon is to wear headphones and turn the music up so you can block out the sound of the wax being stripped. It's a lot easier to get through when your mind's distracted and not anticipating the pain, or hearing the hair being ripped!

in public or the sack. So, nowadays, I simply subscribe to Zazie Beetz's way of thinking. The actress of German and African ancestry, plays Domino in *Deadpool 2* and, unlike her super-heroine counterparts, graces the screen with hairy pits. She also rocks her natural afro, which is another big win for women of colour, Black women in particular. But for a film overflowing with barbs and zingers, the fact that not one is made about her body hair is impressive. Not that Beetz was trying to make a statement, she just decided to not shave after her boyfriend suggested she keep it for the character. That is what we call allyship, lads! In an interview with the *Independent* she discusses her position on body hair in general:

> It depends on how I am, but I feel very sexy when my legs are shaven, right? Where does that come from? So I, sometimes intentionally, will let my body hair grow out so I don't feel beholden to that. I will also intentionally go weeks without wearing [make up], in my personal life, if I'm not on set or something like that. Because I never want to get used to seeing my face with things blotted out. I want to always feel comfortable with me just being naked in front of a mirror.[14]

If cinema is going to continue to be a mirror to the world, our society and culture, here's hoping it will start to reflect more female-identifying characters in all their hairy glory.

---

[14] Loughrey, Clarisse, 'Deadpool 2 interview: Zazie Beetz on why Domino embraces armpit hair' (18 May 2018) https://www.independent.co.uk/arts-entertainment/films/features/deadpool-2-domino-armpit-hair-zazie-beetz-interview-cast-a8354601.html

Chapter 11

'You've never double-clicked your mouse?'

– *American Pie* (1999)

MY FIRST ATTEMPT AT masturbation took place when I was fourteen. I was having a bath, began washing myself downstairs and absent-mindedly gave it a stroke. I felt a tingle and tried to remember what that sex ed teacher told us in assembly about female anatomy and pleasure triggers. I think someone had said to me at school that a showerhead could help, so I turned it on and aimed it in that direction, hoping for the best. The best did not arrive. It tickled a little and I thought about kissing my main crush at the time, but my imagination was too vanilla to knock one out to. But after getting the fright of my life from my dad knocking on the bathroom door, I filed the notion of masturbation away for several years and convinced myself it wasn't for me. Who'd have thought a BBC adaptation of *Tess of the d'Urbervilles* would stir my loins enough to revisit the subject again when I was twenty? Not this girl.

I love a classic book-to-screen adaptation and I studied plenty at university. In fact, I wrote about politeness theory in Joe Wright's *Pride and Prejudice* for a Dramatic Discourse module because I was so obsessed with Matthew Macfadyen's Darcy. I interviewed him once for the first season of *Succession* and awkwardly mentioned it to him. He said very kindly that he would have loved to have read the essay, which was of course nice to hear, but I could see the markers of politeness in his response. Anyway, back to 2008, with me watching Gemma Arterton play the eponymous heroine of Thomas Hardy's 1881 novel opposite Eddie Redmayne's Angel Clare. I binge-watched the series on my laptop as BBC iPlayer was around by then and I was sacking off studying after a particularly rowdy night that required I nurse a terrible hangover. But my senses hadn't been dulled enough because soon a scene arrived that began to arouse me. It starts off quite innocently with Tess in her white dress looking solemnly out of the window where light pours in. The man she loves, Angel, approaches her from behind; he pulls her long hair away from her neck and she tilts her head in response to give him access. Violins play romantically as he proceeds to kiss the bare skin of her shoulder, her neck, and her cheek as she slowly turns towards him for a passionate snog. He grips her head with his hands. Cut to them in bed, the strings swell as the camera pans across Angel's back as he thrusts between her legs, spread wide open for him to enter. She grips his bum, pulling him inside, her breast peaking under his arm, as their lips crash together. She whimpers. The sex scene lasts less than thirty seconds, but I must have rewound it and played it again ten times because my hand had instinctively found my clitoris. I was finally ready to give myself an orgasm for the first time. I ended up giving myself three that day.

It seems ridiculous that I had ever convinced myself that masturbation didn't work on me. I would tell my friends that for me it was like being tickled – it only makes you giggle when someone else is doing it. It wasn't like I was unaware self-stimulation was possible. I'd been to my fair share of Ann Summers parties in my late teens, where colourful dildos were passed around and the host would tell us to turn each on, touch our noses with it, and if we sneezed then we were guaranteed to have an orgasm. The rampant rabbit did inspire a small sneeze, sure, but as if I was going to take one of them home and risk my parents finding it. So I left it up to my romantic partners to help me achieve orgasm and that meant I was faking it for the initial few years of my sex life, sadly. It was only at university, during second year with my boyfriend that I climaxed for the first time. He knew which buttons to push and understood that penetration was often not enough to get women off, but by giving him complete control over my ability to orgasm, I was playing into archaic gender roles that allowed men to be dominant and expect women to be submissive.

Women ceding their sexual pleasure to men has allowed female masturbation to remain a taboo longer than the male equivalent. As early as the seventeenth century, the puritanical influence of a Calvinist view of Christianity in the West deemed self-stimulation a perverse slight on God, especially men who were spilling their seed for non-procreation purposes; the wastemen. Some physicians at the time also believed women produced semen and a build-up could cause 'madness from the womb.'[1] Doctors were using orgasms as a way to treat the so-called nervous disorder 'hysteria', a word derived from the Greek to mean 'that which proceeds from the uterus'. Tanya Wexler's *Hysteria* deals with the subject in rom-com fashion, but as is often the case with historical films based on real people, fiction overrides fact: Hugh Dancy's Dr Joseph Mortimer Granville didn't use his electrical vibrator invention to help women but actually to relieve muscular aches in men, so he's not the feminist ally the film presents.[2] Unfortunately, by the Victorian period, most educated women were peddling the argument for female moral superiority as a feminist position. As academic Lynne Segal notes, 'they fully agreed men were biologically hypersexual, but argued that women's natural

---

[1] Berrios, German E. and Lazare Rivière, 'Madness from the womb' (2006) National Library of Medicine, https://pubmed.ncbi.nlm.nih.gov/17146991/

[2] Tunzelmann, Alex von, 'Hysteria: I'm feeling good vibrations' (31 October 2013) https://www.theguardian.com/film/filmblog/2013/oct/31/hysteria-hugh-dancy-reel-history-vibrator

self-restraint and passionlessness provided them with the type of "moral strength" which society now needed.'[3]

Despite the arrival of second-wave feminism to push back on the sexual purity argument for women, the phallocentric theories of Sigmund Freud and other prominent male thinkers on female sexual anatomy continued the focus on heterosexual sex that required a penis to achieve female orgasm. Cinema has long perpetuated this myth; I've lost count of how many times I've watched films where intercourse begins and ends with a man thrusting his penis into a woman and him climaxing, supposedly her too. A study conducted by Zava in 2019 on sex on screen, found that 30% of the films analysed showed couples climaxing in unison, but a Censuswide survey found only 19% of women said they achieved orgasm every time they had intercourse.[4] I'd rarely see attention paid to the female characters either, especially in spontaneous sex scenes where they are never given time to warm up and get wet let alone achieve orgasm. Foreplay? Not on cinema's watch. The assumption is that she's always wet, ready to go and comes when he does, so for many of us watching that was the expectation we held our sex lives to. We believed there was something wrong with us if we didn't reach those euphoric heights, so faked it until we made it. My university boyfriend proved that wrong, but when it came to female masturbation on screen, the films I'd watched made me feel embarrassed about it.

American Pie (1999) is the first film I can remember ever seeing a woman finger herself and it did not end well for her. While getting changed at Jim's house, on her own, foreign exchange student Nadia finds his porno collection and starts to masturbate on his bed. Except, she's not alone because Jim has turned on a webcam and positioned it so he and his male friends can spy on her getting changed while he waits at his

[3] Segal, Lynne, *Straight Sex: Rethinking the Politics of Pleasure.*
[4] Zavamed, 'How Realistic is Sex on Screen', https://www.zavamed.com/uk/sex-on-screen.html

friend's house. It's a scene reminiscent of *Revenge of the Nerds* except its much worse because Jim manages to broadcast the feed to the rest of the school. Both director Paul Weitz's camera and Jim's webcam are designed with male audiences in mind. This exoticised teen's pleasure caters to their sexual fantasy, not to her own, and the amount of time it spends ogling Nadia's body, reinforces the argument of feminist film critic Laura Mulvey that, 'The presence of a woman is an indispensable element of spectacle in normal narrative film, yet her visual presence tends to work against the development of a storyline, to freeze the flow of action in moments of erotic contemplation.'[5] Mulvey popularised the term 'Male Gaze' which suggests the visualisation of women in front of the camera is inherently masculine. In my opinion, a feminine perspective can be just as objectifying of women. But we have been excluded so much and for so long from the sex conversation, and from the director's chair, that we sometimes are unable to differentiate or extract a sexual gaze from a misogynistic one. But in the case of *American Pie*, Nadia's masturbation scene is clearly delivered through a heterosexual, misogynist male lens that seeks to stimulate men at the expense of a female character. The voyeurism ultimately shames Nadia who is sent back to Slovakia because her private pleasure was made public. Of course the woman is punished for having a sexual appetite; not the men who invaded her sexual space without her consent.

Six years earlier, this voyeuristic approach to female masturbation was viewed in *Sliver* with Sharon Stone's character Carly writhing in a bathtub. The film's writer Joe Eszterhas said the scene was 'classily done' in an interview at the time. 'You can't see body parts,' he said. 'She's in a tub. What you see is her face and her arm is moving.'[6] Makes up for the last time Stone did a film with him where the director, Paul Verhoeven, convinced the

---

[5] Mulvey, Laura, *Visual Pleasure and Narrative Cinema*.

[6] Welkos, Robert W., 'More of This . . . Less of This?' (6 May 1993) https://www.latimes.com/archives/la-xpm-1993-05-06-ca-31955-story.html

actor to take her knickers off and spread her legs for an inter-rogation scene, promising she wouldn't be exposed, only for her vagina to be displayed in the final edit. Imagine only finding that breach of confidence out at a test screening? Can never watch *Basic Instinct* the same way again. In *Sliver*, the action is taken in by a camera's lens inside the room and spliced with CCTV footage of the same scene before a shot zooming out reveals that she is being watched on a television, one of many hooked up to surveillance cameras secretly installed across her apartment building by fellow tenant Zeke. That the film ends with Carly destroying his surveillance room returns some of the power she lost from being sexually consumed without her consent. Though not all voyeurism of female masturbation appears designed to turn the male viewer on. Twenty years later, Francois Ozon's *Young & Beautiful* (2013) opens with a binocular view of teenage girl Isabelle on a beach as she's about to take her bikini top off to sunbathe. The watcher is her younger brother who, later, accidentally intrudes on his sister masturbating on her bed with a pillow. Some women need the added friction of an inanimate object – just ask Amy from *Booksmart* – and the fact that Isabelle still has her night clothes on, and the focus isn't on her cum face, stops the scene from being completely objectifying.

American Pie has some redeeming moments for its female cast. Natasha Lyonne's Jessica imparts some self-stimulation wisdom, asking Tara Reid's Vicky, 'You've never double-clicked your mouse?' encouraging her friend to explore her own sexual appetites before servicing her boyfriend's. While Alyson Hannigan's Michelle is sex-positive about it too – though the 'This one time at band camp, I stuck a flute in my pussy,' sounds as much like a ridiculous male fantasy as Nadia getting the urge to masturbate in someone else's house. *Not Another Teen Movie* (2001) would gender-swap the opening *American Pie* masturbation scene (involving Jim and a tube sock) with its female lead Janey. In a funny bit of intertextuality, she's watching *She's All That* – Rachael Leigh Cook's Laney is the primary inspiration for her character – and is turned on by Freddie Prinze Jr wearing a tux so proceeds to pull out a ginormous, florally decorated dildo and insert it into her vagina under the covers. While Jim is only faced with his parents walking in, this film turns the cringe up to eleven by having Janey's brother, dad, grandparents, a priest and a load of kids burst into her bedroom, but she still has the vibrator inside of her, working its orgasmic magic. The film gets props for showing women masturbating, but it's still an excruciating scene that plays on all our shameful fears of being caught in the act.

Black Swan (2010) is a great yet complicated film when it comes to the subject of female sexuality and the problem with repressing our desires, as it's only metaphorically through dance that Natalie Portman's ballerina Nina can climax, which she inevitably dies for. We learn that the sex scene between Nina and frenemy Lily was actually a wet dream and when she attempts autoeroticism – at the behest of her male director to 'go home and touch yourself' – it is interrupted by the horrifying realisation that her mother is in the same room. Portman said it was 'so disgusting' shooting the scene, 'akin to the experience of watching the movie with my parents sitting next to me.'[7] Not the most sex-positive representation of female masturbation if the actor feels as much shame as the character in the scene. Naomi Watts felt similar unease shooting the tearful masturbation scene in David Lynch's *Mulholland Drive* (2001):

> The masturbation scene was particularly difficult and for obvious reasons. First of all, I had a terrible stomachache that day. I was making many visits to the bathroom and obviously, it was butterflies. I was just kind of freaking out. David created this little tent around me in order to make

---

[7] Dichiara, Tom, 'NATALIE PORTMAN SAYS HER "BLACK SWAN" MASTURBATION SCENE IS "SO DISGUSTING"' (30 November 2010) https://www.mtv.com/news/2438013/natalie-portman-black-swan-masturbation-scene/

me feel comfortable and I would go from crying to being angry. I remember saying, hands down the pants, aware of thirty-five people outside of the black tent. I remember saying, 'David I can't do this. I can't do it!' And being mad at him for making me do it. And he just said, 'OK, Naomi. OK, that's OK.' No cut. Not hearing the word 'cut', not hearing any reloading or anything like that. So I remember being pissed. OK, because I'm supposed to be thinking of my lovely friend and imagining her and then I was like, pissed off, but I had to keep doing it. I did crying. I did anger. I don't know, it was just wildly uncomfortable.[8]

Watts's character is trying to masturbate over the thought of her actress friend, a rising star who doesn't requite her affections, so she arranges to have her killed out of personal and professional jealousy. She is crying her eyes out as she tries to rub one out but, of course, cannot. Once again, female masturbation is wrapped up in despair and shame while the actress performing it articulates the social stigma associated with such an act. It certainly highlights why intimacy coordinators (people who choreograph sex scenes) are such a welcome addition to crew lists nowadays to make sets a safer, more comfortable space for actors to work. That's not to say *Mulholland Drive* isn't a brilliant, tragic reflection on the white female experience of Hollywood and the unruly masculine world. It's just its sex-positive representation of female self-stimulation falls short. Other films might encourage praise for this sort of scene while fail in other areas of presenting female sexuality that counters patriarchal control.

Spike Lee's 1986 film *She's Gotta Have It* is one of the very few Western offerings to show female masturbation from a woman of colour's perspective. Tracy Camilla Johns's protagonist Nola Darling was designed to be an empowering figure of Black femininity and sexual liberation in a country that has a history

---

[8] Watts, Naomi and David Lynch interview (17 April 2020) https://www. youtube.com/watch?v=e_BjbaBEyb4&ab_channel=Josip%C4%90olo

of demonising Black women as promiscuous compared to their virtuous white counterparts. 'Women of colour taking control of their own orgasms can then be symbolic of their rejection of racist and sexist social limitations and prioritisation of their own personal fulfilment and pleasure,'[9] writes women's studies professor Megan Tagle Adams. Initially, the film celebrates the freedom she has in taking multiple sex partners and making herself orgasm. That scene is depicted in artistic, self-loving fashion as Nola, lying back on her bed, plays with her breasts before the overhead camera tracks her right hand under the sheets to find her vagina. The camera pans back up her body to her face where her eyes are closed, and yet, she doesn't climax, rather it cuts to her calling one of her suitors, Jamie, to come over. 'Ironically and unfortunately, Nola Darling's sexual desire is not depicted as an autonomous gesture, as an independent longing for sexual expression, satisfaction, and fulfillment,' notes bell hooks.[10] Soon he is calling her a 'freak', raping her from behind and demanding she tell him her pussy is his to which she responds 'yours' and submits. 'As the spectator watches Nola being sexually dominated, any potential rebelliousness in her previous act of masturbation fades away,' adds Tagle Adams.

Masturbation can certainly be observed as an act of rebellion in cinema against the morality police who would seek to neuter its expression, but censors were more likely to punish films with adult ratings when women reap the sexual benefits. The documentary *This Film Is Not Yet Rated* highlighted the fact that the MPAA's rating system would treat movies that involved female orgasm or non-traditional sexual activities with harsher ratings. Jamie Babbitt spoke about her experience with the censors who forced her to cut a masturbation moment in *But I'm a Cheerleader!*

---

[9] Tagle Adams, Megan "Shaming and Reclaiming Women's Sexuality through Cinematic Depictions of Masturbation" American Shame: Stigma and the Body Politic. Indiana University Press, 2016. Project MUSE muse.jhu.edu/book/45578

[10]Hooks, Bell, *Reel to Real: Race, Sex, and Class at the Movies.*

to be rated R rather than NC-17 and more difficult to distribute. This is a movie mainly about LGBTQ love and sex, with zero nudity and no more graphic scenes than *American Pie* (which was rated R) and Nadia's masturbation scene left in. As that movie was primarily about male pleasure, the MPAA's bias seems pretty evident. But things are ultimately improving.

Park Chan-wook's *Stoker* and Paul Verhoeven's *Elle* push female masturbation to more transgressive heights. In the former, Mia Wasikowska's India takes a shower after an attempted rape, but begins fingering herself and climaxes while thinking about how her hot uncle saved her by breaking her attacker's neck. Isabelle Huppert's Michelle looks through binoculars and masturbates while watching her neighbour Patrick set up Christmas lights in his courtyard and she reaches orgasm when they switch on. It subverted the usual man-watching-woman sexual dynamic, but Patrick turns out to be her rapist and she embarks on a rape fantasy affair with him. Both women are sexual assault survivors and 'imperfect victims' due to their complicated, atypical relationships to sex, as depicted in these scenes, as well as their ultimately immoral reactions to criminal behaviour. Their autoeroticism can both be seen as a celebration and critique of sexual autonomy. Steven Shainberg would present this duality in blackly comedic form in *Secretary*. His masochistic lead Lee (Maggie Gyllenhaal) has mental health issues, including self-harm, and it lays the foundation for her to become a submissive secretary to her dominant boss E. Edward Grey. In the Mary Gaitskill original short story, Lee frequently masturbates at the thought of her lawyer employer and his domineering behaviour. Shainberg gives Lee her sexual autonomy in an upbeat sequence that sees the secretary go from on her front to her back bringing herself to orgasm while fantasising. While some might wince at a taboo BDSM relationship given the happily-ever-after treatment, the masturbation sequence serves female pleasure pretty well.

Jane Campion's *In the Cut* similarly has her female protagonist fantasising about an enigmatic man in power while getting herself off. I can remember the promotional tour of this film and the negative press its star Meg Ryan was getting. From being slut-shamed for her nudity to her past affair with Russell Crowe, and even for a supposedly defensive appearance on BBC talk show *Parkinson*, many used the film as a marker for the end of her career. Critical reappraisal since its 2003 release has seen it and her performance be treated more favourably. It's somewhat ridiculous to think of the backlash Ryan received. This is an actress whose most famous film scene involves her faking an orgasm so well it inspires a fellow diner to say, 'I'll have what she's having.' The idea that seeing her as a forty-something, mousey-haired schoolteacher getting naked, enjoying sex and getting herself off would be frowned upon makes me want to kick a guy in the nuts. Such is the Madonna-Whore binary that Hollywood women can only be seen one way or the other, but at least Campion's defiant casting of an American sweetheart has something to show for it. When Frannie masturbates she's wearing a vest and knickers, lying on her bed front facing and recreating a sexual scene in her mind, placing Mark Ruffalo's Detective Malloy in the position of the faceless male participant. There's no nudity, her toes curl, her bum raises a little as she massages her clit, and when she climaxes she sighs 'oh shit' before turning over to recover from the sensation. It's erotic, but a relatable image of female masturbation that doesn't cater to an over-the-top male fantasy of what women should look like in the throes of self-inflicted passion, unlike, say, Abdellatif Kechiche's *Blue Is the Warmest Colour*. In the early stages of his film, Adèle Exarchopoulos's fifteen-year-old character Adèle wanks while dreaming of the blue-haired student Emma she'd briefly seen on the street. The scene cuts between her playing with her own breasts, grabbing her body, fingering her vagina under her trackies and arching her back energetically, with Emma, played by Léa Seydoux, sucking her body, between her legs, and squeezing her nipples. It's certainly not the most explicit sex scene in the film, or longest, but it's gruelling to the point of, as Mulvey puts it, freezing the flow of action in moments of erotic contemplation that reeks of an overindulgent male director.

HANNA FLINT

Alternatively, Gary Ross's *Pleasantville* uses female masturbation to move the plot forward and signal an immediate change in perspective. This might be the first cinematic representation of sex-positive female wanking I'd ever seen. Joan Allen's unworldly housewife Betty discovers sexual pleasure after a frank conversation with her 'daughter' Mary-Sue/Jennifer, played by Reese Witherspoon, who has been transported with her brother from the present into the world of a 1950s sitcom. 'Well, you know, Mom,' Mary-Sue says. 'There are ways to enjoy yourself without Dad.' Inspired, Betty takes a bath while her husband gets into a twin bed they do not share, and soon enough, with a close-up of her face, we see her utter a fair few 'oh mys' and 'oh my goodnesses'. As she looks around, colourful items appear, juxtaposing with the black-and-white world she has only ever known. Betty's waking up to a new way of life in vivid Technicolor with her climax ultimately symbolised by a tree that erupts into orange flames on her front lawn. Whether it connotes a burning bush or the tree of knowledge setting alight, the reappropriation of religious imagery for Betty's sexual awakening is extremely well placed.

That sort of playful self-discovery is amped up in, my fave, Maggie Carey's *The To Do List*. Aubrey Plaza's Brandy begins on her back frantically trying to flick her bean above and below her panty material before cutting to her sexual fantasy with a local lifeguard applying sunscreen to her back, before returning to the image of her riding a pillow screaming, 'Yes, aloe vera!' as she comes. 'We had blocked the scene, and I was back at the monitor,' Carey recalls. 'Aubrey was like, "Mags, come back in here, I have a question," and she was like, "Is that too much?" and I was like, "We have to do that. Nothing is too much in this movie." Aubrey is game for anything, she'll try anything; she's not afraid to be vulnerable or put herself in awkward positions.'[11]

Speaking of awkward positions, my mind was blown away at the Toronto Film Festival premiere of Claire Denis's *High*

[11] Greco, Patti, 'The *To-Do* List Director Maggie Carey on Casting Connie Britton and Aubrey Plaza's Masturbation Scene' (23 July 2013) https://www.vulture.com/2013/07/to-do-list-director-maggie-carey-interview.html

Life at Roy Thomson Hall, where a packed audience watched a naked Juliette Binoche ride a mechanical dildo in one of the most exuberant autoerotic scenes I've ever witnessed on the big screen. But even as Dr Dibs wildly rides in the 'fuckbox', her character never achieves orgasm. 'The fuckbox, a terrible place to be alone, not like masturbating in a bed,' says Denis. 'The privacy in the fuckbox is horrible, and to try to come is impossible. It looks like a sword! In the fuckbox, you cannot feel enough. It is too mechanical.'[12]

I feel that. I've tried in the past to use a dildo but the noise, the texture and the added effort of having to use both hands has never really appealed. Especially as I mostly masturbate as part of my night-time ritual so *la petite mort* can help me into a state of unconsciousness. Normally, I get into bed, look at Twitter, Instagram, TikTok, then read a comic via the Kindle app on my phone before loading up a porno. I hold my phone in one hand, pay my clit a visit with the other and (thanks to a decade of trial-and-erroring the exact pace and finger-tekkers I require), make myself come seven to eight minutes later. Maybe I should print my own cooking instructions. Masturbation has become an essential sleep-aid to relax my overactive, anxious mind that is frustratingly able to conjure up a million worst-case scenarios before bed, but not strong enough to imagine a sexual sequence that might get me off without a screen stimulant. I guess I'm simply living up to my job title. Still, it's always rather mundane compared to the dramatic autoeroticism of many of the previous films I've mentioned. That's why I love Guillermo del Toro for managing to capture the often-humdrum nature of it so perfectly in *The Shape of Water*. Sally Hawkins's Elise achieves orgasm between waking up, having a bath and boiling an egg for breakfast. The script, co-written by del Toro and Vanessa Taylor, makes masturbation as much a part of her

---

[12] Brameso, Charles, 'Claire Denis on *High Life*' (13 September 2018) https://www.vulture.com/2018/09/claire-denis-on-putting-juliette-binoche-in-a-fuckbox.html

morning routine as shining her shoes. 'We are used to either never depicting female sexuality, or depicting it in a glamorised, artificial way,' del Toro said at the time.

Other film-makers of the last decade have similarly shown that masturbating can be an unromantic part of self-care as well as ensuring it's not laced with shame should a second party interrupt. Hala, the teenage, Pakistani-American Muslim protagonist in Minhal Baig's coming-of-age 2019 film of the same name is pleasuring herself in the bath but stops when her mother calls out to her. The look on her face is not one of embarrassment but one of annoyance as with Alejandra's in Amat Escalante's *The Untamed* when her sons disrupt her shower attempt and Leila's in Channel 4 series *The Bisexual*, where the sexual antics she can hear through the wall kills her mojo. *Sex and the City* really hammered home that flicking my bean was very much an important form of female pleasure and the heroic Samantha, 'I'm masturbating, I told you I'd be doing that all day', Jones was its most ardent advocate. The HBO series really wanked so the likes of *Insecure*, *Sex Education*, and *I Hate Suzie* could rub out welcome, relatable millennial and Gen Z perspectives on the subject. The world certainly needs to see it, especially here in the UK. According to a recent survey, in 2021, men will knock one out 174 times a year, on average, compared with women who will only do so 59 times in what's called 'the masturbation gap'.[13] The figure for that year was 66% but the year before it was 76%, so maybe the increase in representations of female masturbation in cinema is having a positive effect. The history of female self-pleasure on screen has had its ups and downs, but one thing's for certain: the extraordinary can be produced by the ordinary, especially when you do it yourself.

---

[13] Moss, Rachel, 'This Is How Many Times A Year Women Masturbate, Compared To Men' (16 August 2021) https://www.huffingtonpost.co.uk/entry/how-often-do-men-and-women-masturbate_uk_611a2f5ee4b0454ed70f7b27

Chapter 12

'Let me just make sure of something . . . This is a giant cock.'

– Boogie Nights (1997)

FOR MY EIGHTH OR ninth birthday my parents got me a little portable TV. We'd moved from our two-bed flat in Chiswick to a small semi-detached in Isleworth, and for the first time I got a room to myself. My brothers weren't so lucky just yet, but as Nick was at his mum's in Brixton most of the time, Karim mostly had his lay of the land and I couldn't wait to be able to watch my shows without having to share my room. My parents got the little silver number from Currys at a discount because it was a display model and had a few scratches. I didn't care. It was like winning a conveyor-belt prize on the *Generation Game* and I couldn't wait to explore a world of television at my own convenience, especially the shows that aired after my parents sent me to bed. I'd turn the volume down so it was barely perceptible, have the remote in my hand ready to switch it off at the slightest creak outside my room, and tune into whatever was playing. But the show I always stayed awake for was *Eurotrash*.

Do you remember that series, millennials and above? It aired on Channel 4 from 1993 to 2004 and was the most ridiculously camp and, obviously, trashy magazine show filled with bonkers people from across Europe who got up to variously naughty and risqué hijinks and capers. My young eyes couldn't look away. The suited-and-booted Antoine de Caunes was its long-serving, debonair host with his seductive voice. Well, maybe it wasn't seductive, it was just him speaking English with a French accent, but his teasing winks to camera and innuendo-dropping with abandon, was as amusing as the cultural clips from the continent that frequently involved scantily-clad people getting their kink on. I can still hear Maria McErlane's playful voiceover as she narrated the antics, from naked German men to puppet giraffes, with plenty of boobs and bums to boot. In the dark privacy of my little box room, I fed my growing sexual curiosity each night, before I was aware that I was going to become hypersexualised myself, whether I liked it or not. In hindsight, it was probably my first introduction to pornography, albeit, softcore. It premiered pre-Internet and the films I was watching were firmly in the PG and U ratings bracket.

When we moved to Doncaster, the first 18-certificate movie I saw was in year seven at the birthday sleepover of a friend who had chosen *Scream* (and *Arachnophobia*) for us to watch, but the adult rating was for violence and not the tame sex scene involved. I'd see lads' mags in the corner shop, Page 3 girls in the paper and gorgeous models and actresses in various states of undress on boys' bedroom walls. But when it came to video porn, I had limited experience other than *Eurotrash*. Most of us were raised to see pornography as a deviant form of entertainment, and in some ways, for good reason. The industry hasn't historically been too fair to the women involved. Female porn stars may very well be the most desired subject for such sexual imagery, and the gender pay gap tilts in their favour, but too many have been exploited, underpaid and abused by men on both sides of the camera in a system that is hard to regulate. As a young woman in my twenties, I was increasingly cognisant of the problematic nature of the (mainstream) porn world. Feminists I was aware of, including my mum, called it a shameful, unethical racket that both damaged the perception of girls and women and caused an adverse effect on young men's attitudes to sex because of the unrealistic standards the various films set. It's why in movies mothers, not fathers, often get so mad when they find their sons engaging with porn or their collection. Jim's mum gets upset when she sees her son accessing illegal porn channels on his bedroom TV in *American Pie*, while Rory in *Final Destination 2* gives fellow survivor Kim his keys so she can remove any incriminating items from his place in case of his demise. 'Would you take these?' he says. 'And if I die, will you throw out all my drugs, my paraphernalia, my porno, you know, anything that's gonna break my mom's heart.'

There have been several feature films made about adult entertainment and its stars that romanticise the industry. *The Girl Next Door* and *Zack and Miri Make a Porno* endeared adult entertainment to me with its playful depiction of porn stars with hearts of gold and amateur film-makers highlighting the chill, relatable nature of a porn set. Using porn stars to deliver sex education in the former seemed like a pretty great way to mould young minds, especially boys, who were already accessing such material, but according to the British Board of Film Classification (BBFC), 'sex works containing clear images of real sex, strong fetish material, sexually explicit animated images, or other very strong sexual images will be confined to the R18 category.'[1] Paul Thomas Anderson's *Boogie Nights* might be the most celebrated film about porn, and it was my first introduction to him as a film-maker. My parents had the VHS tape and I remember watching it when they were out in maybe year nine or ten and being sucked into this grainy counterculture world of carnal pleasure. The opening one-shot of the camera gliding through the night club, like the Copa shot in *Goodfellas*, introduces the key

---

[1] https://www.bbfc.co.uk/about-classification/research/classification-guidelines-report-2019.

players through a seductive haze soundtracked by The Emotions' 'Best of My Love'. You wanted to know these people, be friends with them – Heather Grahams's roller girl was particularly entrancing to me and I think about her every time I put my own skates on. But Anderson doesn't entirely glamourise the industry. The latter section gets dark as it enters the drug-fuelled excess of the eighties, but it certainly shows an affection for the seventies' Golden Age of Porn, where people consumed pornography together in a theatre and directors like Burt Reynolds' Jack Horner wanted to make films for more than guys to jerk off to.

JACK HORNER

How do you keep them in the theater after they've come? The beauty and the acting. No, I understand you've got to get 'em in the theater. You know, you've got to get the seats full. But I don't want to make a film where they show up, they sit down, they jack off, and they get up and they get out before the story ends. It is my dream, it is my goal, it is my idea to make a film where the story just sucks them in. And when they spurt out that joy juice, they've got to just sit in it. They can't move until they find out how the story ends. You know, I want to make a film like that. And I understand, they have to make films . . . I've made them myself, you know where there's a few laughs, everyone fucks their brains out. And that's fine. But it's my dream to make a film that is true and right and dramatic.

Boogie Nights is as much a film about porn as it is about the slow death of cinema. The dawn of the video tape and the anxiety felt by film-makers who saw the cheaper technology as an affront to their artistic integrity. Still, it's a film that bottles the essence of porno chic that became somewhat aspirational for film-makers taking bolder steps when it came to sex on screen. It began in the US with Andy Warhol's *Blue Movie*, released in 1969, the first film to get a wide theatrical release across the country despite its explicit sexual content. The notorious Linda Lovelace-led *Deep Throat* followed in 1972 after American national treasures Johnny Carson and Bob Hope referenced the film on television. It was a commercial success. Critics and journalists were covering the releases in newspapers because it was edgy, popular and seemed to get the people going. For a hot minute, many in the film and adjacent industries believed porn and cinema could get it on. 'In this imagined future, explicit sex acts would be naturally integrated into narrative films, not to deliver the regular doses of pleasure and requisite numbers of "money shots" required by the porn genre but to expand the representative power of the medium into the realm of the "performance" of sex,' Linda Williams writes. 'In this imagined future pornography as such would disappear, porn stars would cross over to the mainstream, and respected actors would consider the performance of sex acts part of the challenge of their craft.'[2]

Alas, that didn't materialise thanks to a Supreme Court decision in 1973, Miller v. California, where the definition of obscenity changed from 'utterly without socially redeeming value' to lacking 'serious literary, artistic, political, or scientific value'. This led to porn across the board being targeted and, in many cases, banned by local governances from being produced and distributed into the mainstream. The cinematic quality of porn films dipped too, the stars were not taken seriously as actors and, as with *Boogie Nights*, the arrival of home video meant artistry came secondary to the money shot.

---

[2] Williams, Linda, 'Cinema and the Sex Act' (2001) *Cinéaste,* https://www.jstor.org/stable/41689431

FLOYD GONDOLLI

I'm not a complicated man. I like cinema.
In particular, I like to see people fucking on film.
But, I don't want to win an Oscar and I don't want
to re-invent the wheel.

It's easy to forget that while the sex is un-simulated, porn scenes are just as contrived as mainstream cinema. They involve lots of takes, cuts, edits, acting, directing, hair and make-up, costume, lighting, production design and other such film-making detail to achieve scripted sexual fantasies to varying degrees of exaggeration, intensity and violence. Visit YouPorn or PornHub and you will see videos involve some seriously gruelling, aggressive or violent versions of sex for the benefit of its targeted male viewers. It's one thing to be dominated, another to be practically assaulted with a dick or three smashing into every orifice. The less romantic options focus on women giving head or being penetrated. Sometimes a scene will open with the female actor masturbating, but that's less about her pleasure and more about the male viewer, as a guy often shows up before she's had the chance to climax. Unless it's a rape fantasy. She'll be depicted as a willing participant: agreeing to be slapped, spanked, choked, gang-banged or receive any sexual punishment or injury before taking the notorious cum-shot. In her mouth, in her vagina, on her back, on her ass, in her ass, on her tits or on her face? Take your pick with one click!

She might passionately moan and utter epithets of enjoyment, but does she actually orgasm? A man ejaculating almost always marks the end of a scene. Unless it's two women getting each other off. With such a prominent focus on male desires, it's no wonder many men fail to deliver women pleasure in bed or even know how to do it. Especially when a female partner doesn't react the way the performer does in a video. Joseph Gordon-Levitt tackled the subject of porn addiction in his 2013 directorial debut *Don Jon*, where he plays a Catholic bartender from New Jersey who can't maintain a relationship with a woman because of his obsession with porn. 'The message *Don Jon* is trying to bring to light—and make fun of—is reducing people, especially women, to nothing but sex objects,' Gordon-Levitt said of the film,[3] in which he plays the titular character involved in a love quadrangle between Scarlett Johansson's bombshell, Julianne Moore's worldly older woman and his laptop.

Non-pornographic film-makers delivering sex scenes certainly have the acceptability of avant-garde/Hollywood gloss to fall back on. That and its mostly non-graphic, simulated sex to ensure it gets wider theatrical distribution with a lower age rating. Still, there have been a fair few directors who have chosen to feature un-simulated sex in order to add some artistic authenticity to their narratives. *Bad Luck Banging or Loony Porn* begins by showing an energetic, smartphone-shot sex tape between a teacher (Katia Pascariu) and her husband (porn actor Stefan Steel) that will become the subject of contention for the rest of the film after he uploads it to a private fetish site and it gets downloaded and published to wider porn sites. That I closed my blinds to watch a review copy at home one afternoon only highlights the societal shame associated with the sex acts embedded in the film. Film-maker Radu Jude is asking us: what is obscene? The porn video or a society that sees sex acts between two consenting adults as obscene?

For *Nymphomaniac I & II*, Lars von Trier hired porn actors to perform intercourse that was later superimposed on the scenes of cast members faking the same act. 'We shot the actors pretending to have sex and then had the body doubles, who really did have sex, and in post we will digitally impose the two,' producer Louise Vesth said. 'So above the waist it

---

[3] Rottenberg, Josh, 'The Real Don Jons: How online porn has affected a generation' (26 September 2013) https://ew.com/article/2013/09/26/real-don-jons-porn/

will be the star and below the waist it will be the doubles.'[4] Von Trier had previously hired porn stars for his 1998 film *The Idiots*, to stand in for a couple in a group sex scene, shown having vaginal intercourse for a few seconds. Linda Williams suggests 'a raw primitivism emerges in contrast to romantic prettiness' out of the film,[5] while British critic Mark Kermode was famously booted out of the Cannes film for shouting 'il a merde!' several times. It's unclear whether his removal was down to the disruption or his bad French but there's no sex scene in Von Trier's wheelhouse that has earned quite so much ire as that depicted in his 2009 film *Antichrist* which takes genital mutilation to graphic new levels. I'll take an erect penis over a sliced clitoris, thank you very much, Lars!

Elsewhere, French film-maker and novelist Catherine Breillat has become synonymous with the cinematically explicit in her interrogation of female sexuality under the shadow of patriarchy through such works as *Fat Girl*, *Anatomy of Hell* and *Romance* which starred bona fide Italian porn star Rocco Siffredi. It was thrilling to see him in action having climaxed to some of his more *exotic* work. What's striking about *Romance* is nothing seems that gratuitous: it has a naturalistic, honest feel to sex as a young woman pushes the boundaries of her sexual freedom through adultery because her partner refuses to fuck her. 'Pornography was a manifesto. I have the right to make pornography,' Breillat says. 'And it's not pornography; it's art because it tells something and it removes preconceived ideas; and these preconceived ideas that have been repeatedly hammered into us need to be removed.' The seventies porn films *Behind the Green Door* and *The Devil in Miss Jones* and their ability to

---

[4] Roxborough, Scott, 'Cannes: "Nymphomaniac" Producer Reveals Graphics Are Used in "Groundbreaking" Sex Scenes' (20 May 2013) https://www.hollywoodreporter.com/movies/movie-news/cannes-nymphomaniac-producer-sex-scenes-525666/

[5] Williams, Linda, 'Cinema and the Sex Act' (2001) *Cinéaste,* https://www.jstor.org/stable/41689431

connect 'sex and fiction' were a massive influence on Breillat overcoming shame in herself and her work: 'The porn industry separates sex from fiction, therefore from the soul. Which means there's sex and there's pornography, therefore there's no soul, no person, no characters anymore; there's only flesh.'[6]

The first time I accessed a porn site it was with my boyfriend at uni as part of a night of passion. He suggested it, of course, so we clicked on one of the more romantic-looking offerings to ease me in and within ten minutes he was easing himself into me. It was a turn on for sure, but once I taught myself how to masturbate and became a single woman, I was increasingly looking to understand myself better and my desires on my own terms. And once I realised I couldn't make myself come with just my imagination, both erotic cinema and porn became an exploratory avenue to work out my kinks. I began searching YouTube and Google for cinematic sex scenes that might provide the visual stimulation I needed. It's funny how many movies there are where I've only seen the sex parts: *Embrace of the Vampire*, *Original Sin* and *Raw Justice* were a few I stumbled upon, but I'd also revisit erotic thrillers like *The Devil's Advocate*. OK, maybe it's not an erotic thriller, but there's one sex scene that was pretty thrilling to me. I'm surely not the first, or the last, person to knock one out to a bit of simulated sex from a movie. In Karen Maine's *Yes, God, Yes*, Natalia Dyer's Catholic schoolgirl ends up masturbating to the car sex scene in *Titanic*. We've all been there, Alice!

As a curious sexual being, living without the worry of people barging in or scouring my browsing history, I slowly graduated from erotic movie scenes to hentai. Maybe it's the *Pokémon* fan in me, but the animated form allowed me to explore a wider, more graphic array of pornographic videos that didn't see a

6   Maas, Sofie Cato, 'The Gaze of Shame: A Conversation with Catherine Breillat' (21 October 2019) https://mubi.com/notebook/posts/the-gaze-of-shame-a-conversation-with-catherine-breillat

real-life woman being exploited for it. There were giggling
schoolgirls having sex with a male classmate in a locker room,
a boss having sex with his secretary against his office window
that was not unlike that scene in *Shame* where Michael
Fassbender is banging Nicole Beharie against the floor-to-ceiling
glass of his hotel room. I was a particular fan of this medieval
scene between a long-haired lothario who would shag a beer
maiden against a cave wall. Couldn't understand a word they
were saying but at least these animated videos offered the foreplay that most live-action videos weren't supplying. The
suggested videos on the side did send me down several hentai
rabbit holes. I watched centaurs fucking, zombies fucking and
tentacled monsters fucking that made me wonder if the directors
behind *The Untamed* and *Elle* had come across the same videos.
When I rewatched *Boogie Nights* in my twenties I was inspired
to check out more vintage offerings, and the cinephile in me
very much appreciated the production value and the more
natural bodies of men and women that seem so foreign to the
hard, hairless bodies of today's industry. I love me a moustache,
I love me a hairy chest and I love to see a full bush on a woman
too because it made me less willing to adhere to a bare standard.
'Lesbian' porn taught me more about the different types of
sexual pleasure for women than any heterosexual offering,
although I've never had a real-life inclination to have sex with
a woman. Apart from that one threesome. Neuroscientist Ogi
Ogas says 'sexual fantasy obeys its own set of rules that have
nothing to do with propriety, common sense, or even the physical laws of the universe.'[7] This explains a lot about my evolving
porn-viewing habits because I was able to navigate an online
world and cut through the more negative sexual depictions to

7 Khazan, Olga, 'Why Straight Men Gaze at Gay Women' (8 March 2016) https://
www.theatlantic.com/health/archive/2016/03/straight-men-and-lesbian-porn/
472521/?utm_campaign=the-atlantic&utm_medium=social&utm_source=face
book&fbclid=IwAR0CtpbxHWFMrx7yk-NoYcLbNiCGHjItgrgu9ixETF6U
W9nqfvpXJD38wLc

find videos more in-keeping with what I desired. As the late porn star, director and sex-positive feminist Candida Royalle once said:

> Porn can deliver you there at best, or disgust you at worst. It all depends on what you choose to watch. With the availability of porn online, it's possible to sample enough porn quickly that you don't have to find yourself watching wall-to-wall hard-core sex if it's plot driven erotica that appeals to you. You're only a victim of bad porn if you let yourself be.[8]

That's certainly easy to say as an adult viewer of porn with the shame around sex and female desire very slowly being dismantled, but what if you're the actor? The documentary *Hot Girls Wanted* explores the problematic reality of young women wanting to escape depressing home lives or banal jobs for a more exotic career in pro-amateur porn that almost always ends with disappointment. The film argues that for many women entering the industry, via Craigslist ads, it is out of financial necessity. That shadow hovers over their decisions to undertake scenes and performances they feel uncomfortable with, and the monetary compensation is never as much as they were led to believe. 'Being a porn star was very expensive,' former porn actor Tressa Silguero says in the film. 'Rent, nails, makeup, food, flights, and then 10 percent for Riley [her agent]. I only made $25,000 in four months. And after I got out, I had $2,000 in my bank account.'[9]

Ninja Thyberg's *Pleasure* observes 'Bella' (newcomer Sofia Kappel) a young Swedish woman trying to break into the LA porn industry. This film might be fictional but it's very much

---

[8] https://www.nytimes.com/roomfordebate/2012/11/11/does-pornography-deserve-its-bad-rap/pornography-can-be-good-for-consumers

[9] *Hot Girls Wanted*, https://subslikescript.com/movie/Hot_Girls_Wanted-4382552

immersed in the reality of adult entertainment that features recognisable members of the industry playing characters or themselves. One sequence really stuck out when I saw it as part of Sundance film festival. Bella takes part in a BDSM shoot with a female director where emphasis is placed on consent, comfortability, choreography and ensuring the set was a safe space for both her and the male actor to work in. It's almost a dreamlike scenario that screams sex positivity for those involved and those watching this sort of consensual sexual roughness. Next, the film shows the harrowing contrast when a male director is in charge of a scene where 'rough' is an understatement. Thyberg's intimate camera has you wincing at every hit, slap and choke Bella is dealt without warning and is completely overwhelmed by.

It represents every abusive, violating scene female performers are expected to undertake and is grotesque to watch. It's the type of scene that legitimises the aggressive violence employed by men towards female-identifying women in the real world in the guise of sexual pleasure. I remember being choked out of the blue during a one-night stand with the brother of a guy I knew. I was shocked by it, told him I couldn't breathe and he removed his hand immediately, but the damage was done. Another guy I dated tried it and I was more confrontational, asking him why he choked me. He said another girl was into it and I pointed out that just because one person enjoyed it, not everyone does. We certainly need to stop assuming that everyone has the same sexual appetites and get better at articulating our preferences without being caught off-guard by sexual violence. It's a team effort and while I hope women reading this might develop the confidence to speak up in the bedroom and say 'no' where necessary, I want men to remember as much as cinema and porn have positioned your pleasure as dominant, in real life it should never be the sole rule for sexual engagement. And, of course, 'no' means 'FUCKING NO, STOP, I DO NOT CONSENT.'

Maybe my biggest takeaway from *Pleasure* is the porn industry – and most industries actually – would be a lot safer, less negatively influential and exploitative for everyone involved if women were in charge. Personally, after years of watching the good, the bad and weird of porn I've come to the point where I only visit sites like Bellesa, a female-run company that produces its own films and curates other female-made, ethically-sourced videos. Erika Lust's streaming sites XConfessions, Lust Cinema, and Else Cinema similarly promote the ethical tenets of fair pay, diversity, transparency, safe sex and equal pleasure. They maintain that there is nothing wrong with having sex, kinks or carnal appetites that might diverge from societal expectations,[10] at a time when the very natural activity of sex continues to be shrouded in shameful secrecy. If we can extinguish the associated taboo and have a public dialogue then maybe people would demand more from pornography and its imperfect industry instead of expecting the BBFC to classify as 18 'the strongest sex references, in particular those that use the language of pornography';[11] to be less exploitative of women and marginalised individuals; to reduce the criminality that too frequently overlaps (e.g. sex trafficking and revenge porn). Because pornography can and has taught many of us about our sexual selves that conventional sex education outlets just haven't. In fact, a recent study into women watching porn found that 'more frequent pornography use was generally associated with more favorable sexual response outcomes during masturbation, while not affecting most partnered sex parameters.'[12] If cinema can provide a reflection of the world

---

[10] Except, of course, bestiality, rape or paedophiliac content.

[11] BBFC Annual Report and Accounts 2019.

[12] McNabney, Sean M., Krisztina Hevesi and David L. Rowland, 'Effects of Pornography Use and Demographic Parameters on Sexual Response during Masturbation and Partnered Sex in Women' (2020) *International Journal of Environmental Research and Public Health*, https://www.mdpi.com/1660-4601/17/9/3130/htm

we live in, why can't pornography reflect our sexual worlds too? Done the ethical, consensual and compassionate way, porn could provide the further education every single one of us needs in order to enjoy full, happy and healthy sex lives without the stigma.

Part Four

Workplace Drama

Chapter 13

'My native habitat is the Theater.'

– All About Eve (1950)

IF THERE WAS EVER a Flint-Cole family pastime to be passed on to future generations, it would be watching movies. There was truly no more unifying act in our household than sitting down at the local cinema, or in front of our telly with a rental, and escaping into cinematic realms of action, adventure, horror, comedy, romance, you name it! Our ardent affection was communally felt and we'd get just as much enjoyment debating the merits of a film after the credits rolled as we did watching. If the film was particularly bad, even more so. We'd record films off the TV onto blank video tapes – and I'm pretty sure my childhood appearance on *Playdays* was recorded over to make room for some eighties actioner – but my favourite had *Krull, Teen Wolf* and *Die Hard with a Vengeance* awkwardly cut without the advert breaks into a triple bill. Dad has been a subscriber to *Empire* magazine since its first issue in 1989 and Karim and I would fight over who got to read it after he was done. When it was my turn, I'd always go to the back of the mag first to read which classic scene had been featured that month. Every week, we'd watch *Film* with Barry Norman, then with Jonathan Ross when he took over, and tuned into Mark Kermode's film reviews on the radio to find out what was worth watching at the weekend. I'd spend many an hour browsing the shelves of HMV and Blockbuster to see which films released before I was born, or before I was old enough to watch, might be worth spending a few pounds to buy or rent. Though it wouldn't be until I was into my twenties that I would entertain the idea of becoming a film critic myself.

I did dream of becoming an actress, though. Didn't we all? It all looked so marvellously glamorous. Surely making films would be just as much fun as watching them; certainly rom-coms where you'd get to kiss hot dudes and get paid a pretty penny for the privilege. My cinematic tastes as a teen were not as broad as they are today, but the idea of getting to put on a character's clothes and personality for a living, to pretend to be someone else entirely, was desirable to me as a kid. I got an A* in GCSE Drama, which I put down to my stirring performance as Gail in John Godber's *Teechers*, but honestly, going on to act was not something I took that seriously. In Doncaster the opportunities for amateur dramatics, let alone with British Arab girls, weren't exactly bountiful. That and an early rejection from being in the first *Harry Potter* film. There was an open call on *Newsround* to submit your picture and details to audition to play Hermione Granger, and after proudly posting mine in the letterbox at the end of my road I never heard anything back. Not even a generic letter saying thanks for sending your pic! I imagine it was a dark period for a sea of would-be Hermiones in the early noughties, but, you know, good for Emma Watson and her eyebrow acting.[1] That's showbiz, eh? I resigned myself to taking performing arts classes at school, sixth form and university as a way to feed the drama queen within without setting myself up for disappointment.

When I moved down to London to complete my postgrad, that's when my movie watching turned up a notch. I bought

---

[1] I will say her acting as an adult was distinctly better, especially in *Bling Ring*.

a Cineworld Unlimited membership and for the next few years, whenever I wasn't studying or working, I'd be down West India Quays to watch as many films as possible per month. I'd plan movie marathons around my days off, working out how many I could see in one visit and supplying a bag full of food accordingly. I loved the freedom of going to the pictures on my own. You could see what you want, when you want and not have to deal with someone overly chatting in your ear, or getting their phone out because they don't respect the theatrical experience as much as you do. Go see an 11am movie on a Thursday and the place is empty, or at the most have a few OAPs, students or shift-workers filling seats. You'd sit back in silence and as a small collective take in the latest studio blockbuster, indie flick, or foreign-language film you might have overlooked if not for the all-access card. Like critic Addison DeWitt in *All About Eve*, 'My native habitat was the theater', albeit the movie theatre; a place where I could switch off my mind and be transported into an endless stream of new realities that scared me, excited me, inspired me, shocked me, moved me, humoured me, angered me and educated me to no end.

There's a scene in *The Souvenir Part 2* where Richard Ayoade's film-maker Patrick is trying to get feedback from his editor about the scenes of his film they just watched. Exasperated by their one-word responses, he roars, 'What does it make you feel?' Cinematic empathy has long informed my understanding, enjoyment and critical assessment of films and when done right, it can cause a palpable reaction. I might leave the venue experiencing a flurry of emotions and need several minutes to acclimate myself back into the real world. I remember seeing *Beasts of the Southern Wild* in 2012 and being so overwhelmed that I walked the thirty minutes home in tears and called Dad to tell him how much I loved him. It was the same year I realised that maybe the reason I picked a career in journalism was because I wanted to talk about the world. As cinema was the world to me, then why not talk about it?

181

I was working a paid intern gig at a marketing agency after completing my MA with Commendation because I had rent to pay and was being rejected from every bloody journalism job I applied to. Luckily, one of our company clients was AOL who owned *HuffPost* at the time. I was doing some campaign copywriting for one of its sister outlets and decided to contact *HuffPost*'s UK editor-in-chief Carla Buzasi via LinkedIn and pitch myself to do some user-generated blogging for free. I probably should have pitched for paid work as a junior reporter or journalist, but I was too scared she might report back to my marketing manager that I was using work contacts to job hunt. Thankfully, Carla was no grass and put me in touch with the blogs editor who set me up with an account. My first film review was published in 2012 for Roman Polanski's *Carnage*,[2] and soon followed up by some equally unrefined assessments of *The Vow*, *This Means War*, *21 Jump Street* and *The Devil Inside*. Still, it was a start and it got me thinking about cinema in a more analytical way to help me pinpoint what did or didn't work for me. Emphasis on me, for there is one thing that I knew pretty early on: art is subjective, taste is subjective, and to be a critic worth her salt I had to go with how I felt about a film rather than what the critical consensus was. Which is nerve-wracking when you're not coming into the field with a degree in film studies or a childhood with only French New Wave cinema for company.[3] So I reminded myself that there is a lot of narrative and visual storytelling crossover between cinema and broadcast journalism, (especially documentary-making),[4] that I spent three years analysing literature, drama

---

[2] In the years since I've learned the harrowing detail of his rape conviction against a thirteen-year-old and have chosen not to review another movie of his again.

[3] I wish I had spent my youth watching French New Wave so wouldn't need to catch up now!

[4] Not to brag, but absolutely to brag, I got a distinction for my final documentary project on the Mandaeans.

and critical theory within my American studies and English undergrad, which also included a module on television narratives in my third year. That knowledge was transferrable. Combine all that with the twenty-two years of movies I'd already watched and reviews I'd read, I had a decent enough foundation to build on my craft, but it would take another decade for me to call myself a professional critic.

Some critics and film journalists I know walked out of university into jobs at film magazines. *Total Film*, *Sight & Sound*, *Empire* and *Little White Lies* are the UK's magazines and some are still there because one of the hardest things to get around is that there are so few job opportunities because no one leaves. Most people don't have the fortuitous timing to leave school and find a cushty job like that, so whenever I saw or heard about people swooping into these roles I'd think about that line from the 2009 rom-com *He's Just Not That Into You*: 'You're the rule, not the exception.' They were the exception, and I was the rule who was going to have to work my opportunities to my advantage and use them as a stepping stone to where I wanted to be as a critic. Over seven years, I went from brand marketing to working every day for six months while additionally freelancing as an assistant producer at LBC and TalkSport. I then began online showbiz reporter shifts at *MailOnline* where I'd never been so bullied by an editor in my life, but I sucked it up. After two years I moved to *Metro Online* as acting entertainment editor, but it was a toxic work environment; I was getting underpaid and was sexually harassed, so I quit. I ended up as entertainment editor at *OK!* online for five months until I was sacked because I wasn't hitting their required traffic figures. No bother, the work was mind-numbing[5] and my gut was telling me now was the time to go freelance again to really focus on film. So I began pitching and doing shifts on the diary desk at the *Evening Standard* and Yahoo

---

[5] I had to write SEO stories about the lyrical meaning of Ed Sheeran's 'Supermarket Flowers' in order to get traffic hits.

Movies to keep a steady income flow for rent and, you know, everything that comes with living in London. All the while, I was unsuccessfully applying to every film journo staff job going. When I was at *Metro Online*, I applied to one film magazine to be their news editor. I had two interviews, but I was told by their deputy editor that they went with someone with richer section edit experience. That's fair enough, I thought. I might have run an entertainment desk and managed a team of reporters, but I hadn't worked on a magazine before, so I'd probably be learning a lot on the job. When it was later announced that they had promoted their own online writer to the position and then hired another white dude to replace him, I was briefly salty about it.

As with the film industry, the respective field of journalism today and criticism within it, is a white male-dominated place. A recent study conducted by Dr Martha Lauzen, executive director of San Diego State University's Center for the Study of Women in Television and Film, showed in early 2022, men wrote 74% of the 4000 reviews examined and women just 26% – an 8% decline from 2020.[6] When the movie business was seen more as fluff than the high-brow culture of theatre, literature and art, female critics, white women at least, did boast higher numbers. Dilys Powell, Judith Crist, C.A. Lejeune, Pauline Kael and Janet Maslin are among the most celebrated names in film criticism of the twentieth century, but when cinema continued to receive more gravitas their female comrades were being overlooked in favour of male writers – just as pioneering female directors had been pushed out of the industry before. The dawn of the Internet created more space to talk about cinema, but data continually shows how limited it was and still is for women to claim it – where every dude and his dog set up a blog to wang on about the mise-en-scène in an Amblin production or how hot a topless Vinessa Shaw

---

6 Rubin, Rebecca, 'Film Criticism Continues to Be Dominated by Men, Study Shows' (24 May 2022) https://variety.com/2022/film/news/film-critics-male-female-study-1235276110/

looked in *3:10 to Yuma*, while their female counterparts were made to feel like their opinions were not as important. There's also something of a circle-jerk between some male critics and male film-makers whose conscious and unconscious bias has meant female film-makers have suffered for it. In Amy Adrion's documentary *Half the Picture*, Chris Hegedus says that journalists only ever want to interview her husband and partner, DA Pennebaker, despite the fact they've spent forty years making Oscar-nominated documentaries as a team. Mary Harron recalls how critics assumed her male editors and cinematographers 'saved' her films. 'I didn't sit around doing nothing!' she laments. Her 2000 film *American Psycho* ran the gamut of critiques, from extreme delight to extreme repulsion from mostly male critics (and to be fair a lot of feminists who didn't get it) but even the ones who liked it didn't deem it worthy enough to warrant end-of-year praise:

> [The movie] didn't get nominated for anything, obviously. It also didn't make a single ten-best list, which is really funny now, because today it's got this revered position. But at the time, even people who liked it wouldn't have considered it an important film.[7]

As someone who has read the book, watched the film and the musical, I can easily say Harron's adaptation is an iconic piece of film-making; a feminist masterpiece that has rightly earned cult classic status in the twenty years since its release, and that's partly thanks to the increase in female critics offering retroactive reviews. Lauzen's 2018 study[8] found that critics of the male persuasion were harsher on female-made and -led movies. 'For

---

[7] Shapiro, Lily, 'In Conversation: Mary Harron' (22 April 2020) https://www.vulture.com/2020/04/mary-harron-american-psycho-in-conversation.html

[8] Lauzen, Martha M., 'Thumbs Down 2018: Film Critics and Gender, and Why It Matters' (2018) https://womenintvfilm.sdsu.edu/wp-content/uploads/2018/07/2018_Thumbs_Down_Report.pdf

decades, many male directors have benefited from reviews in which they have been described in larger-than-life, almost mythic ways,' she said at the time. 'Few women, with the possible exception of Kathryn Bigelow, have enjoyed this same kind of critical treatment.'[9]

A month earlier, another report[10] similarly highlighted the imbalance by analysing the gender and ethnicity of writers whose reviews[11] were hosted on the reviews aggregation site *Rotten Tomatoes*. The data found 77.8% were written by men and 22.2% by women. In terms of ethnicity, 82% of reviewers were white and broken down even further: white males wrote 67.3% of reviews, white women 21.5%, non-white men 8.7% and women of colour a pitiful 2.5%. Even today, the four major UK film mags have completely white writing staff, the majority of which are male too. Dr Stacy L. Smith, co-author of the study, founder and director of the Annenberg Inclusion Initiative, said:

This report reveals the absence of women of colour working as reviewers [. . .] We have seen the ramifications of an industry in which the content sold to audiences is created and reviewed by individuals who are primarily white men. Creating inclusive hiring practices at every stage of the film-making and review process is essential to meeting business imperatives and ensuring that we see diverse perspectives reflected in society.

This was the same year *Ready Player One* came out, a film I enjoyed less than the book but did remind me just how white,

[9] Buckley, Cara, 'Male Critics Are Harsher Than Women on Female-Led Films' (17 June 2018) https://www.nytimes.com/2018/07/17/movies/male-critics-are-harsher-than-women-on-female-led-films-study-says.html

[10] Choueiti, Marc, Stacy L. Smith, Katherine Pieper and Ariana Case, 'Gender and Race/Ethnicity of Film Reviewers Across 100 Top Films of 2017' (June 2018) https://assets.uscannenberg.org/docs/cricits-choice-2018.pdf

[11] The report analysed 19,559 reviews for the 100 top-grossing films at the US box office in 2017.

male-focused a narrative it really is. In order to win a virtual egg hunt, players need to have an encyclopaedic knowledge of eighties pop culture beloved by the white dude who designed the VR world in which the prize (his vast fortune and control of said VR world) resides. From *Monty Python* to *War Games*, it's a white fanboy's wet dream where the protagonist is also a white boy, of course, and his BFF presents as a white male for most of the book and film, despite being a Black lesbian. Nothing symbolises how much non-white and non-male people have to get with the programme of white male tastes more than *Ready Player One*, and that sort of cultural gatekeeping is reflected in a film industry that continues to be over-represented by cis white men and under-represented by everyone else. Every time I go to a press screening or a junket interview you can guarantee the journalists and critics in attendance will mostly be white men, then white women and often I'm the only ethnic minority in the room. Unless it's a film made by a person of colour then you'll likely see a few more journalists or critics from that ethnic background – but why aren't they always this diverse? Why is it still the case that white critics, male especially, have free rein to review every type of movie going, but most under-represented critics are still forced to stay in their lane and commissioned to review themselves?

Before I was getting booked as a critic, I'd pitch film op-eds and critical essays with a feminist or ethnic angle because a) I felt it was important to show just how often cinema has maligned, erased or discriminated in terms of gender and race, and, b) these hot takes were far more likely to get commissioned by white editors who needed to outsource their diversity. Taking an activist approach to my critical work certainly raised my profile and improved my ability to look at films more shrewdly to determine how film-makers' methods might be positively, or negatively, promoting certain attitudes or stereotypes about cultures. This led to more editors reaching out to me hoping I might knock out 700 words on whatever controversial film or industry topic that was trending that day, and eventually my film culture commentary led to me getting official, paid reviews. But just because I'm a woman of colour it doesn't mean I can't offer a critical assessment of *Avengers: Endgame* as easily as I could *The Man Who Sold His Skin*. I had to awkwardly mention that to an editor once because after seven films, he had only given me ones made by ethnic minorities and not even film-makers with the same background as me. It's honestly wild to me that I've been asked to review movies about Black, East Asian, South Asian and Jewish minorities, but not once have any of my regular outlets asked me to review a MENA movie, especially given how often I bang on about MENA representation. In fact, the only way I've been able to review MENA films is via *The New Arab* and you can guess why they might have commissioned me!

Luckily this editor was cool (though embarrassed, bless him) about me pointing out the bias and apologised for pigeon holing me. I was glad to be in a position, financially and professionally, that I felt confident enough to raise the issue, but in such a competitive field women and minorities often don't for fear of losing future work. I have one critic friend who would get contacted to only review Black films and after a while she simply ignored their emails. If you're good enough to review films made by people with similar backgrounds then you are qualified, dare I say overqualified, to review films made by the homogenous group you've spent most of your life watching.

We are not simply boxes on your diversity quota to be ticked. Even when you do get paid for reviews, sometimes it's a pittance. There was an animated series called *The Critic* with Jon Lovitz voicing its onscreen reviewer and in the pilot episode he mentions he earns over $200k, which made me chuckle. The most I've ever been paid for a review is £300 at 50p per word. The least is free and anything else depends on the outlet's budget and, in some cases, your status. Mainstream print always pays more than online, despite some of these outlets relying on their digital platform and ad sales to support its print costs. It's always a shame to hear how many critics I have come across who are writing for outlets that don't pay them at all or offer the bare minimum. While the majority of independent blogs are run by white men, others like *Scream Queenz* and *Film Daze* have popped up to offer platforms for diverse writers to cut their teeth and build their published portfolio of work.

If you're in the infancy of your critical career these places can prove beneficial, but writing for free for a blog that you don't own should be a stepping stone. The first review I was paid for was by *Time Out* to cover *An Elephant Sitting Still*, a bleak four-hour movie that earned me £100.[12] It was one of two paid review commissions I got that year and it barely covered a third of a month's rent. Today, I'm a Tomatometer®-approved critic who has written reviews for *Empire*, *Time Out*, *IGN*, *Radio Times*, *SyFy Fangrrls*, *The New Scientist*, *The New Arab*, *The i*, *The Big Issue* and *Stylist* magazine, but it's only a fraction of what I earn a year. I continue to supplement my income by penning features, op-eds, columns, interviews, profiles and securing broadcast work that has helped to establish my position as a sought-after voice in film. Although it did take me three tries to get accepted into London's Critic Circle and the second time I was rejected, in 2019, was because I didn't have enough traditional reviews in my application.

It's taken me over a decade of hustle as a journalist, in newsrooms, studios and working from home to get to this point. I even had the middle-class privilege of my parents being able to put money towards my postgrad tuition fee at a time when they were far lower than they are today in the UK. A lot of critics don't have that early financial support or still rely on full-time jobs while critiquing as a side gig, which limits how much they can cover. If you're a UK-based critic outside the M25 that makes it even harder when the majority of screenings take place in the capital. What about film festivals? How do you cover Cannes or Sundance when you're not based in that country, or nearby, and there isn't always a guarantee that you'll earn enough to offset that personal investment? I only felt

---

[12] The editor gave me an extra £20 because it was so long!

financially comfortable attending the Toronto Film Festival in 2018 and 2019 because they offered a stipend to female critics as part of a Share Her Journey initiative that covered four days' accommodation and flight costs. I didn't have the disposable income to risk losing money just so I could tweet about movies before their theatrical release.

I managed to secure work with some of my established outlets once I knew I could go, and that still didn't add up to what the stipend took care of. More film festivals are offering this type of monetary support to marginalised and young critics which is amazing to see. It not only helps people from low-income backgrounds to get ahead of the curve when it comes to critical opportunities, it fosters more diverse perspectives coming out of the festival. Festival coverage is a major part of which films get bought for distribution and if the critical gatekeepers are more diverse, then diverse film-makers get a fairer shake too. A small positive of the pandemic was festivals moving online, allowing critics to access titles across the world as well as locally. Even studios and distributors were providing virtual screening links so that writers could cover weekly releases during lockdown, which gave more opportunities for regional critics, as well as differently-abled writers who can't always access cinemas. Sadly, once the world opened up, these gatekeepers closed a lot of these avenues.

In 2020, I joined *Time*'s Up Critics Committee as a co-chair to advise and support fellow female-identifying film writers and critics. We advocated for fairer pay, and in one instance managed to secure actual payment for contributors to one podcast. There is, however, only so much a small group of freelancers can do, but I know greater transparency on rates and using your platform to speak up about inequality can change the perspective of people in charge of commissioning. Wider, long-lasting progress needs to be spearheaded by those inside the gates, by editors, commissioners, PRs, studios and distributors who can ensure a broader spectrum of critics are able to write about the ever-increasing roster of movies coming out weekly. Things are slowly improving and I'm grateful to every single editor who continues to commission me. That I'm now featured regularly in *Empire* magazine certainly makes the little girl who used to steal her dad's copies smile every time she sees her name in its pages.

I go back to this idea of cinema being a mirror to the world because it is one of the few things I believe in, and so far that reflection has been distorted to prioritise one walk of life. Now, as we make slow but sure steps to diversify the people in front of and behind the camera, it's just as important that the people writing about it make similar gains. I think about what Brie Larson said about wanting perspectives beyond the established:

> If you make a movie that is a love letter to women of colour, there is an insanely low chance a woman of colour will have the chance to see your movie and review your movie. I don't need a 40-year-old white dude to tell me what didn't work about *A Wrinkle in Time*. It wasn't made for him! I want to know what it meant to women of colour, to biracial women, to teen women of colour.[13]

This isn't to say a Black woman reviewing *A Wrinkle in Time* has to like the film just because Ava DuVernay made it. I hate this expectation that just because a marginalised movie made by marginalised film-makers has come out, marginalised critics have to automatically support it because if it doesn't do well it will prevent future films about or by marginalised film-makers being made. Hanna, say 'marginalised' one more time. MARGINALISED! *Bitch Media*'s Jenn Jackson said, 'the fantastic journey through space and time was as engaging visually as it was narratively,'[14] while Monique Jones for *Slash Film* prefaced

---

[13] BBC News, 'Brie Larson wants more diversity among film critics' (15 June 2018) https://www.bbc.co.uk/news/newsbeat-44495537

[14] Jackson, Jenn, 'No Need for Superheroes' (14 March 2018) https://www.bitchmedia.org/article/a-wrinkle-in-time-needs-no-superheroes

her review with a note on the push she felt to do right by a Black female film-maker:

> I distinctly feel the pressure I'm under as a Black woman to like and laud *A Wrinkle in Time*, to support director Ava DuVernay. But I can't honestly do that. The film has a multitude of issues that must be addressed.[15]

Jones wasn't alone in her negativity. After a tally of 344 reviews on *Rotten Tomatoes*, the sci-fi adventure was certified rotten with a 42% approval rating. It was a studio production that marked the first time a woman of colour had directed a live-action film with over a $100m budget.[16] Despite it also being a financial failure, DuVernay's career was not curtailed. She followed it up with the critically acclaimed miniseries *When They See Us* and has several TV and film projects in the works with streamers like Netflix and HBO. Subsequently, female film-makers and film-makers of colour haven't suffered either: Cate Shortland directed *Black Widow*, Niki Caro directed *Mulan* and Chloé Zhao directed *Eternals*. Each one had a production budget north of $200m – go on, gyals! – but I agree with Larson. I want to read reviews from people who might be able to offer insight that comes from their lived experience as well as their critical craft, and maybe poke holes in films the dominant critical body might overlook.

Some people like to think they watch movies in a bubble, that they aren't political, but I don't believe we can compartmentalise our experiences from how we view the world in real life and onscreen. There is no objectivity in the arts, so the best we can hope for is a diversity of subjective voices

---

[15] Jones, Monique, '"A Wrinkle In Time" Spoiler Review: A Heartbreaking Misfire With A Powerful Burden' (12 March 2018) https://www.slashfilm.com/556838/wrinkle-in-time-spoiler-review/?utm_campaign=clip

[16] There are only nine women in the history of cinema to have had the privilege of directing a film with a $100m+ budget.

that readers can choose from and trust, as well as artists who might want to take constructive criticism into their future projects. Although read reviews of your own work at your own peril!

The best thing I can do right now as a critic is to read as much as I write. I love hearing what Mark Kermode has to say as much as Candice Frederick, Angelica Jade Bastién, Clarisse Loughrey, Simran Hans and Roxana Hadadi. Every time I read one of their reviews (cue Jack Nicholson voice) it makes me want to be a better writer. Even when I don't agree with their assessment, these women introduce me to new ideas about cinema. Although, I did a book of Pauline Kael's collected writing and came across this troubling paragraph in her review of Laurence Olivier's *Othello*:

> Part of the pleasure of the performance is, of course, the sheer feat of Olivier's transforming himself into a Negro; yet it is not wasted effort, not mere exhibitionism or actor's vanity, for what Negro actor at this stage in the world's history could dare bring to the role the effrontery that Olivier does, and which Negro actor could give it this reading? I saw Paul Robeson and he was not black as Olivier is; Finlay can hate Olivier in a way Jose Ferrer did not dare—indeed did not have the provocation—to hate Robeson. Possibly Negro actors need to sharpen themselves on white roles before they can play a Negro. It is not enough to be: for great drama, it is the awareness that is everything.[17]

Nothing like a critical blind spot, Pauline! Sidney Poitier won a bloody best actor Oscar two years before she committed these racist remarks to paper.

---

[17] Kael, Pauline. The Age of Movies: Selected Writings of Pauline Kael. United States: Library of America, 2011.

Criticism is an art form, a craft, and it needs to be constantly nurtured with study and practice. It needs more than just the dominant cis white male voice dictating what's hot or not, especially when it comes to critiquing art by film-makers they have historically maligned. It's a battle and not everyone will achieve that goal. It's been a struggle. Sacrifices were made. Blood, sweat and a lot of tears were shed along the way, but it's been worth every minute. I can only hope that the next generation of under-represented critics get to walk an easier path than the ones that came before.

Chapter 14

'When an Arab sees a woman he wants, he takes her!'

– The Sheik (1921)

IF YOU'RE ARAB, MIDDLE Eastern, North African or a Muslim covering Western cinema there are two academics that will earn a nod of approval, a mutter of, 'Oh, of course!' every time their name is referenced: Edward W. Said and Jack G. Shaheen. These guys have taught me about the artistic representation of people from the Arab diaspora more than anyone else. They've helped me become more finely attuned to the ways Hollywood has influenced my internalised racism and the Arabophobia I held towards people of my heritage. In a professional capacity, my eyes were opened to the myriad ways Western film-makers and writers have marginalised, maligned and, frankly, made up what they want about how Arab people live their lives and these are the dudes I wish I could have thanked for waking us up to these fictions.

Edward Wadie Said was a Palestinian-American professor of literature and cultural critic who applied his bicultural interrogation of Western and colonial texts to examine how the academic field of 'Orientalism'[1] contributed to a condescending

---

[1] That is, the academic study of art history, literature and culture, derived from the Eastern world, but depicted by writers, designers, and artists from the West.

and inaccurate depiction of MENA societies as uncivilised. Arab, Persian and Turkish civilisations have massively influenced the rest of the world, from economics to philosophy, but instead the degradation of Orientalist literature contributed to the justification of homogeneity and the imperial conquest of MENA regions. In 1978, Said reclaimed the term 'Orientalism' and made it the title of his seminal book that redefined the phrase to reflect the patronising, monolithic attitude towards these 'Other' diverse cultures mostly created by Europeans as a way to position the Occidental world (the West) as superior. 'Too often literature and culture are presumed to be politically, even historically innocent,' Said wrote, arguing that Orientalist literature has helped establish 'a belligerent collective identity' which has influenced social and geopolitical discourse and calcified negative stereotypes in the public consciousness and policy-making. His book mostly examines various works of European authors, like Joseph Conrad and Gustave Flaubert, but he also reflects on the contemporary mediums through which such manufactured archetypes have been maintained:

> One aspect of the electronic, postmodern world is that there has been a reinforcement of the stereotypes by which the Orient is viewed. Television, the films, and all the media's resources have forced information into more and more standardized molds. So far as the Orient is concerned, standardization and cultural stereotyping have intensified the hold of the nineteenth-century academic and imaginative demonology of 'the mysterious Orient.' This is nowhere more true than in the ways by which the Near East is grasped.[2]

Jack George Shaheen was an American writer and lecturer of Lebanese Christian heritage who wrote *The TV Arab*. It examined the troubling portrayal of Arabs on screen after

---

[2] Said, Edward W., *Orientalism.*

seeing the gross stereotypes in the cartoons his children were watching. 'Daddy, Daddy, they've got bad Arabs on TV,' they'd tell him. It was published in 1984 after receiving dozens of rejection letters from publishers unwilling to support such a candid review of harmful tropes used in American television programmes. Seventeen years later, he would deliver an expansive study on cinematic portrayals in over 1000 films, in his hefty tome *Reel Bad Arabs: How Hollywood Vilifies a People*. The revised and updated 2012 copy I swear by – and had me going 'what the fook?' when realising just how many films I had grown up on featured both subtle and substantial preju-dicial statements – incorporates all the additional post-9/11 stereotypes that have kept the Arab and the diaspora in a cycle of negativity. From one-liners to entire storylines, 'reel images have real impacts on real people', Shaheen wrote in the preface to the third edition:

> Regrettably, stereotypes of Arabs and Muslims persist, replayed and revived time and time again. Sweeping mischaracterizations continue spreading like a poisonous virus. One of the first lessons that our children learn from their media about Arabs, and one of the last lessons the elderly forget, is: Arab equals Muslim equals Godless enemy . . . There are some bad Arabs and Muslims out there – but that goes for people of all races and religions. No one group has a monopoly on the good and innocent.[3]

The stereotypes of Arabs are commonly referred to as the Three 'B' Syndrome: 'bombers, belly dancers and billionaires.' How fun! Let's start with billionaires. The Sheikh trope portrayed men as greedy, perversely obsessed with Western women, violent and/or sneaky with archaic values. This, Shaheen says, contrasted linguistic origin of 'sheikh' as a signifier of respect for a wise leader, chief or head of a tribe, family, or village.

---

[3] Shaheen, Jack G., *Reel Bad Arabs: How Hollywood Vilifies a People*.

The 1921 silent film *The Sheik* has every Orientalist trope going with Italian silent film star Rudolph Valentino playing the Algerian sheikh Ahmed Ben Hassan, who kidnaps the Western heroine Lady Diana (Agnes Ayres) with exotic maidens, belly dancers, Arab slavers and barbaric desert nomads and rapists wielding sabres, making up the rest of this Arab world. 'When an Arab sees a woman he wants, he takes her!' Ahmed says, except, plot twist, he is not actually Algerian, rather a tanned British-Spanish orphan raised by the old sheikh in the backward ways of his people. When Stockholm syndrome leads Diana to fall in love with her captor-turned-rescuer, by the end his white origin is revealed so any heroic association with Arabs is retconned, which played into the already prevalent exclusion of interracial relationships in Hollywood films between non-white and white characters.

The Song of Love (1923) and *The Son of the Sheik* (1926) would continue this fetishised depiction of sheikhs, while later films *Raiders of the Desert* (1941), *Samson Against the Sheik* (1962), *Ilsa: Harem Keeper of the Oil Sheiks* (1976) and *Jewel of the Nile* (1985) would position them as far more dark and evil. Film-makers responding to the disruption of the oil crisis and the 1973 Arab embargo reconfigured the sheikh trope as billionaire oil barons still hell-bent on kidnapping western women, as with the American-Israeli-made *Ashanti* (1979), Hollywood comedy *Protocol* (1984) as well as the French-made drama *Harem* (1985). Omar Sharif actually got himself on the Arab Boycott List[4] for several years for playing a Westernised Prince in *Ashanti*, who cannot shake off his Arab predilection for enslaved women, while white actor Peter Ustinov played sleazy Arab slaver Suleiman. *Slavers* (1977) had previously used this evil Arab stereotype, positioning the Sheikh as less humane than Western slavers, while *Utz* (1992) referred to an 'Arab oil sheikh' who collected dwarfs. Never one to let historical or

---

[4] Sharif, Omar, and Miriam Rosen, 'The Making of Omar Sharif: An Interview' (1989) *Cinéaste,* https://www.jstor.org/stable/23803061

racial accuracy get in the way of a good story, Sir Ridley Scott's AD 180-set *Gladiator*, penned by David Franzoni, John Logan and William Nicholson, threw in some Arab slavers to kidnap Russell Crowe's Roman general Maximus near his Spanish home, even though none operated in the area at the time. Harvard University professor Kathleen Coleman was a consultant on Roman history for the film and told Shaheen:

> I'm quite sure Arab slave-traders would not have penetrated Spain [where the scene was set] to kidnap Maximus . . . I was not present during any of this process, so when I saw the preview I was unpleasantly surprised. I was under the impression that although the plot was fictitious, DreamWorks wanted the atmosphere to be authentic. But that is evidently not the case.[5]

Scott isn't the first British film-maker to tweak history to fit his epic white saviour narrative. There is no denying that *Lawrence of Arabia* is an incredible feat of film-making; rightly earning its praise as one of the most breathtaking movies ever made. David Lean's biographical epic launched Omar Sharif in Western cinema as the fictional Bedouin sheikh Sherif Ali, though led by Peter O'Toole as the titular English soldier leading Arabs against the Turkish-Ottoman Empire. The film manages to give him far too much credit, perpetuate Orientalist images, historical falsehoods, with Alec Guinness and Anthony Quinn browning up to play Arab leaders Prince Faisal and Auda abu Tayi. In his 1926 autobiography *Seven Pillars of Wisdom*, on which the film is based, T.E. Lawrence admits to exaggerating his role in the events of the Arab revolt of 1916–18: 'My proper share was a minor one but because of a fluent pen, a free

---

[5] Shaheen, Jack G., '"The Gladiator": How in the World Did Bad Arabs Happen to This Roman on His Way to the Forum?' (14 August 2000) https://www.wrmea.org/000-august-september/the-gladiator-how-in-the-world-did-bad-arabs-happen-to-this-roman-on-his-way-to-the-forum.html

speech, and certain adroitness of brain, I took upon myself, as I describe it, a mock primacy.'[6] Even when a subsequent biography penned in 1955 questioned his claims and determined Lawrence to be 'at least half a fraud'[7] the prevailing perception of the film is one of a superior white knight unifying inferior sheikhs and their Bedouin tribes against the Turks and each other for the sake of Arab independence. The film depicts these Arabs as prone to internal conflicts and unable to maintain order of Damascus for long, before the British swoop in to take control. In reality, Lawrence's Bedouin guide was never shot by a rival tribesman for drinking from a well without permission; the Arab Revolt was bolstered not by a disparate group of Bedouin guerrillas, but by a more sophisticated Sharifan army and regular Hashemite[8] soldiers; pan-Arab enthusiast Prince Faisal's rule of Damascus lasted two years before he was expelled by the French and Lawrence was actively involved and fully aware of the British army's dishonest plans to usurp power to protect their interests. 'My own ambition is that the Arabs should be our first brown dominion and not our last brown colony,' he wrote in 1919.[9] 'It's almost as if Bolt had to fall back on such colonialist cliches in order to provide a neat dramatic conclusion to the film,' concluded *Cinéaste* founder and editor-in-chief Gary Crowdus, about that late scene depicting Lawrence's attempts to convene the Arab sheikhs, too temperamental and aggressive to overcome petty rivalries in order to sustain order:

> In perpetuating Lawrence's inflated claims to leadership of the Arab revolt the film caters to the same old self-flattering

---

6 Quote from Letter to Lord Curzon quoted in John E. Mack, A Prince of our Disorder. The Life of T. E. Lawrence, London, OUP, 1990, p. 280.

7 Aldington, Richard, *Lawrence of Arabia: A Biographical Enquiry.*

8 Royal family descendants of the prophet Mohammed.

9 Louis, William Roger, 'The Great Middle East Game, and Still No Winner' (27 August 1989) https://www.nytimes.com/1989/08/27/books/the-great-middle-east-game-and-still-no-winner.html

Western prejudices about Third World peoples, those benighted colonial subjects incapable of ruling themselves.[10]

More recently, *Wonder Woman* and its 2020 sequel would do a U-turn on Arab representation through the sheikh trope. The first film, set during World War I, treated Saïd Taghmaoui's Moroccan ally Sameer so well, but *Wonder Woman 1984* really lived up to its title by revisiting the eighties Arab oil baron through Amr Waked's Said Bin Abydos. He is tricked by antagonist Maxwell Lord into wishing to return Cairo back to the fictional kingdom of Bialya,[11] his ancestral realm and 'for all the heathens who dare trod upon it to be kept out forever.' I wish the Arab cliches had stopped there. Patty Jenkins' film also sees Egyptian soldiers beaten up by the Amazonian hero while she saves children, clad in traditional Arab garments. It later shows a Middle Eastern sniper wishing for nuclear weapons. Because heaven forbid an Arab might desire more in life than mutually assured destruction! Patty, girl. Why you gotta do us like that? But it's not just her. The film's co-writer Geoff Johns, who is half-Lebanese, must share responsibility. I guess we should be grateful the film didn't have any belly dancers.

If Arab women aren't treated as submissive, devout women then they signify the Exotic Other. You can guarantee any movie inspired by *Arabian Nights* or Ancient Egypt will depict women as scantily-clad, sensual, or sexually promiscuous. There have been over 160 films with sheikh characters and most of them feature a harem of mostly mute exotic-looking women serving as window dressing to the regressive Arab male characters as with, *Carry On Follow That Camel* or the 2004 remake of *Around the World in Eighty Days*. Even when they have been given agency, these female characters are still fetishised

[10] Crowdus, Gary, 'Lawrence of Arabia: The Cinematic (Re) Writing of History' (1989) *Cinéaste*, https://www.jstor.org/stable/41687645.

[11] A made-up DC Comics country originally located in the Middle East near Iran and Saudi Arabia, not North Africa.

like Princess Jasmine or Cleopatra. Silent film star Theda Bara became known as 'The Vamp' because of a string of exotic roles including Cleopatra, and studios claiming she was 'the daughter of an Arab sheik and a French woman, born in the Sahara'.[12] She was a white woman from Ohio. In 1917 Bara played Cleopatra in J. Gordon Edwards's erotic silent film where it depicts her seducing Julius Caesar in a barely-there costume; reinforcing the temptress impression cemented by Ancient Roman historians trying to tarnish her name. 'You have to remember, the information that we have about her was written by the people who defeated her – her enemies,' biographer Duane Roller says. 'They saw her as a dangerous threat to the Roman Republic and [built] her up as this horrible woman who led men to their doom.'[13] Most portrayals of the Egyptian ruler have seen her played by white women as exotic and sexually charged with Elizabeth Taylor delivering the defining porcelain performance in the 1963 epic, though at least her white handmaidens avoided the typical midriff-baring outfits. The James Bond franchise would use the exotic seductress stereotype with Beirut belly dancer Saida in *The Man with the Golden Gun*. In a not-at-all-ridiculous scene, Bond sucks out and accidentally swallows a gold bullet she keeps in her belly button for safe keeping. Sometimes I really do wonder if screenwriters are OK.

In 1999, *The Mummy* was released with a horde of Orientalist tropes including the exotic villainess. I'd be lying if I didn't admit to being a die-hard fan when I was eleven and didn't know any better, but as I've found with most movies I loved growing up featuring Arabs, they ultimately disappoint.

---

[12] *Montreal Gazette*, 'Famous Silent Screen Vamp Theda Bara Dies of Cancer' (8 April 1955) https://news.google.com/newspapers?id=qYEtAAAAIBAJ&pg =7227,1426917&dq=arab-death+theda-bara&hl=en

[13] NPR, 'Forget The Temptress Rep: Here's The Real Cleopatra' (25 April 2010) https://www.npr.org/2010/04/25/126195946/forget-the-temptress-rep-heres-the-real-cleopatra

Welcome to Hollywood; sorry if I keep ruining your faves! Every Egyptian character is treated like dirty, uncivilised, disgusting, murderous and/or perverted savages, with none actually played by Arabs either. The good Arabs, the supposedly half-Egyptian characters Evie and Jonathan, are whitewashed by Rachel Weisz and John Hannah. As discussed by critics Dave Ansen and Roger Ebert at the time:

> **Ansen:** *The Arab-bashing of this movie is kind of unforgivable. They're smelly and they spit and there's the kind of condescension and contempt that Hollywood would not dare with any other group.*

> **Ebert:** *I notice that in a lot of movies these days. They and the Nazis are the only two villains Hollywood feels comfortable with.*[14]

These lads still gave it two thumbs up! Anck-Su-Namun, meanwhile, is played by Venezuelan actress Patricia Velasquez, the Pharoah's cheating femme fatale wife and mistress of eponymous baddie Imhotep (white Afrikaner actor Arnold Vosloo). She is naked throughout the film save for body paint and a strategically placed loin cloth. The 2017 remake would place French-Algerian actor Sofia Boutella in the eponymous role so, at least, there was some North African representation this time, but it's still a terrible movie that relies on white saviours like Ethan Hunt, sorry Tom Cruise, to save the day. Boutella's Ahmanet is still exoticised in flashback scenes depicting her sauntering naked in her rooms. In present daydreams she attempts to seduce Cruise's Nick, her skin-tight, mummy-wrapped costume unravels to reveal more of her flesh as the story unfolds, and how does she suck the souls out of other men? With a Vampiric kiss. Boutella is one of the

---

[14] McNab, J.M., '"The Mummy" Is Not A "Perfect Film," It's Racist Garbage' (21 March 2022) https://www.cracked.com/article_33077_the-mummy-is-not-a-perfect-film-its-racist-garbage.html

few Arab actresses to have penetrated the studio system and every day I wonder why this absolute badass and beautiful performer hasn't led her own film already. Before *The Mummy*, she played the sexy femme fatale sidekick to Samuel L. Jackson's antagonist in *Kingsman: The Secret Service.* After she played sexy femme fatale love interest in *Atomic Blonde* and, in *Hotel Artemis* she played, er, the sexy femme fatale ex of a bank robber. I'm all about sexy action stars, but there's an awkward layer when this typecasting affects Arab women in real life. The amount of times I've been called 'exotic', 'spicy' or some other ethnically-charged sexual epithet by a man – one dude said to me in bed, 'I can tell you're dirty' – is all to do with how Arab women and women of colour are overtly sexualised in the art we consume.

Bombers today might be the most prevalent and fear-mongering representation. Arab terrorists replaced the Red threat of communism in Hollywood and Irish freedom fighters in British cinema as the go-to villains. Film-makers and screen-writers respond to what they read in newspapers, see and hear on TV and radio, as well as use military departments, consult-ants and veterans to advise on geopolitics that regularly position American and British soldiers as heroes. Whenever there is coverage of US and British efforts in MENA conflicts, as well as heavy focus on fringe terrorism, a stereotype of *all* Arabs as untrustworthy, bloodthirsty, West-hating, religious fanatics prevails, and is reused on the big screen ad nauseum. Libya and Palestine were country-checked in various films during the eighties and nineties because of the political animosity towards Palestinian and Libyan leaders Yasser Arafat and Muammar Gaddafi. Remember *Back to the Future*? The opening scene reveals Doc Brown tricking a Libyan terrorist group into providing the plutonium for his time travelling DeLorean that they thought he would use to build a nuclear bomb. When two turn up at the Twin Pines Mall parking lot to confront Brown over his deception, one is wearing a red and white keffiyeh, both utter nonsensical dialect that is meant to be Arabic, and are played as inept, violent men by two non-Arab actors. As

Shaheen points out, the only Middle Eastern country with nuclear weapons at the time was Israel. The Israel-Palestine conflict really kicked off with the catastrophic British-backed events of the Nakba in 1948, which saw the violent expulsion of 80% of Palestinian Arabs and the deaths of 13,000, during the establishment of the state of Israel in Mandatory Palestine where 78% of their land was siphoned off. Over 500 Palestinian villages were destroyed[15] and the Palestinian right of return was denied, leading to between 2,700 and 5,000 Palestinians killed by Israeli forces as they tried to return to their homeland.[16]

Over the years, Palestine continues to shrink in size and aggression affects both nations, but one side has almost always suffered more losses than the other and it's not the one Hollywood has historically depicted as the underdog. 'Never do movies present Palestinians as innocent victims and Israelis as brutal oppressors,' Shaheen wrote.[17] Otto Preminger's 1960 film *Exodus* about the foundation of the State of Israel, starring Paul Newman as Jewish hero Ari, has been credited as inspiring US support for Zionist claims to the land and firmly establishing Israelis as the good guys in this conflict, the rabid Arabs as baddies and the British as far more sympathetic despite doing significant harm to the Holocaust survivors on the original *Exodus* ship featured in the film. The only good Arab is Ari's friend who is ultimately killed by Palestinians as a sort-of race traitor. Most of the critical community celebrated the film and accepted the events at face value, as did an American public relishing the romanticised plot, epic nature and idealistic overtures

---

[15] Al Jazeera, 'Palestine Remix: Destroyed Palestinian Villages', https://interactive. aljazeera.com/aje/palestineremix/maps-and-data-visualisations.html

[16] Morris, Benny, *Israel's Border Wars, 1949–1956: Arab Infiltration, Israeli Retaliation, and the Countdown to the Suez War.*

[17] Shaheen, Jack G. "Media Coverage of the Middle East: Perception and Foreign Policy." The Annals of the American Academy of Political and Social Science, vol. 482, 1985, pp. 160–75. JSTOR, http://www.jstor.org/ stable/1046388. Accessed 25 Jul. 2022.

of liberty and self-determination. German-born film-maker Gideon Bachmann who grew up in Israel, called it a 'propaganda' film. 'Considering the fact that *Exodus* is dishonest as far as facts are concerned, it is hardly surprising to find that it is also – and perhaps more drastically – dishonest on the higher level.'[18] Even the first Israeli Prime Minister David Ben-Gurion described Leon Uris's novel the movie is based on 'as a piece of propaganda, it's the greatest thing ever written about Israel'.[19]

Exodus paved the way for anti-Palestinian sentiment to manifest as the terrorist trope in *Black Sunday* (1977), *The Soldier* (1982), *The Little Drummer Girl* (1984), *Scorpion* (1986), *The Delta Force* (1986), *Snake Eyes* (1998) and plenty more during this period. *True Lies* (1994) is one I once watched fondly as a kid. James Cameron's spy game was funny, action-packed and had Arnie in super dad mode trying to rescue his daughter and the US from a terrorist threat. When I look back at it now, putting aside the misogynistic subplot where Arnie's hero uses CIA resources to stalk and intimidate his own wife, it's clear to see how caricaturist the depiction of the Islamist threat Crimson Jihad is, led by Art Malik's Salim Abu Aziz. Malik is not even Arab, he's British-Pakistani. Many Arab-Americans protested the film upon its release.[20] Maybe we should be thankful that an Arab actor didn't have to sully their name by appearing in such dehumanising roles, but for a very long time, and still today, villainous roles like these are one of the few guaranteed ways for actors of our heritage to earn a living in this industry. Omar Sharif, who had a lot of gambling debts, says financial necessity was part of the reason for taking *Ashanti*

---

[18] Bachmann, Gideon, 'Review: Exodus by Otto Preminger' (1961) *Film Quarterly.*

[19] McDowell, Edwin, '"Exodus" in Samizdat: Still Popular and Still Subversive' (26 April 1987) https://www.nytimes.com/1987/04/26/books/exodus-in-samizdat-still-popular-and-still-subversive.html?smid=url-share

[20] *New York Times*, 'Arab-Americans Protest "True Lies"' (16 July 1994) https://www.nytimes.com/1994/07/16/movies/arab-americans-protest-true-lies.html

because despite his romantic roles in *Doctor Zhivago* and *Funny Girl*, he says there weren't many good roles for actors like him after the sixties. 'There was a rise of young, talented directors,' he said in 1995, 'but they were making films about their own societies. There was no more room for a foreigner, so suddenly there were no more parts.'[21]

Just a lot of roles for Arabs to be killed by Western military or government agencies as part of jingoistic storylines. The 2000 film *Rules of Engagement* might be one of the grossest examples. Hussein Ibish of the American-Arab Anti-Discrimination Committee said at the time it was as comparatively racist as the D.W. Griffith's anti-Black *The Birth of a Nation* and Fritz Hippler's antisemitic Nazi propaganda film *The Eternal Jew*. 'The basic plot is not problematic. What's problematic is the treatment of and depiction of an Arab society. There aren't any positive images.'[22] The film centres on the trial of Samuel L. Jackson's military veteran over a rescue mission in Yemen that saw his squad massacre locals protesting the US embassy. As it turns out, he was completely justified in telling his soldiers to 'waste the motherfuckers' because the Yemeni were all toting guns and took the first shot. Yes, even children! I've never been so sad to hear Samuel L. utter 'motherfucker'. What's even more pernicious is that the original script didn't even involve Arabs. It was set in an unnamed Latin American country, which suggests the reason they moved it to Yemen was to avoid backlash from the larger Hispanic community in the US compared to the smaller Arab one. We're fair game!

Post-9/11 cinema saw an increase in Arabs as jihadi terrorists with films like *Zero Dark Thirty*, *Body of Lies*, *Rendition* and *The Kingdom* presenting them as far more sophisticated

---

[21] Berkvist, Robert, 'Omar Sharif, 83, a Star in "Lawrence of Arabia" and "Doctor Zhivago," Dies' (10 July 2015) https://www.nytimes.com/2015/07/11/movies/omar-sharif-a-star-in-dr-zhivago-dies-at-83.html

[22] https://www.adc.org/arab-americans-denounce-paramount-s-racist-film-rules-of-engagement-br/

than the bumbly bombers of the eighties. The mercenary-terrorist character Georges Batroc played by Canadian UFC fighter Georges St-Pierre was introduced in *Captain America: The Winter Soldier* and in the Marvel Comics he was simply a French adversary called Batroc the Leader. Yet the film makes a point of saying he is not a French criminal through Robert Redford's Alexander Pierce. 'For the record, he's Algerian,' which reads as particularly malicious given the torrid history between the two countries. We have small-screen series like *24*, *Homeland* and *Jack Ryan* to thank for that, as well as the British drama *Bodyguard* for increasing the image of the female jihadi bomber. I'm all about gender equality, but not like this! Because of the meek feminine traits women are expected to exhibit, they have been portrayed as more unnaturally evil. In Clint Eastwood's adaptation of *American Sniper* starring Bradley Cooper as Iraq vet Chris Kyle, the deadliest marksman in American military history, the opening sequence sees a woman give a Russian-made RKG-3 anti-tank grenade to a young boy and pushes him to run towards a US convoy. In Kyle's book, no child was ever involved.[23]

After the movie came out, the American-Arab Anti-Discrimination Committee reported an increase in 'violent threats [that are the] result of how Arab and Muslims are depicted'[24] because every Arab Kyle takes out is presented as a righteous kill. According to a report on Muslim representation in films, roughly one-third of Muslim characters are perpetrators of violence, and more than half are targets of violence.[25] When you couple that with the fact 66.7% of these characters were

[23] Tunzelmann, Alex von, 'Is American Sniper historically accurate?' (20 January 2015) https://www.theguardian.com/film/filmblog/2015/jan/20/why-american-snipers-historical-dishonesty-misleads

[24] BBC News, 'American Sniper film "behind rise in anti-Muslim threats"' (25 January 2015) https://www.bbc.co.uk/news/entertainment-arts-30972690

[25] Khan, Al-Baab, Dr. Katherine Pieper, Stacy L. Smith, Marc Choueiti, Kevin Yao and Artur Tofan, 'Missing & Maligned: The Reality of Muslims in Popular Global Movies' (June 2021) https://assets.uscannenberg.org/docs/aii-muslim-rep-global-film-2021-06-09.pdf

MENA it perpetuates the synonymous depiction of Arabs and Muslims, so even if a character is a Muslim villain of another ethnicity, like in *Bodyguard*, Arabs get the hit too. There has been a modern awareness to not totally malign us in these scenarios by adding a token good Arab or two as a buffer to the negative terrorist portrayals. In *Salmon Fishing in the Yemen*, Amr Waked plays another sheikh, although this one's goodness is coded by his pro-British and Western stance. Recently, *All the Old Knives* had Ahd Kamel playing the role of CIA operative Leila Mahoof, but she's in barely any scenes. There's also been a few films focused on Guantanamo Bay where Arab men have been rounded up and tortured by US forces. Films like *The Report* and *The Mauritanian* always have a white saviour as a way into the story and the graphic torture shown can create an empathy gap between the audience and the Arab characters. Well-intentioned or not, it can dehumanise Arabs even further and continue the cycle of associating us with despair and trauma.

Not all Western representation of Arabs uses them as a stock villain; if you squint you can see films that broke away from that problematic mould. The stunning *Ben Hur* and *13th Warrior* present nuanced Arab men, although you can always count on white actors bogarting these juicy roles. *The Prince of Egypt* is a wonderful musical that doesn't simply portray Egyptians as bad and Jews as good, but the entire voice cast is white. Ridley Scott defended his decision to whitewash his retelling of Moses' story *Exodus: Gods and Kings*, by saying:

> I can't mount a film of this budget, where I have to rely on tax rebates in Spain, and say my lead actor is Mohammed so-and-so from such-and-such. I'm just not going to get it financed. So the question doesn't even come up.[26]

---

[26] Foundas, Scott, '"Exodus: Gods and Kings" Director Ridley Scott on Creating His Vision of Moses' (25 November 2014) https://variety.com/2014/film/news/ridley-scott-exodus-gods-and-kings-christian-bale-1201363668/

There is a little, tiny, incy bit of petty satisfaction when white-washed movies like this one tank. Who can forget *Gods of Egypt* which saw Gerard Butler, among other white actors cast as the main Egyptian gods and civilians? I remember doing the press junket for *Geostorm* a few years after its release and asking Butler if he regretted playing a whitewashed role:

> No because I think that was . . . I understand the movement generally, but you consider our movie, also one of our leads was based on an Egyptian god who is not Black. We had Ethiopians, we had Egyptians, we had all different actors from all over the place. It was never really . . . They were from everywhere. So I thought that was a little too much to try and damage a movie like that. I don't know. I disagree, but I got the point.[27]

Did you though? I'm not sure who the Egyptian or Ethiopian actors are who he is referring to, but the sentiment here reinforces one of the most frustrating falsehoods when it comes to race: that it exists in a binary of black and white. A Hollywood diversity report found that, in terms of film leads, 'Black persons, about 13.4 per cent of the U.S. population in 2020, were over-represented in this important employment arena (19 per cent). By contrast, Latinx (5.4 per cent), Asian (5.4 per cent), Native (1.1 per cent), and MENA (1.1 per cent) persons were all under-represented among film leads.'[28] I've seen actors with sub-Saharan heritage prioritised for casting in North African roles like Djimon Hounsou as a Numidian slave in *Gladiator*,

[27] Flint, Hanna, 'Gerard Butler praises Geostorm's diversity, thinks Gods of Egypt "whitewash" backlash was "too much"' (20 October 2017) https://uk.movies.yahoo.com/gerard-butler-praises-geostorms-diversity-thinks-gods-egypt-whitewash-backlash-much-095603184.html

[28] UCLA, 'Hollywood Diversity Report' (2021) https://socialsciences.ucla.edu/wp-content/uploads/2021/04/UCLA-Hollywood-Diversity-Report-2021-Film-4-22-2021.pdf

Chadwick Boseman as Egyptian god *Thoth* and most of the Fremen characters in *Dune*. Cinema too has normalised the representation of Moors as primarily Black. Jamie Foxx played a Moorish version of Little John in 2018's *Robin Hood* after Morgan Freeman played the Muslim Moor Azeem in *Robin Hood: Prince of Thieves*. In the movie adaptation of *Othello* starring Laurence Fishburne as the Spanish Moor, and Mehki Phifer in the high-school adaptation *O*.

The Shakespeare play is rarely performed with Arab, Amazigh or North African actors despite the tragic hero believed to have been inspired by the olive-skinned Abd el-Ouahed ben Messaoud ben Mohammed Anoun, the Moorish ambassador to the Arab King of Barbary who was present in Queen Elizabeth's court. The 'Moors' was the name given to the indigenous Imazighen by European Christians and later broadened to include Maghrebi Arabs, but the few mainstream occasions Othello has been depicted as an Arab-African Moor is with brownface by actors Anthony Hopkins in 1981 and Michael Gambon in 1991, a precedent set by Laurence, 'never a role he wouldn't paint his face for', Olivier who played him in blackface in 1965. Could Black, Arab and Afro-Arab actors all get an equal turn? Even watching the BBC series *Noughts and Crosses* felt like I'd been confronted by a government form asking me my ethnicity but only offering Black African or White African as an option. In this dystopian world where African nations colonised Europe, and Black 'Crosses' rule over white 'Noughts' there appear to be no Egyptian, Tunisian, Moroccan or other North African characters and actors to be found. It's kinda like doing a film about the Latin-American community and not casting anyone Afro-Latinx. I welcome the increasing opportunities afforded to the wider BIPOC community, but I wish it didn't always feel like Arabs were the minority not being heard at the back of the queue.

Take the controversial casting of Javier Bardem in both *Dune* and *Being the Ricardos*. When the Latin community questioned the decision of the Spanish actor playing Desi Arnaz, the white

Cuban other half of Lucille Ball and co-lead of Aaron Sorkin's biopic, there was widespread coverage. News outlets reported on the backlash and when interviewed, a journalist put the casting question to Sorkin directly. Comparatively, there was next to no noise about the decision to cast Bardem as Stilgar, a Fremen character from Frank Herbert's *Dune* who lives on a planet that is not only coded Arab-North African, but is part of a nomadic desert community highly inspired by Bedouin culture, the writings of Tunisian philosopher Ibn Khaldun, his book *The Muqaddimah*, and whose language is Arabic. Despite online criticism from a faction of the MENA community, it did not become a trending topic or earn mainstream coverage. Sparse MENA critics, including myself, Roxana Hadadi and Leila Latif broached the subject in our critical analyses while the rest of the critical community remained silent. Journalists with access to director Denis Villeneuve failed to push him on the exclusion of Arab and MENA people from key roles. It felt like I was screaming into the void because no one really cares and despite some critics, academics, film-makers and advocacy groups using our online platforms and writing to raise awareness, the Western diaspora of MENA people is just too small to inspire much support or demand of Hollywood gatekeepers. Where Black Twitter, Latinx Twitter and Asian Twitter can be formidable forces for change and conversation starters, we just don't have the presence, unity or expectation that our concerns about representation will be answered.

That's how we've got to a point where Dwayne 'The Rock' Johnson can play Black Adam, Hollywood's first Middle Eastern superhero to lead a solo movie on the big screen. As a superhero movie fan I've been especially aware of how Arabs appear in this widely popular genre. Comic books have long relied on Orientalist tropes to depict some of their more mystical superheroes like Marvel's Iron Fist and Doctor Strange, whose white heroes' powers derive from East Asia, and Ancient Egypt for Moon Knight as well as DC's Doctor Fate, Hawkman, Hawkgirl and, sigh, Black Adam. OK, let me preface this by saying I am a fan of Johnson and his ability to counter his outwardly machismo image with endearing depth and comedic looseness in films like *Central Intelligence*, *Pain & Gain*, and the *Fast and Furious* franchise. As an actor of Samoan and Black Nova Scotian descent, he has claimed space for the people of colour on screen and through his part in *Moana*, has helped to establish a new precedent for the artistic and cultural benefits of having authentic representation in telling culturally rich and diverse stories on screen.

It's in the action genre that he has made a significant impact by positioning people of colour as leads, as heroes, after decades of the world watching mostly white heroes battling brown villains. It's exactly because of that norm, that he was cast in his first film role as the villainous Scorpion King in *The Mummy Returns* where it didn't matter that his character hails from the Ancient Mesopotamian city of Akkad,[29] he was big and brown enough to play the foreboding baddie. You can forgive him for taking the role as he was new to Hollywood, where there was a one-ethnic-minority-fits-all directive. Today? Sorry, pal. I cannot give you that benefit of the doubt. Johnson was cast in 2007 off the back of his *Scorpion King* solo film to play this villain-turned-antihero who was originally the son of the ancient Egyptian Pharaoh Ramesses II corrupted by the magical powers of Shazam. His origin story was later changed to being the protector of the fictional North African city of Kahndaq. He's had over a decade to recognise that by remaining in this role he has taken the opportunity away from an Arab actor to play the first Arab superhero.

Ryan Coogler's *Black Panther* and Daniel Destin Cretton's *Shang-Chi and the Ten Rings* went to great lengths in front of and behind the camera to ensure that cultural richness and representation was felt in every facet of their movies, and neither leads were box office draws. Apart from being hench, Johnson looks nothing like Black Adam. He didn't even bother doing

---

[29] Nowadays, the region occupies modern Iraq and a bit of Kuwait.

213

Teth-Adam's statement black hair, and if the *Men's Health* covers of Kumail Nanjiani, Chris Pratt and Zachary Levi prior to appearing in *Eternals*, *Guardians of the Galaxy* and *Shazam!* are anything to go by, an Arab actor could easily buff themselves up to fit the role they are already ethnically and culturally suited to. Marwan Kenzari just appeared in *The Old Guard* as the hot and buff-as-fuck immortal Yusuf Al-Kaysani but only as a supporting role. I remember when Johnson tweeted that the Dutch-Tunisian actor was joining Black Adam and you know what, my hand slipped. 'Marwan should have been cast as Black Adam and if his secret role is villainous I will not be impressed,' I tweeted because of the frustration at seeing a great North African actor sidelined in a North African story by a non-North African star. Johnson replied, 'Haha well pretty much means you won't be impressed.'

I'm not the only one. 'I was really annoyed with DC when they set Black Adam in a fictional Middle Eastern country as an excuse to cast non-Egyptians when it was obviously meant to be in Egypt,' said Egyptian film-maker Mohamed Diab. 'Representation opportunities shouldn't be wasted.'[30] Diab didn't waste his opportunity when asked to direct the *Moon Knight* series. The white Marvel hero imbued with the powers of an Ancient Egyptian god has all the Orientalist trappings on the page, but Diab and his wife-producing partner Sarah Goher managed to push back against completely whitewashing the series by replacing the white female love interest Maurene with archaeologist Layla El-Faouley played by Egyptian-Palestinian actress May Calamawy opposite Guatemalan-Cuban-American actor Oscar Isaac as the eponymous hero. The show cast only MENA actors as MENA characters, including F. Murray Abrahams, Antonia Salib, Amr Al-Qadi, Zizi Dagher, Ahmed Dash and Hazem Ehab and Calamawy's character

---

[30] Barnhardt, Adam, 'Moon Knight Director Takes Shot at Dwayne Johnson's Black Adam' (22 March 2022) https://comicbook.com/dc/news/moon-knight-director-takes-shot-dwayne-johnsons-black-adam/

becomes the superhero Scarlet Scarab herself, making her the first Arab superhero in the Marvel Cinematic Universe. Watching the finale where Layla confidently replies, 'I am,' when a young girl asks, 'Are you an Egyptian Superhero?' was a simple, beautiful thing that I wish Jack and Edward had seen. After a century of bombers, belly dancers and billionaires, Layla truly broke the mould as a curly-haired Arab heroine that my younger self would have absolutely looked up to. She is just a normal, resilient woman, neither painted with a sexual or religious brush, that speaks to many of us in the diaspora who similarly don't fit into the Western canon's narrow view of Arab people.

Calamawy is no stranger to this sort of TV role thanks to Ramy Youssef's self-titled comedy series that's now in its third season. It hilariously captures the normality of the bicultural Arab-American experience of a Muslim Egyptian family in New Jersey. She plays Ramy's sister Deena, a graduate student dealing with the familial double standard as a woman compared to her brother who lives a millennial lifestyle that doesn't always seem compatible with his faith. Shaheen lamented the lack of films and TV shows showing Arabs doing normal things, working normal jobs and dealing with normal hang-ups, but with Ramy and the Rami Malek-led *Mr. Robot*, finally, the show captures that sort of mundane reality for many children of North African immigrants in the West more used to micro-aggressions than Molotov cocktails. Of course, Deena and Layla cannot possibly represent all Arab women, but both are a step in the right direction. And who knows, maybe Layla will be the first female Arab character to lead a studio movie. We're still waiting for any Arab woman to earn that honour in Hollywood; MENA women are still vastly under-represented. 2019's *Aladdin* is still the only one to feature a leading man, ever, which is rather tiring when sci-fi franchises like *Dune* and *Star Wars* borrow so heavily from Arab culture. Luke Skywalker's home planet Tatooine literally stole its name from a Tunisian city near to where *A New Hope* was shot and

HANNA FLINT

featured the Tusken Raiders, coded nomadic aliens who wear masks and speak in unintelligible grunts. Still today, space Arabs are only allowed in a galaxy far, far away if they are played by anyone other than Arabs!

So where else to look for Arab stories? European independent cinema has made promising steps that offer a diversity of Arab leads and characters beyond the one-dimensional stereotypes. Danish thriller *Sons of Denmark* (2019), French crime drama *Un Prophète* (2009), family drama *Lullaby* (2019) and terrorism biopic *You Resemble Me* (2021), as well as Scottish refugee comedy *Limbo*, are all fantastic, intriguing films, but are still awfully wrapped up in traumatic storylines. Even the American rom-com *Amira & Sam* (2014) manages to Other Dina Shihabi's female lead by making her an illegal immigrant from Iraq. In Canadian-Lebanese-French drama *Memory Box*, the film centres on a teenager trying to learn more about her mother through notebooks, tapes, and photos from her time in 1980s Beirut during the Lebanon War. British-Egyptian film-maker Sally El-Hosaini follows up her powerful debut *My Brother the Devil* with *The Swimmers*, based on the true story of the Mardini sisters whose heroic refugee journey led to one of the young Syrian women going to the Olympics.

This is not to say these stories aren't phenomenally made or worthy enough to be told. We certainly need more empathetic understanding of the Arab world to combat the dehumanising stereotypes that the media loves to reuse. The occupation of the West Bank, including East Jerusalem, and the Gaza Strip that Amnesty International says has 'resulted in systematic human rights violations against Palestinians living there' so documentaries like *Eleven Days in May*, *Mayor* and *Tantura* are providing more balanced coverage of the Israel-Palestine conflict. We need these films to remind the world that 'Reel bad Arabs' are vastly outnumbered by those who are good and complicated and deserve as much empathy as any other person in the world.

Arab cinema might have issues with government censorship when it comes to the way it presents politics, religion and sex, but there are more than enough film-makers who have produced films that capture the unfiltered realism and diversity of the Arab world. Haifaa al-Mansour's films *Wadjda* and *The Perfect Candidate*, despite the rigid Saudi laws, grant her female protagonists living in suburban Riyadh confident and progressive attitudes. Al-Mansour tackles feminist issues concerning autonomy, gender inequality, religious hypocrisy and family life with a lighter touch and without religious prejudice. I loved the frothiness of Manele Labidi's comedy *Arab Blues* about a Tunisian psychotherapist returning home from France to open a practice. Thanks to Netflix, you can find the iconic Egyptian classics of Youssef Chahine, like *The Blazing Sun* and *Cairo Station*, as well as contemporary female-led series like *Al Rawabi School for Girls* that prove stories can be set in Jordan and about Jordanians rather than simply serving as a historical or sci-fi backdrop to American movies.[31]

I've lived my whole life in the West and believe I have just as much right to see myself reflected on screen as any other person. Arab actors deserve more than the dregs of characterisations left by lazy screenwriters. After nearly 100 years of vilification, hasn't Western cinema made Arabs suffer enough? Please, I beg. Give us joy. Give us Arabs leading stories where their race isn't a punchline or a punch in the face. I'm a critic who wants to be entertained by every type of story going, but I'm also just a British-Arab girl, sitting in front of a screen, asking the movies to love her.

---

[31] *Dune, The Rise of Skywalker, Lawrence of Arabia, The Martian* etc., have all used Wadi Rum as a shooting location.

Chapter 15

'Be hashtag 'blessed' because the whole world is watching.'

– Assassination Nation (2018)

EVERY MORNING, AFTER I wake up, I pick up my phone and do four things. First, I check the time in case it's actually too early and I can get more sleep. I'm something of an insomniac who hasn't been able to remain unconscious through the night longer than five hours since 2013. A combination of anxiety and weird working hours has probably done it, so I regularly wake up in the small hours, and force myself to catch a few more winks. I know I should see a doctor, I have. And a psychiatrist. And a therapist. Alas, the antidepressants didn't work so I'm all for other suggestions. When it is an acceptable time to start the day, I check my email in case there's some emergency matter that needs sorting. Then I look at my bank balance. I'm paid sporadically, often late, and it can feel like Russian roulette every time I sign into my banking app. Finally, before it's time to shift from my covers and remove myself to the toilet seat, I enter the endless rabbit hole of social media to see what's whatting.

I've long convinced myself it is a requirement of my job to include a Twitter browse as part of my morning routine. I don't think I'm entirely wrong. When I was doing my postgrad, my course leader said a good journalist wakes up listening to

BBC Radio 4 and always checks the papers for the day's stories. She also described entertainment coverage as 'fluff' for the end of a news broadcast when I once pitched a cinema story, so I didn't take all her little tidbits of wisdom to heart. But she's absolutely right about keeping abreast of the news from the moment you wake and social media has become an essential part of news gathering, distribution and consumption. As a freelancer, especially, keeping up to date with trending topics disseminating online is a valuable way to inspire my work's content because of an announcement I've gleaned from a morning scroll. Ah, the scroll. That silent flickering of your eyes across a screen as you glance at a glut of posts until something captures your brief interest before continuing your descent into past thoughts and reports. Pale light refracts off the contours of your face as videos, images and memes whiz in and out of your phone's frame of vision. Lots of films and TV shows nowadays incorporate how much social media has become an everyday function in our lives; from the origins of Facebook in *The Social Network* to a dad looking for his missing daughter, presented entirely through a computer screen in *Searching* and even via Jennifer Lopez's meta popstar influencer in *Marry Me* who is always red-carpet ready and 'on' for the 'Gram.

Eighth Grade acutely captures social media exploration and expectation through the eyes of a fourteen-year-old girl, but you don't have to be a fourteen-year-old girl anymore, or at all, to recognise just how normalised this obsessive process has become in our daily lives. As someone whose rise to fame was on YouTube, and was once told that he was a 'comedian for thirteen-year-old girls,' it's no surprise that Bo Burnham[1] was able to encapsulate the angst and anxiety of adolescence when every facet of your life is meant to be airbrushed to within an inch of its life on Snapchat, TikTok, or whatever the young

---

[1] Burnham, Bo, Spirit Awards acceptance speech (25 February 2019) https://www.youtube.com/watch?v=IHHLiS0tttU

kids are fucking with these days. Social media has fast become a compulsory extension of the school environment and not to get all geriatric millennial, but I'm so glad that the only cool thing my mobile phone was expected to do when I was fourteen was play Snake and recreate pop songs as ringtones. Burnham consistently focuses the camera on Elsie's dispirited face illuminated by the bluish light of her phone as she scrolls and scrolls and scrolls across her various social feeds, peeking into the carefully curated lives of her school peers while rarely ever feeling part of these social circles herself. I love the opening sequence which is really an update of the opening scene of *Bridesmaids* for the social media age. In the 2011 rom-com, Kristen Wiig's Annie wakes up, sneaks to the bathroom to do her make-up before returning to bed to convince Jon Hamm's Ted that she, in the words of Beyoncé, 'Woke up like dis'. In *Eighth Grade*, Elsie does her make-up with a YouTube tutorial then returns under the covers to capture the perfect selfie, with the addition of a filter, to convince her followers she woke up like dis too. I don't think I've gotten out of bed to put on make-up for a guy, brushed my teeth maybe, but I've added a filter here and there for a social media post. When it comes to spots, I subscribe to the Andy Warhol school of thought. 'When I did my self-portrait, I left all the pimples out because you always should . . . Pimples are a temporary condition and they don't have anything to do with what you really look like. Always omit the blemishes – they're not part of the good picture you want.'[2]

I'm not going to tell you whether you should retouch your photos or not. Your aesthetic and beauty practices are a personal thing you need to work out and we all come to it with our own baggage. But I appreciate films like *Eighth Grade* and *Bridesmaids* that at least don't try to demonise girls and women with insecurities who might feel more comfortable presenting themselves online or offline with a few enhancements. Unlike Gia Coppola's *Mainstream*, which can't decide whether it wants to shame

---

[2] Warhol, A. (2018). Fame. United Kingdom: Penguin Books Limited.

women for wearing make-up or not. In one scene, Alexa Demie's character Isabelle is brutally pressured into posting a photo without make-up that shows the large birthmark on her face. Andrew Garfield's influencer No One Special delivers a diatribe against vanity and for self-love with zero compassion and Isabelle is visibly humiliated. He later attacks beauty influencers for making women feel insecure but he himself has no qualms exploiting people for clicks. It's all a bit eye-rolling and judge-mental and as critic Jessica Kiang points out, 'the idea that the worst damage social media can do is to exploit the insecurities of vulnerable individuals or heroize the ravings of the occasional mentally unstable loner, seems a little old-hat.'[3]

Whether it's through pics, vids or tweets, our authentic selves rarely ever make the transition to socials. They will only ever be facsimiles, like René Magritte's painting *The Treachery of Images*, with the drawing of a pipe and the words 'Ceci n'est pas une pipe.' The self-iterations we present are mostly designed to make us look attractive to other people. Of course, there are people who like to share everything, the ups and the downs, but unless you're living your life like *The Truman Show*, where every aspect of your world is streamed live without your knowledge, we can never get the full picture. Most of us are focused on capturing our best selves. That's what Elsie is doing with her motivational YouTube videos and her edited selfies: aspirational images of the girl she wants to be rather than who she is right now.

In *Assassination Nation*, Sam Levinson taps into the distor-tion between our offline and online selves, specifically the pressure on women to conform to certain ideas about how they should behave and act. Bringing a new witch hunt to the Salem setting, Odessa Young's high-schooler Lily offers a cynical perspective on the toxic masculinity that feeds the hypocrisy of this small town when a hacker puts the town's

[3] Kiang, Jessica, '"Mainstream" review: Internet Fame Eats Itself in Gia Coppola's Satire' (5 September 2020) ://variety.com/2020/film/reviews/mainstream-review-gia-coppola-1234759713/

private phone data online, and among other secrets, it is revealed she had an affair with a married man:

LILY

They tell you that if you're honest, and you say what you feel, then you'll get what you want. The truth is no one wants the real you. So you stop telling the truth. You lie to your friends. You lie to your family. You lie to everyone who says they love you for being you. Because guess what? They're lying too. They only want pieces and parts. They want to pick and choose. They want that laugh with that smile. That pic, with that confidence. That girl, with that willingness . . . but not her, not like that. And to be honest . . . he's perfect. He's sweet. He's gorgeous. And you're lucky. So be happy. Be grateful. Be hashtag 'blessed'. Because the whole world is watching. And waiting. And it's only a matter of time before you fuck it all up.

That sentiment is touched upon in Magnus von Horn's *Sweat* where Polish fitness influencer Sylwia (Magdalena Kolesnik) presents a stream of positivity, happiness and motivational zest to her 600,000 followers and maintains an image of a hard-bodied Barbie doll that she says they could achieve if they just follow her lead. Of course, sustaining this body is her job and there's tough slog, strict dieting required and significant time invested into this aesthetic. She gets paid loads to promote products, is sent amazing freebies, lives in a swish apartment and gets invited to glitzy events. But in reality she's living a lonely, loveless life with only her 'loves' (her followers), for moral support and positive affirmation. Some take that parasocial relationship too far, demanding more than she can give or have any right to take after she breaks the positivity cycle with a video of herself crying over her single status. The first time she was authentic, she ended up admonished for it. Magnus von Horn compassionately captures the dichotomy of a person's public and private persona as well as the struggle for people, whether they be fitness influencers or an average joe, to have only the online world as an outlet to be vulnerable in lieu of real-world connections. The Internet can be a lifeline, but also a chokehold, especially for women who are often expected to be accessible and carry the emotional burden of people they don't know.

The curated image that I want to present is that of a successful, intelligent, hardworking, knowledgeable, funny, grateful, compassionate, desirable, you know, self-deprecating woman and writer. For some people it works, others it irritates, but as my online presence has evolved, so has the professional position I'm in for the better. 'Personal brand' sounds so gauche, but isn't that the reality of what we are all trying to sell, at least in the pursuit of professional achievement? If I'm not posting links to articles or appearances, I'm sharing thirst traps with punny captions as though it will make the narcissism of each posy photo less potent. I rarely post about my mental health unless it's underscored by a joke because I feel that I'm too privileged in life to whine about my sadness or anxiety in public. Just here, in my book. I also find it odd that we click 'like' on pretty depressing stuff. Maybe we need another button for that situation, something like 'Acknowledge' or 'Nod' that lets you show someone you see and hear them without the buoyant tone of a like. I'm still workshopping that idea. I mostly aim to write witty or sincere observations about movies, my life and the things going on in the world to garner engagement that might boost the online awareness of me and the things I care and write about. My Instagram, Twitter and TikTok are all shops in the strip mall that is me and I'm hoping to convert browsers to buyers and by buyers I mean editors or employers who might read my stuff and want me to work with them. Most of the new commissions I get now are from DMs or people contacting me via my website link in my social media bios. That's how I was asked to become a host for MTV Movies; a development producer had been following me for a while and thought I would be a good fit.

Being online, in my case at least, also has a lot to do with ego and validation. I worry a lot about what people think of me, whether I'm a good person or a good writer, and I've been a people pleaser since I was a kid, so the need for likes and to be liked has become an inconsistent way to boost self-confidence. Even after turning off my push notifications, I find myself refreshing my social feeds several times during the day, almost robotically checking to see if there's a new bit of engagement I can get a dopamine hit from. *The Social Dilemma* documentary is right; these tech companies have designed these sites to keep you hooked in and it's a time-consuming addiction. This is why I love watching movies in a cinema even more than before smartphones became the standard. I put the world on airplane mode until the film is over. At home, it's a nightmare trying to break the habit of checking my phone every ten minutes. At this point, it's almost an involuntary reflex. The amount of times I've had to stop a film or episode and rewind because I've been hypnotised by the scroll. On occasion I have to physically put my phone in another room just so I can focus and find myself reaching towards the empty space it once filled. Living alone has only made me more reliant on this kind of social gratification. I can go days without uttering a single word to another soul, during lockdown especially, so being able to chat and catch up with people online gives me an energy boost to combat the loneliness when I'm feeling low mood or anxious. Some of my best friends came into my life via social media and I'm so grateful that it has provided a space to connect with people you might never have had the opportunity to do so. Yet the shifting dynamics of online relationships and community interactions can exacerbate anxious feelings to a detrimental degree.

I couldn't get through the *Black Mirror* episode 'Nosedive' the first time I put it on. Its dystopian world of endless personal rankings that affect your socioeconomic status sees Bryce Dallas Howard emit the barely-concealed stress of being extremely online through her well-meaning but desperate loner Lacie. The way her perky Stepford Wives persona slips as her rating begins to plummet following a series of unfortunate events had me clicking pause and having to come back to it a few years later. It was too triggering. It made me think too much about my own online presence which always causes negative thoughts to cloud my head as I think about my own perceived ranking compared to friends, peers and nemeses. OK, nemeses might be too strong a word, but we all have those mutuals who annoy us and do not want to see succeed, or at least, succeed more than ourselves. It can trigger some awful spates of self-loathing where instead of recognising that someone else's triumphs do not make you a failure, you lean into the toxic choice of beating yourself up for not being where you want to be in your life. Nothing feeds a sense of inadequacy like logging on and 'Nosedive' taps into the way social media can have an adverse impact on your career when one of Lacie's colleagues loses his jobs because he's lost too much social clout. It's so bleak!

In Laurent Cantet's *Arthur Rambo*, the world of a young French-Algerian writer implodes when problematic tweets resurface from a defunct satirical account he used to run as a teen. Loosely based on the controversy surrounding media personality Mehdi Meklat, Rabah Nait Oufella plays this Gen Z cause célèbre who came up from a low-income housing estate and earned critical acclaim for his debut novel until everyone dropped him the minute the ugly extent of these youthful tweets were revealed. Like *Assassination Nation* it shows the lack of empathy brewed by online practices, while also highlighting the fickleness of the Establishment figures, like his white publisher who swiftly goes from praise to pulping his new book instead of supporting their writer. Cantet creates a meaningful space in the grey area of social media life for this complex debate about identity, racism, class and outsiders to take place.

The gender-swapped *She's All That* sequel, aptly titled *He's All That*, replicates the insecurity of social media as a career through a TikTok influencer who pretends to live an affluent life when, in truth, she's providing financial support to her single mother nurse. After being humiliated in a livestream, she begins losing her followers and sponsorship deals which damage their household income. It poses an interesting premise given the societal and generational friction concerning influencer culture. Derision is often reserved for social media personalities because of the lavish lifestyles some of these high-profile users promote despite not having any particular expertise or talent. But, it allows those from low-income backgrounds, who haven't benefited from class privilege, to tap into a contemporary entre-preneurial endeavour that allows them to do what they love. Not everyone has the financial support to enter further educa-tion or certain connections to make it into creative industries. So whether it be beauty, fashion, science, film, maths, baking or any other area they are passionate for, I can respect social media influencing as a viable income resource.

But there's no denying how often follower count carries more weight than actual talent and *He's All That* provides that example too by casting TikTok influencer Addison Rae as the lead. She has cast a wide net for what she promotes,[4] but her acting failed to impress viewers after seeing the first trailer or most critics when the film was released. 'Rae struggles to modulate her camera-ready bubbliness in moments that require pathos,' wrote Devika Girish for the *New York Times*,[5] while the *Guardian*'s Adrian Horton said, 'While Rae offers flashes of promise, especially when she pops her genuinely winning smile, she doesn't make the case for TikTok-to-film-stardom here.'[6] I stopped the

---

[4] Rae started off doing dance numbers to popular songs and now has a beauty line, a Spotify podcast, released a pop song and has done various endorsement deals from Pandora to Reebok.

[5] Gerish, Devika, '"He's All That" Review: Much Ado About Nothing' (27 August 2021) https://www.nytimes.com/2021/08/27/movies/hes-all-that-review.html

[6] Horton, Adrian, '"He's All That review – Netflix's dull TikTok teen remake lacks charm' (27 August 2021) https://www.theguardian.com/film/2021/aug/27/hes-all-that-review-netflixs-dull-tiktok-teen-remake-lacks-charm

film after twenty minutes because if I've learned anything as a critic it is to not sit through ones you are not enjoying unless you are getting paid for it. Had Rae delivered a fine performance it would have quieted most of the criticism surrounding her casting. Celebrity status has moved well beyond traditional media and into digital marketing, which means the casting process will continue to see the hiring of popular influencers or actors with platforms that rarely match the size of their talent in order to tap into their audiences. Of course, Hollywood has already seen the casting of mediocre actors through nepotism for decades, so while there are obviously truly talented people working in the industry, it has not and will never be a meritocracy. Still, the loud and negative reaction to Rae's casting and acting shows just how much scrutiny you face as your public profile rises.

Even with my much, MUCH, smaller presence, I've noticed an increase in the amount of criticism, abuse and trolling I've been met with. There's something rather ironic about a critic struggling with criticism, but over the last few years I've experienced vitriolic pile-ons because of my film opinions and it admittedly has had an adverse impact on my mental health. According to Amnesty International, one in five women in the UK have suffered some form of online abuse and '55% experienced anxiety, stress or panic attacks as a result' while 'many faced other psychological consequences, such as loss of self-esteem and a sense of powerlessness in their ability to respond to the abuse.'[7] I once tweeted 'white men in power can't be trusted' using four images from the MCU to point out a bureaucratic character trope they reuse and among the misogynist insults thrown at me in quote-tweets and replies, one guy created a seventeen-minute YouTube video to insult me and questioning my identity. When Sean Connery died I

---

[7] Amnesty International UK, 'Online abuse of women widespread in UK', https://www.amnesty.org.uk/online-abuse-women-widespread

posted a tweet that reconciled my love for him as an actor, but unease with his personal admission of hitting women:

> Sean Connery was a fine actor, an even better Bond. A Bond that was suave, dapper and charismatic but defined by a toxic masculinity that he sadly seemed to exhibit offscreen. A problematic fave. RIP.

The tweet was ratio'd with sexist insults and derision from predominantly men that, even when I blocked and muted the conversation, negative comments managed to slip through the gaps, in my DMs and on other platforms. To be a woman writing about film comes with an overwhelming amount of unsolicited replies from men that can range from condescending, overfamiliar, rude and abusive. One guy went on a rant about me because I tweeted I didn't like *Paddington 2*. A few weeks later, he DM'd me asking me out for a drink. It's why I really got on with *The Columnist* about a feminist writer who goes on a killing spree against the misogynist trolls who post shit about her. We're told to not engage and take the high road, but this film provides the revenge-fantasy of meeting verbal abuse with physical abuse even if its commitment to interrogating the real issues faced by women online is only really used as a jumping-off point.

It's not always men – it's mostly men – but sometimes it can be young women with a lot to say about you if you mention their fave. I've felt the wrath of Harry Styles fans over the years. One time a stan tweeted 'WHOS COMING WITH ME TO SHOOT THIS HANNA FLINT' after I wrote about the One Direction wax figures in Madame Tussauds. More recently when I suggested the overpraise Olivia Wilde gave Styles, her boyfriend, for accepting a supporting role opposite Florence Pugh in her movie *Don't Worry Darling*, was one for 'bare minimum Twitter'. I got a litany of offended responses calling me various insults, a white feminist too, and a few DMs including one asking me to 'c word in ur sleep'; I assume they meant 'choke' and not 'climax'. Another said, 'I know your address and you should take care of yourself because I will go for you.' The worst pile-on was when I wrote an op-ed about Gal Gadot's casting as Cleopatra. Given the long history of the Egyptian queen being played by white women and Hollywood frequently using Egypt and North Africa as a backdrop to tell mostly white saviour stories without actors from the region in the lead, I lamented the missed opportunity once again. That even if you did or didn't agree with the position that Cleopatra may have had North African heritage through her unknown mother, this could have been a chance to counter Hollywood's colourism of favouring light-skinned actors. When the *Guardian* published the piece with the headline 'Gal Gadot as Cleopatra is a backwards step for Hollywood representation', I received an onslaught of trolling from people accusing me of antisemitism including high-profile actors and media personalities. One mutual subtweeted the article with the suggestion I hated Jews. It was a shock to the system. I had earnestly asked a Jewish friend to read the article before filing it as I was conscious of avoiding any antisemitic language. I couldn't sleep for four days because of the endless accusations, and despite asking the editor – who is Jewish – to change the headline and the reference to Gadot's Jewish heritage, which was added during the sub-edit, my requests were not met. It was only after posting a note on my own website providing the context that the trolling ended.

In all of these situations, regardless of many people supporting me, I can find myself obsessing over the negative reactions rather than the positive. Our brains really don't have our back sometimes. It also made me realise that over the years I may have contributed to pile-ons. When we respond to things we disagree with online we only consider it a drop in the ocean, but when a lot of drops get whipped up it becomes a wave that can swallow a person up. I've been drenched too many times to want anyone else to experience that for something as innocuous as a hot take about movies. I'm trying to tweet less, browse less, be less snarky and take negative responses less to heart. I don't need to respond to every opinion I don't agree with. Instead I might text a friend or, if it's film related, discuss it on my weekly podcast in our Hot Take section. It's not that I'm going to silence myself. I will speak about things I don't agree with even if I lose followers and gain vitriol. I'm just limiting the people who I am willing to engage with. Fighting for people to understand nuance on Twitter is a battle not worth entering into when bad faith is the only argument that a lot of users want to respond with. And it's certainly not my responsibility to respond to every person who might contact me, be it positive or negative.

I'm trying to no longer be an extremely-online person, more of a sometimes-online person, and remind myself that I don't need to ascribe self-worth to strangers on the internet. I began therapy after the Cleopatra saga and it has made me face the fact that as much as I want to control the narrative about who I am, I cannot control what others might say or feel about me either. I can report, block, mute, unfollow all I want, but there will be people hiding behind Internet anonymity to say unpleasant things and I don't need to give time to that when I can be spending it doing things that matter, that make me feel good, maybe watch a movie or read a book. Or write a book! Oh wait, I guess the plan's working.

Part Five

Strong Female Character

Chapter 16

'Grow up, Heather. Bulimia is so '87.'

– Heathers (1989)

THE FIRST TIME I made myself sick was because I had drunk too much alcohol. It was a Friday night in Nottingham, my second year of uni, and I was out with some girlfriends at Ocean nightclub. We'd done pre-drinks at mine and Glen's Vodka followed by a string of cheap colourful cocktails and Bacardi Breezers had done quite a number on my head and my balance. One of the girls guided me to the loos and suggested I perform what was commonly known at my uni as a 'tactical chunder'. She instructed me how to make myself vomit so my dizziness would clear. Lo and behold, the booze and remnants of a mushroom stir fry exploded out of me into the toilet below. My head did clear, briefly, and I washed away the nauseous taste with another Breezer. Nothing like a hack to keep the party going, right? Unfortunately, I'd soon be using this hack to enable an eating disorder that would plague me throughout my adult life.

My first cinematic introduction to eating disorders was the 1999 movie *Drop Dead Gorgeous*, a Christopher Guest-esque mockumentary, written by Lona Williams, about a small Minnesota town beauty pageant and it's still one of the most biting satires about unrealistic beauty standards, American nationalism and civic corruption ever made. It also has Ellen Barkin and Allison Janney appearing as trailer-park BFFs and their no-nonsense double act is a joy to watch. But the contest's previous winner, Mount Rose American Teen Princess Mary Johansen (Alexandra Holden) represents the many girls and young women, who in their pursuit of achieving the perfect female body to win a crown, become overwhelmed with an eating disorder and in Mary's case anorexia. A study conducted in 2003 found that over 25% of pageant contestants had developed an eating disorder from the age of sixteen[1] – an unsurprising stat given the ridiculous expectations set by these competitions – but what I remember when seeing this film in my teens was how unattractive anorexia looked. Mary looks emaciated when they meet her in hospital, bedridden because she is too weak to stand and barely looking like she's in the room with a hazy smile. Later in the film, she returns to the pageant, as tradition dictates, to perform her winning routine from the year before and she gets pushed around in a wheelchair in awkward fashion. It's a darkly funny but tragic scene that captures how unglamorous and detrimental anorexia can be. It made me hyper aware of not wanting to develop an eating disorder, oh sweet summer child, but everywhere I looked, thinness was the goal.

From the women's magazines offering 'Lose a stone in two weeks!' diets in every issue, to size-zero models in shop windows and pretty much every single movie featuring a slender white girl or woman as its lead, my generation was raised on images that said, 'Go girl, hate your body!' According to a 1997 study, 'as many as 90% of women find fault with some aspect of their body and approximately 70%

---

[1] Thompson, S.H. and K. Hammond, 'Beauty is as beauty does: body image and self-esteem of pageant contestants' (September 2003) National Library of Medicine, https://pubmed.ncbi.nlm.nih.gov/14649788/

of all women are preoccupied with their weight'.[2] So if you're a millennial woman and didn't have size hang-ups during your teens then I envy you, because even though I was objectively slim and had an athletic build from playing sports five times a week, I always felt I was fat in comparison to my skinnier friend who was only a size smaller than me. I used to be embarrassed about my fatter butt because it would protrude compared to hers, my hips were wider and I developed bigger boobs. Of course now I recognise these are enviable assets to have, but when you can't borrow your friend's clothes because your ass is too big it can certainly give you a complex. *Love Actually* derided the idea of having a big rear. Even at the time, I was confused by the sentiment that Martine McCutcheon's Natalie was a 'chubby girl'. This woman is normal sized and yet she's body-shamed throughout by having her suggest she was dumped because 'nobody wants a girlfriend with thighs the size of tree trunks'. Her svelte colleague Annie says she has a 'sizeable arse there . . . huge thighs', while her dad calls her 'plumpy'. It gives the impression that Hugh Grant's PM is some sort of white knight able to look past the flaws of her weight, despite her not being at all fat or oversized. The film really gave fresh meaning to the camera adds ten pounds. Similarly, *Bridget Jones's Diary* and the surrounding press made a massive deal about Renée Zellweger's weight. Media outlets were obsessed with the fact the actress gained thirty pounds for the role, lost it and then gained it again for the 2004 sequel, which still only made her 136lbs. Throughout the films her goal is to constantly lose 20lbs and there's a brutal scene where she walks in on Hugh Grant's Daniel cheating on her with Lara from the US office. Her only line is: 'I thought you said she was thin.' A dagger

---

2   Anderson, Lisa, Jill-Marie Shaw and Linda McCargar, 'Physiological effects of bulimia nervosa on the gastrointestinal tract' (1997) https://downloads. hindawi.com/journals/cjgh/1997/727645.pdf

through every woman's heart! Even though the film is articulating the very real weight obsession women have through
a normal-sized woman like Bridget, who has been conditioned
to believe she is overweight, there's never a moment of real
bodily self-acceptance.

When I got to university, boozing became a more frequent
activity. I was responsible for my own food too which mostly
revolved around two-for-one pizzas from Dino's after a night
out, packet noodles and meal deals from the Sainsbury's Local.
I was such a lazy bitch I used to have a leaning tower of pizza
boxes near my bedroom door. So even though I was playing
basketball throughout this period, the training was no longer
offsetting my calorie intake and I gained a pot belly that I
haven't been able to shift since and averaged out my weight
at about eleven stone by the time I graduated. I'd try diets on
and off but, like most women, just accepted that the pursuit
of the perfect body and weight would be a never-ending story.
I used to watch the TV show *Supersize vs Superskinny* and be
grateful that I was on neither end of the spectrum, yet always
took mental notes of the superskinny woman's plate and sometimes tried to replicate her meal plan in the hopes of losing a
few pounds. These attempts only lasted a day before hunger
won out. I loved to eat. I still love to eat so when my eating
disorder developed, it was the supersized woman's meals that
my plates began to look like.

It started at Camp Che-Na-Wah. I'd saved up from a gap
year job at Topshop to afford the trip to upstate New York
and work as a basketball coach at a girls' summer camp. I was
twenty-two, still getting over the break-up that crushed me a
year earlier, but *Wet Hot American Summer* this was not. In
fact, it was after watching the bonkers comedy during my trip,
about sexually frustrated counsellors at a sleepaway camp in
the eighties, I thought maybe I wasn't having the full camp
experience. I was older than the usual counsellors, most of
whom were former campers themselves. I felt a bit of a distance
between myself and my seventeen-to-nineteen-year-old peers

and I was saving all my earnings for the month I planned to spend in New York after. I often volunteered as designated driver so the others could get drunk and merry. Meals were provided all-you-can-eat-buffet-style, and I couldn't resist the yellow food: pasta, fries, bread and other deep-fried options. When the kitchen was closed, I could munch on the sweets my thirteen-year-old bunkers brought with them in massive storage boxes. It was the first time I was introduced to the concept of a cookie cake. One girl's parents sent her to camp with one that had wrapped sweets stuck on to the cookie base with icing which might have been the most American thing I have ever seen. If the job didn't require me to be on my feet and active all day, I would probably have gained even more weight, but I still felt bloated. My clothing was getting snug and I felt less comfortable in my swimsuit compared to the younger girls and their tiny bodies. When I checked my weight on the scales I'd gained half a stone and I panicked. I tried to eat less, run more, started to sneak back to my bunk toilet during meals to make myself sick if I overindulged (the Romans did it, right?) and counted the days until I could escape to Manhattan, away from the temptation of food.

I had already begun stocking up on porridge oats sachets that I stole from the canteen so I wouldn't need to waste money on food later in the city. Plus, by the end of my time there, I'd finished reading this vegan book with the awful title of *Skinny Bitch*. It basically put me off eating a lot of American food because of its description of the additives and chemicals pumped into various animals. Honestly, it's a wonder the X-Gene hasn't been triggered in the populace already.[3] Once in New York City, on my own for the first couple of weeks until my friend Ana arrived, I was able to control my eating out of necessity, really. I'd spent a good chunk of my money renting a studio flat on 148th Street in Harlem, so I needed to count every penny and make sure I had enough to tick off

---

[3] One for the X-Men fans.

every activity on my to-do list. The porridge diet and trying to walk everywhere helped to shift the weight I'd gained over the summer, but I'd also developed a deep sense of guilt for anything bad that I put in my body. When I eventually returned to London, weighing less than when I left, I resorted to fad diets in a bid to maintain that weight.

One of them was the Maple Syrup diet. Pretty much every celebrity and woman's magazine relied on the dieting tips offered by famous women to sell issues. They began recommending this particular ten-day fast widely after a then twenty-four-year-old Beyoncé revealed she'd used it to lose weight for her role in *Dreamgirls*. The movie musical – based on the stage musical the creators said was not about the rise of Diana Ross and The Supremes but very much is about the rise of Diana Ross and The Supremes – saw the Destiny's Child singer cast in the role of Diana, sorry, Deena. Despite her already being slim in a way that accentuated her natural curves, she felt the need to lose 13lbs by fasting and only consuming a concoction of lemon juice, maple syrup and cayenne pepper for ten days before filming. She revealed the details in a 2007 interview with Oprah and obviously every media outlet became obsessed with getting their own soundbite on the subject because of our cultural preoccupation with women's bodies, especially those in the public eye. From Judy Garland and Sandra Dee to Charlize Theron and Beyoncé, Georganne Scheiner comments, these women are 'part of an industry in which the female body is constituted as an object of spectacle, fetishized, and often hacked apart and dismembered by the editing process.'[4] Beyoncé's extreme weight loss was just another by-product of working in Hollywood that she saw as requirement for doing a good job. 'It was no-one's suggestion I lost weight for the film, it was me who wanted to make a physical transformation,' she told BBC Breakfast.

[4] Scheiner, Georganne, 'Look at Me, I'm Sandra Dee: Beyond a White, Teen Icon' (2001) *Frontiers: A Journal of Women Studies,* https://muse.jhu.edu/article/12013.

In *Dreamgirls*, my character starts at 16 – and then 20 years pass. Normally they'd change your make-up or your clothes but I wanted to go the extra mile. Back in the Sixties, models like Twiggy were popular and I knew Deena would have been thin then. So even though I really love eating, it was necessary to lose weight really fast because we shot Deena at 16 and Deena at 36 two, weeks apart. My nutritionist suggested the only way to do that was the fast. As soon as it was over I gained the weight back. I would never recommend it to anyone unless you are doing a movie and it's necessary, and you have proper help. There are ways to lose weight healthily if you want to lose weight, but this was for a film.[5]

Of course, Beyoncé's warning was heartily ignored and even after doctors and nutritionists spoke out against the diet, the recipe and endorsements remained online forever. It came up when I Googled 'weight loss tips' in September 2010 and I managed to maintain it for longer than ten days while beginning my postgraduate programme at City University London. It felt good to be under ten stone for the first time since my early teens, never mind the fact that I couldn't stand up without feeling light-headed and seeing spots. Like Kate Moss at the time, I thought, 'nothing tastes as good as skinny feels.' I was doing Broadcast Journalism because I wanted to be on TV covering movie premieres, interviewing film stars and knew that being slim and attractive was something of a prerequisite for female entertainment journalists or presenters. Holly Willoughby, Alexa Chung, Tess Daly and Jameela Jamil were all models before becoming presenters, so I knew that simply being an excellent journalist wouldn't be enough.

For a month or so, I was all good. I started eating again and joined the local gym; feeling confident about this new stage of

[5] *Irish Examiner*, 'Beyonce warns against her maple syrup diet' (16 August 2006) https://www.irishexaminer.com/lifestyle/arid-30272483.html

my life and the first step I was making towards a career covering film. But then on a night out at a rave with my old university friends, I was unfortunately reunited with my ex, slept with him and all the mental work I'd done to rebuild myself after he dumped me crumbled. The anxiety rushed back as well as the memories of how he made me feel about myself. In arguments he would call me 'fat', 'dirty' and other such awful insults. When it became clear this was just a one-night stand and he had no interest in rekindling our relationship, I was left with rejection and shame to combat once more. Now I just wanted to fill the hole and food was the easiest choice. I'd go to the gym and on my way home visit the supermarket to buy the cheapest biscuits, cakes, crisps, snacks and fast food I could find. I knew the store layouts of several in the area and timed my visits to coincide when the reduced section would be filled because binge-eating can be an expensive habit and I was on a student budget.

During the Christmas break I spent most of it in my bed watching *Grey's Anatomy* and only left the house to replenish my stock, sneak most of it to my room and stuff my face until I felt sick enough to puke. Then I would. I bought laxatives to purge the food through the other hole, taking triple the recommended dose, and sometimes I couldn't even have a drink without needing to run to the loo. I can remember setting up work experience at a production company for a week during spring break. I was feeling depressed, unwell but showed up to the office which was located opposite an all-you-can-eat Chinese restaurant. During lunch I went there, stuffed my face and felt too sick to come back. I went home and sent an apology email to my host that I wouldn't return for the rest of the week. My course tutor gave me a bollocking over it. She called me in for a meeting and I was too embarrassed to admit the real reason. I said I left because I was ill and that it was not going to be valuable experience anyway. All I was doing was cutting out newspaper stories. She told me it was unprofessional. She was right, but I'd rather live with that shame than admit I had an eating disorder. I couldn't even admit it to myself. I was living in a flat near Brick Lane, with a girl I went to Nottingham University with and her best friend, and at my lowest point I would steal their food too. I'd replace what I took but they knew what was going on. They once mentioned vomit in the toilet bowl and I'd never felt so ashamed in my life, but rather than open up about my issues I closed myself off and tried to operate more carefully. I couldn't get myself out of the binge-eating and purging cycle.

Bulimia is not a word I knew the meaning of when I heard it for the first time in *Heathers*. Eating disorders were so normalised in teen culture by the eighties that the nonchalant reaction of Heather Duke's friend to her bulimia is not an endorsement but a realistic reflection. 'Grow up, Heather. Bulimia is so '87,' queen bee Heather Chandler tells Duke as Veronica files her nail down to help her fellow brunette with the purging in the girls' bathroom. The line isn't designed to tell Duke to stop having an eating disorder; it's dismissing her for having one that's out of fashion, which is exactly the sort of sharp satirising that continues to position *Heathers* as a high-school classic. But the term 'bulimia' went straight over my head as a teen. Anorexia? Sure, I knew that term. Looking 'anorexic' was a common descriptor for girls or women who appeared too skinny, but no one I grew up around was using 'bulimic' in the same way. What is it to look bulimic? The NHS definition of bulimia nervosa is a mental health and eating condition where 'people go through periods where they eat a lot of food in a very short amount of time (binge eating) and then make themselves sick, use laxatives (medicine to help them poo) or do excessive exercise, or a combination of these, to try to stop themselves gaining weight'. I ticked all these boxes; I even ran a half-marathon during this period, but I never lost any weight. I actually gained three stone and to be honest I felt a bit cheated! All that binging and purging and all it gave me was lower self-esteem, a terrible relationship with food and an even worse relationship with my body, plus a puffy face and acid reflux.

It was because I wasn't losing weight that it took me so long to accept what I had. Eating disorders were associated with thinness, right? And as I wasn't getting any thinner I obviously didn't have one! A psychological glitch had formed in my brain where after twenty-two years of being able to eat three, mostly healthy meals a day I was no longer able to experience negative emotions without needing a binge-and-purge session. This is why they call it a mental health issue because my mind was in full denial mode for several years, especially because screen depictions of eating disorders revolved around skinny white girls.

In *Skins*, Cassie's a manic pixie dream girl type[6] with anorexia. It defines her character. I remember the scene where she teaches Sid how to make it look like you're eating food on a plate without actually eating it. It reminded me of that little moment in *Clueless* where Cher tells Dionne that you can lose weight by cutting food 'really small'. *Pretty Little Liars'* Hanna had an eating disorder for one season, while *Gossip Girl* included a bulimic storyline for Blair Waldorf, whose in-patient treatment is mentioned a few times in season one and shown explicitly in a Thanksgiving episode. Stress is her trigger and after a barny with her mum she devours an apple pie then throws it up after because of the guilt. Both *The Crown* and *Spencer* would visualise a similar scene with Princess Diana scarfing and barfing food from the Royal kitchen and dinner table, with both offering rather dramatic depictions. Ballet movies *The Best Little Girl in the World*, *Center Stage* and *Black Swan* highlight the commonality of anorexia and bulimia in the competitive world. I never saw a correlation between my disordered eating and theirs, certainly not the pre-2020 characters, because they were specifically white and super thin,

---

[6] A trope defined by Nathan Rabin in 2005: a 'bubbly, shallow cinematic creature that exists solely in the fevered imaginations of sensitive writer-directors to teach broodingly soulful young men to embrace life and its infinite mysteries and adventures.'

whereas I felt an uncomfortable mess buying clothes with stretch and elasticated waists so I didn't have to feel or see the body I hated. These depictions all feed into the myth that eating disorders are a specifically middle- to upper-class, skinny-white-female problem, rather than it being a disease that can affect anyone. Historian Angela Tate has written about her experience growing up with an eating disorder without the language or literature that focused on Black millennials:

> If you look at the popular Black celebrities of the '90s, the thin, modelesque figures of Halle Berry, Whitney Houston, Lela Rochon, Tyra Banks, and others don't appear too different from their white contemporaries (Julia Roberts, Claudia Schiffer, Shania Twain, et. al). Yet the myth persists that Black women do not suffer from eating disorders—and that if they do, they are perceived and treated in the same manner as white women.[7]

A YouGov poll commissioned by eating disorder charity Beat found that nearly 39% of people believed eating disorders were more common amongst white people than other ethnicities.[8] No doubt stereotypes play a part in that perception. Eating disorders also occur at similar rates across all levels of income and education, yet Beat also said that nearly 30% of respondents believed low-income people were less likely to develop them compared to affluent people. Marti Noxon's 2017 film *To the Bone* might be the first ED film to break that cycle. It still positions a white female character suffering with anorexia amongst a lot of white female archetypes, but it did include a

---

[7] Tate, Angela, '"Eating disorders are for white girls."' (16 June 2021) https://annehelen.substack.com/p/eating-disorders-are-for-white-girls?s=r

[8] Beat, 'New research shows eating disorder stereotypes prevent people finding help', https://www.beateatingdisorders.org.uk/news/beat-news/eating-disorder-stereotypes-prevent-help/

male ED patient in dancer Luke[9] as well as Kendra, a Black woman with a binge-eating disorder who was plus size. While she didn't purge through vomiting, she does use laxatives and enemas. She represents a type of woman who's not in treatment because she's in danger of getting too thin. I recognised myself in Kendra more than any other fictional ED character even if her character was barely fleshed out.

The height of my bulimia was during 2011 to 2013 and it's probably not a coincidence that it was right when I was transitioning from education into full-time employment. My stress levels had massively intensified, but I can also look back at it now and recognise just how lonely and depressed I felt too. I had moved into my third flat in three years, in Dalston, and for the first time with housemates I had no prior relationship with. It turned out to be a terrible fit; they'd party into the wee hours on weekends when I would have to work the early morning shifts. I'd rarely see them in the week because I'd often have to do night shifts too. In the alone-time I binged and purged and binged and purged until my eyes went red with retching. Then one day a personal trainer called Nick contacted me on Twitter. He had some clients that often got papped while they were working out in the park and was hoping I might be able to credit him in the pics if they popped up. It was no skin off my nose. I obliged and accepted his invite for a coffee to chat about maybe doing a fitness story with one of his clients. After about fifteen minutes of chatting over green tea and a latte I told him my entire disordered eating sob story. I might have sobbed too. Maybe it was because he was a stranger that I unburdened myself in his company. It felt less shameful to admit it to him than my friends who I'd tried to hide it from, or my parents who I'd argue with.

---

[9] At least 1.5 million people in the UK – of which 25% are male – have an eating disorder, according to experts. https://www.bbc.co.uk/news/newsbeat-54343453

I'm glad I did speak to Nick because he generously offered to write me a meal plan and do a session with him each week for free and it was exactly the support I needed to get me out of my funk. I had someone to talk to now and directives to adhere to. It was like playing sports again, and as ever I wanted to please my coach. The change didn't happen overnight, but I started to binge less, purge less, socialise more, work out more too and changed my environment by moving across London to Kensal Rise to be closer to work and a crew of people I got on with very well. After a year I had lost the weight I'd gained from binge-eating and was no longer an emotional slave to the binge-purge cycle. The stresses in my life had not changed, but I'd found new ways to process them and they weren't all necessarily healthy. Smoking became a new crutch for handling my anxiety triggers and it would take me a decade to get out of that daily habit. I was partying more regularly too. The more I was getting back to my old self, the more I wanted to dress up and go out and maybe grab a guy's attention.

It wouldn't be until my thirties that I'd feel comfortable discussing my eating disorder with loved ones. I needed the perspective and time to understand what was really going on with me during my twenties. I was in denial about a lot of things concerning my mental health because all my problems seemed pretty first-world compared to everything else that was going on in the world. But we've benefited from a cultural shift to share our internal struggles and it wasn't much of a surprise to find that some of my friends I knew had similar experiences. It was reassuring to hear their stories and share mine too but watching *Freddie Flintoff: Living with Bulimia*, a documentary about the former cricketer's struggles, confirmed to me that you're always in recovery. 'I've had periods where I've not done it for a long time and I've had periods when I've done it,' he says. 'I've done it this year. It's not right. I know it's not right. But I can't say for certain when it's going to stop or when it will happen again.'

Ditto, Freddie. I've overcome so many of my bad eating habits and finally got to a point where the positive inner voice about my weight and body drowns out the negative. I have had relapses that I've struggled to admit, but here it is on paper, in ink, and I can't hide from the fact that I'll probably be wrestling with this part of my mental health for a lot longer. I spoke to a therapist about my anxiety and insomnia for the first time in 2020. Maybe, after twelve years, I should bite the bullet and speak with a professional about the hangover of my bulimia. For too many people, eating disorders are an elephant in a room that only they can see. Only when we share our struggles and bring them into the light can we begin to mend.

Chapter 17

'Look, when you get that drunk, things happen.'

– Promising Young Woman (2020)

I WAS SIXTEEN WHEN the incident happened, but the details are murky. They say that can happen when you've been through a traumatic incident. You're so focused on the darkest, most immediate aspects that the time, the place and what existed in the periphery fade further each time you think of it. I'd spent many years suppressing that memory, pushing it back into the far reaches of my mind. I wanted to get on with my life and not feel shame coursing through my brain like there's that nun with a bell from *Game of Thrones* running riot. Yes, nun! I am shamed! Be quiet! But I had managed to get on with my life as most young girls and women have been conditioned to. For over a decade, I'm not sure that I ever thought of it again. Then the #MeToo hashtag began to trend and the bell started ringing.

Here's what I remember. Let this be your trigger warning. I was at a house party at my best mate's boyfriend's house in a neighbouring area to where we lived. I think it was in his house. It could have been one of his mates' houses, but as I said, the details are murky. All the lads there were older than me and my best mate. They didn't go to our school either.

Except one. He was two years above us and we all had a crush on him. But he's not the one I needed to worry about. We're in the house and the music is blaring. I think my best mate and I are the only girls there, plus the older sister of another of our friends. I have to assume I'd lied to my parents about where I was because there is no way in hell Mum or Dad would have let me attend a party with older boys and booze. But such is the secret life of teenagers we all know to be true. I must have been knocking back some vodka and cranberry because beer has never been a taste I've easily acquired. Maybe there were a few swigs from a mammoth bottle of White Lightning or Strongbow that was going around, but how much I actually drank is a mystery to me. The details are murky. All I know is that it was enough to have me crawling up the stairs for a lie down in a spare room. There was no bed, so I pushed the door ajar and turned the light off before lying down on the floor on some jackets. I think it was jackets. The details are murky. My head was spinning. I tried closing my eyes, but it just made it worse. I just waited there in the near dark, trying not to puke and unable to move. I'm not sure how long I had been lying there before the door opened.

It was a familiar face. A male face. One of the older lads who hadn't gone to my school but was one of the quieter, nicer guys I'd recently been acquainted with. I can't remember his nickname, the details are murky, but it began with a 'D'. D said something. 'Are you OK?' maybe. I'm not sure if I formulated the words to utter, 'I'm too drunk,' but that's what I wanted to say. D came in and closed the door. He laid down next to me and, probably because I was drunk and naive and D was a nice guy, I thought he was going to keep me company while I rode out this booze coma. But then D unbuckled my belt. The panic quickly set in, but I couldn't move. D unzipped my jeans. I said 'No' but I'm not sure if it translated that well or he just didn't hear me. I'm pretty sure D heard me. Still, he put his hand inside my underwear and pushed down further. I was internally screaming for my body to move, to flinch away, to nudge him off me, but it wouldn't respond. How dare my body leave me hanging this way? During my time of need! Just when I needed her most! If only I had the sheer will power of Beatrix Kiddo to wiggle my big toe. I'm a child full of alcohol; not a deadly trained movie assassin. I'm wiggling on the inside. My skin is squirming and just when his hand goes deeper, light fills up the room. My friend's older sister standing in the doorway. I could have cried. Maybe I did. The details are murky. Her lingering presence was enough to stop his assault. D got up and shuffled out of the room. What happened after his departure I couldn't tell you, but I'll always remember my friend's older sister as the white knight who'd arrived just in time to save my drunken damsel from further distress. That detail is never murky.

In the following days, I would tell a couple of people what happened. My best friend, of course. I told one of D's mates about it too. They both agreed it was bad but nothing more. It was an uncomfortable truth about someone in our lives and they wanted to forget the incident as quickly as I did. I thought about telling my mum but we weren't close like that. Not yet. And I thought she would blame me for getting too drunk and lying about where I was. I've only recently told her what happened and she was horrified that I thought she might victim-blame me. My sixteen-year-old brain couldn't comprehend that sort of response. I couldn't get past the guilt and shame. I'd put myself in danger. That's what society loved to tell girls, still loves to tell girls. It's why survivors continue to be reluctant in reporting sexual assault. They fear they won't be believed and ultimately shamed by the situation. A 2020 study found that fewer than one in six (16%) of victims who experienced sexual assault by rape or penetration (including attempts) since the age of sixteen reported the assault to the police. Of those that told someone other than the police, 40% stated embarrassment as a reason for not telling them, 38%

did not think the police could help, and 34% thought it would be humiliating.[1]

No one could blame me for what happened that 2003 night more than I blamed myself. I was a smart girl. I did well at school. I played basketball for England! I thought I knew better. It wasn't that bad, I rationalised. He hadn't fully assaulted me, right? It was only on the precipice. He had touched my vagina, but he hadn't put his fingers *in* my vagina. It was a near-miss, I told myself. Wasn't I lucky to not be fully molested? Just a little bit molested! My assault wasn't a capital R rape story, not even a lower case. It, like a million others, existed in the grey area where it was far easier to internalise the shame than acknowledge the violation took place. After a while I shrugged it off like I was a female character in an eighties teen comedy; where drunk women are fair game to nerds looking to assert their manliness like in *Sixteen Candles*, when perfect guy Jake Ryan passes his inebriated girlfriend Caroline off to The Geek. She's a party girl with boobs and a slutty air about her compared to innocent Samantha, so it was OK for Jake to so callously hand her off. 'I could violate her 10 different ways if I wanted to,' he says after finding her collapsed in his room where you'd think she'd be safe. 'I'm just not interested anymore.'

There's the long-running fallacy that women who binge-drink must be sexually promiscuous. That when they are physically unable to articulate their consent because they are so paralytic, they are always willing participants. Jake passes Caroline to The Geek, tells her the nerd is actually him and heads off. 'Have fun,' he says. The next morning, Caroline wakes up, sex is implied, and she's asked if she enjoyed herself: 'You know, I have this weird feeling I did.' Hughes's muse and *Sixteen Candles*

[1] Office for National Statistics, 'Nature of sexual assault by rape or penetration, England and Wales: year ending March 2020' (18 March 2021) https://www.ons.gov.uk/peoplepopulationandcommunity/crimeandjustice/articles/natureofsexualassaultbyrapeorpenetrationenglandandwales/yearendingmarch2020

lead, Molly Ringwald has since spoken out about the troubling images of rape culture embedded in the film and other eighties comedies. 'If attitudes toward female subjugation are systemic, and I believe that they are, it stands to reason that the art we consume and sanction plays some part in reinforcing those same attitudes,' she wrote,[2] and she's right.

Stanley Kubrick's 1971 film *A Clockwork Orange* sees Malcolm McDowell's droog leader Alex lead his young cohorts in a home invasion which results in the brutal assault and rape of an innocent woman to the tune of 'Singin' in the Rain'. In 1973, a seventeen-year-old Dutch girl was gang-raped by a group of men in Lancashire singing the same song. We cannot possibly blame one fictional film for the real-life actions of men, but it is one among a vast number of cinematic stories that use rape and sexual violence toward women as a plot device in gratuitous, exploitative or ambiguous terms, and that surely has a knock-on effect. Sam Peckinpah's *Straw Dogs*, released the same year as Kubrick's dystopian thriller, features a barbaric rape scene that suggests the victim enjoys it. The main female protagonist, Amy, is sexualised throughout the film. When her ex-boyfriend rapes her, pleasure appears on her face before he holds her down so his friend can rape her too.

Where some movies rape, others ravish. *Gone with the Wind* paved the way for romanticised non-consensual sex disguised as lovemaking. When Rhett Butler sweeps Scarlett O'Hara up the stairs to their bedroom in anger he does so because his ego has been bruised by the fact that his wife loves another man. She is not a willing participant, but as the scene cuts to Scarlett smiling the next morning as she wakes up, it confuses the audience into thinking, oh maybe she was into being ravished all along. 'The reality of rape is rendered invisible by the many novels and films, such as *Gone with the Wind*, which romanticize and mystify it,'

---

[2] Ringwald, Molly, 'What About "The Breakfast Club"?' (6 April 2018) https://www.newyorker.com/culture/personal-history/what-about-the-breakfast-club-molly-ringwald-metoo-john-hughes-pretty-in-pink

wrote feminist philosopher Marilyn Friedman in 1990. 'They portray the rapist as a handsome man whose domination is pleasurable in bed, and portray women as happy to have their own sexual choices and refusals crushed by such men.'[3] Many feminist critics have shared the assessment that this scene is one of marital rape, which may well have been inspired by the original novel's author Margaret Mitchell whose first husband Berrien 'Red' Upshaw once beat and raped her so violently she was bedridden for a month. But this was written at a time when the idea that a husband could rape his wife was unthinkable. As recently as 2018, one in four Britons believed that non-consensual sex within marriage did not constitute rape.[4] I often think of that quintessentially British saying commonly attributed to one Lady Hillingdon's 1912 journal that women have gotten used to demonstrating: 'Lie back and think of England,' paraphrases her feeling of resignation over having to be fucked by her old husband whenever he comes a-knocking and it's now become a statement for the female obligation to be sexually dominated by men whether they want to or not.

From the romantic spin on marital rape of Daenerys by Khal Drogo in *Game of Thrones* (a show overflowing with sexual assault) to the shocking moment in *Crank* where Jason Statham's assassin rapes his girlfriend in public (it's OK, guys, it's so he can keep his heart rate up or die from a deadly serum and she gives in to him!) and let's not forget the date rape scene in *Observe and Report* where Seth Rogen's mall cop penetrates Anna Faris's passed-out cosmetic counter worker. Too often rape has been legitimised through male antiheroes

[3] Kuntz, Tom, 'Word for Word. A Scholarly Debate; Rhett and Scarlett: Rough Sex Or Rape? Feminists Give a Damn' (19 February 1995) https://www.nytimes.com/1995/02/19/weekinreview/word-for-worda-scholarly-debate-rhett-scarlett-rough-sex-rape-feminists-give.html

[4] End Violence Against Women, 'Major new YouGov survey for EVAW: Many people still unclear what rape is' (6 December 2018) https://www.endviolenceagainstwomen.org.uk/major-new-survey-many-still-unclear-what-rape-is/

and the lines between rape fantasy, eroticism and violent assault have been blurred to reinforce misogynistic ideas of manhood and the submissive position of women. Do women want to be dominated or ravished or is it that we've watched so many films and series made by men that have told us that's how we should like it? In an otherwise groundbreaking neo noir, *Blade Runner* has Harrison Ford's rugged investigator aggressively 'ravish' Sean Young's replicant Rachael as she tries to leave his apartment. The saxophone underscoring the scene is telling us its meant to be sexy, but without the music its simply showing the demanding, forceful behaviour of Deckard and the fear on a woman's face who already lacks agency as an underclass of citizen. That director Ridley Scott allegedly pushed Ford to be more violent towards Young, because she claims she declined his dating proposition, makes it even more problematic:

> Well, honestly, Ridley [Scott] wanted me to date him. He tried very hard in the beginning of the show to date him, and I never would. I was like, nah. And then he started dating the actress who played Zhora, Joanna Cassidy, and I felt relieved. And then we do this scene, and I think it was Ridley. I think Ridley was like, 'Fuck you.' I was thinking, 'Why did this have to be like that? What was the point of that?' and I think it was Ridley's none-too-subtle message that he was getting even with me.'[5]

The film industry has a torrid history of male film-makers putting women in uncomfortable positions; it literally launched a global reckoning, but 'auteurs' frequently get a free pass. *Last Tango in Paris* is considered one of the greatest films

---

[5] Ferme, Antonio, 'Sean Young Says Her Career Was Derailed by Ridley Scott, Oliver Stone, Warren Beatty and Others' (22 March 2021) https://variety.com/2021/film/news/sean-young-ridley-scott-oliver-stone-warren-beatty-1234935883/

committed to celluloid and a top-tier outing from Marlon
Brando, but the then forty-eight-year-old and director Bernardo
Bertolucci did not get consent from nineteen-year-old actress
Maria Schneider before shooting the 1972 film's infamous rape
scene. Brando's character uses a stick of butter as lubricant
to anally rape his young lover, a direction that wasn't in the
script, but they chose not to tell Schneider so they could
capture a real reaction. 'I was so angry,' she said in 2007. 'I
should have called my agent or had my lawyer come to the
set because you can't force someone to do something that isn't
in the script, but at the time, I didn't know that.'[6] No one
batted an eyelid until 2016 when a 2013 video of Bertolucci
confirming the incident, and his lack of regret for his method,
went viral.

Alfred Hitchcock has long been considered one of cinema's
greatest directors of all time. His films *The Birds* and *Marnie*
are heralded, but the British film-maker terrorised his lead
actress off-camera as much as on. Tippi Hedren had spoken
of her fraught experience shooting the films for years and
reflected on the psychological warfare, verbal and sexual
abuse, he waged against her in a memoir[7] published a year
before the *New York Times*' exposé on Harvey Weinstein
triggered the Hollywood mogul's long-awaited downfall. 'I
had to be extremely strong to fight off Mr Hitchcock,'
Hedren said:

> He was so insistent and obsessive but I was an extremely
> strong young woman and there is no way he was going
> to get the better of me. I admired Hitch tremendously for
> his great talent and still do. Yet, at the same time, I loathed
> him for his off-set behaviour and the way he came on to
> me sexually. He was a great director – and he destroyed

[6] Das, Lina, 'I felt raped by Brando' (19 July 2007) https://www.dailymail.
co.uk/tvshowbiz/article-469646/I-felt-raped-Brando.html
[7] Hedren, Tippi, *Tippi: A Memoir.*

it all by his behaviour when he got me alone. He wanted to possess me completely.[8]

Brigitte Auber appeared as Danielle Foussard in *To Catch a Thief* and told Hitchcock biographer Patrick McGilligan about her experience of the director lunging at her without her consent. McGilligan also noted his gross habit of groping women and for 'thrusting his tongue inside [a woman's] mouth.'[9] Hitchcock's offscreen misogyny towards women can be traced in his films, but his 1972 film *Frenzy* might be the most potent manifestation of his toxic desires. The London-set film focuses on a rather unpleasant man falsely accused of being a serial killer-rapist, but it's his likeable greengrocer friend Bob who's the real criminal, exacting revenge on the women who won't date him. The rape and murder of Brenda, who runs a dating agency, is prolonged and uncomfortable to watch. Bob comes to her office and finds her putting on make-up which 'offers an opening for the "women are always asking for it" male erotic fantasy that provides the rationale for sexual aggression,' suggests writer Jeanne Thomas Allen.[10] Bob tries chatting her up and gets angry when she declines his advances or to set him up on dates based on his 'preferences'. So he attacks and molests Brenda then strangles her with his necktie with the camera closing in on her various body parts including her crotch and breasts, to objectify her as she suffers. Hitchcock's voyeuristic eye means at several moments audiences

---

[8] Todd, Ben and Dennis Cassidy, 'Tippi: My fears that Sienna Miller's portrayal of me in Hitchcock biopic won't show how I stood up to legendary director' (13 March 2012) https://www.dailymail.co.uk/tvshowbiz/article-2114161/Tippi-Hedren-fears-Sienna-Millers-portrayal-Hitchcock-biopic-wont-stood-director.html

[9] McGilligan, Patrick, *Alfred Hitchcock: A Life in Darkness and Light.*

[10] Allen, Jeanne Thomas, 'The Representation of Violence to Women: Hitchcock's "Frenzy"' (1985) *Film Quarterly,* https://online.ucpress.edu/fq/article-abstract/38/3/30/40491/The-Representation-of-Violence-to-Women-Hitchcock?redirectedFrom=fulltext

might empathise with this rapist, which several male critics noted at the time, including Roger Ebert, who said viewers 'sometimes cannot help identifying with him . . . We know he is a slimy bastard, but somehow we're sweating along.'[11] *New Yorker* critic Pauline Kael didn't review *Frenzy*, but said she 'found that film rather offensive' in an interview years later: 'the woman is made to look ridiculous right at the point where she was being killed. I thought there was something very ugly – spiritually – about that. It's very odd that no one protested that.'[12] Well, one woman did in the *New York Times*. 'I'm tired of going to movies and seeing women get raped,' English professor Victoria Sullivan responded to the film and the paper's critical assessment. 'Some of the meanings this film suggested to me include: 1. Woman are naturally victims. 2. Psychopathic rapists are basically nice guys [. . .] screwed up by their mums.'[13]

I turned thirty not long after the #MeToo reckoning but the fourteen-year-old incident wasn't the only memory replaying. There was the nice guy who tried to finger me in the backseat of the taxi after a night out in Peckham. There was the nice guy I worked with at a news outlet who sent me Facebook messages after a staff night out saying he wanted to fuck me. There was that nice guy who tried to choke me during sex. There was the other nice guy who also tried to choke me during sex. And who can forget the nice guy who posted a video of me giving him head on Snapchat? Rape culture has conditioned women to give nice guys the benefit of the doubt, but *they* are the type of men to be most worried about. Whereas *Frenzy*

[11] Ebert, Roger, *Frenzy* (1 January 1972) https://www.rogerebert.com/reviews/frenzy-1972

[12] Kael, Pauline, 'Talking Out of Turn #4: Pauline Kael (1983)' (26 November 2010) https://www.criticsatlarge.ca/2010/11/talking-out-of-turn-4-pauline-kael-1983.html

[13] Sullivan, Victoria, 'Does "Frenzy" Degrade Women?' (30 July 1972) https://archive.nytimes.com/www.nytimes.com/library/film/073072hitch-frenzy-comment.html

seems to want you to empathise with nice guy Bob, who today might be considered an incel, films like *Colossal*, *Unsane* and *Rose Plays Julie* serve as a warning that niceness doesn't come for free with these guys either. It comes with a sexual expectation that a woman must go along with or they get hurt. Emerald Fennell's *Promising Young Woman* continued this theme by employing the nicest comedy guys of film and TV – Bo Burnham, Adam Brody, Chris Lowell and Max Greenfield – to play the butter-wouldn't-melt, predatory opportunists against Carey Mulligan's grieving, avenging heroine Cassie.

You can imagine how cathartic this movie might have been for me even if its ending was more anticlimactic than Coralie Fargeat's *Revenge*. That film subverts the rape-revenge narrative popularised by the 'roughie' sexploitation subgenre by both limiting how much the audience sees of her protagonist Jennifer's sexual assault (compared to her namesake's in *I Spit on Your Grave* which combined receives over twenty minutes of screen time)* and exaggerating her powers as a survivor and hunter, able to make bloody mincemeat of the men who wronged her. In *Promising Young Woman*, Cassie's late-night activities involve exposing supposedly friendly dudes who actually prey on drunk women, as a way to deal with her grief over her friend who was a victim of one such fiend. Her BFF got drunk at college, was taken advantage of, and killed herself after the video evidence went viral on campus. I felt Cassie's pain, anger and need to not feel helpless to the whims of men. It's a brilliant antidote to the way the world likes to stereotype sexual abusers and harassers as these beastly anomalies of the male species. It's saying, 'Hey not every bad guy looks like Harvey Weinstein,' more often than not they are the nice guy next door too. And sometimes another nice guy is filming.

---

* Full disclosure: There are certain films with violent, excessive rape depiction that I refuse to watch, like *I Spit On Your Grave* and Gasper Noe's *Irreversible*. I'd rather rely on other writers and critics to give me their graphic insight instead!

HANNA FLINT

These films counter the overwhelmingly white trope seen in films like *Love Actually*, *500 Days of Summer*, *Say Anything*, and *Knocked Up*, which frequently position average dudes as romantic, heroic figures just trying to secure the hard-to-get girl. In reality they often profess their love to unavailable women, get unhealthily attached, stalk, or stealth their way into having unprotected sex. That latter move is what the story of *Knocked Up* hinges on, where Rogen's character Ben (I know, another one!) chooses not to put a condom on while having drunken sex with Katherine Heigl's Alison, without her consent, after she tells him to hurry up. She ends up pregnant and bizarrely chooses to keep the baby despite having a meltdown over losing her career. It's a pretty disturbing situation that happens far too often; leaving women with unwanted pregnancies, sexually transmitted diseases, trust issues and sometimes all of the above. But films like this sanitise the behaviour with people not truly understanding a criminal act has taken place. That's why *I May Destroy You* sparked a vital, global conversation about the nuances of consent. Based on her own experiences, creator and star Michaela Coel plays Arabella, a writer who is drugged, date-raped and striving to work out who her attacker was. If that wasn't a heady enough thing to process, in the fourth episode, she has sex with a fellow writer called Zain who removes the condom halfway through without her knowledge. When she questions him he plays dumb. 'I thought you knew,' he says, as though women's vaginas are designed to detect whether a guy is raw dogging her or not. After hearing on a podcast that actions like his were criminal, Arabella outs him onstage at an industry event. 'He gaslighted me with such intention,' she says. 'I didn't have a second to understand the heinous crime that had occurred. He's not rape-adjacent or a bit rapey, he's a rapist under UK law.'

The thing about nice guys is that they're everywhere. They're sons, fathers, husbands, boyfriends, uncles, colleagues, bosses, coaches, teachers, doctors, best mates, you know, just one of the lads. But you shouldn't have to know an assault victim, be fathers of daughters, brothers of sisters, or husbands of wives, to acknowledge the risk that women face on a daily basis. Until we stop constantly minimising the experiences of those who identify as female, the reality and the scale of who is committing these misogynistic crimes is just going to allow rape culture to thrive as this unbearable societal norm. '#NotAllMen!' I see you tweet and let me tell you if you say that to me you sacrifice your right to a polite response. Because we know it's not literally all men. No one is actually saying all men are rapists or every nice guy has a sexual ulterior motive, but there are enough men who are! Too many nice guys who do! Plenty of men have played the part of the abuser, or the harasser, or not done something when they've witnessed or heard about these men in action, and it's enough for nearly every woman to consider nearly every man a potential threat. I would love that not to be the case. What a privilege it would be to go for a run after dark without worrying a man might grab you from behind. Or dance with your girls in the club without worrying that a man will see it as an invitation to grind on you from behind. Or leave a drink at the bar without worrying a man will spike it. Or pick up some food from the Sainsbury's Local during a pandemic without a man checking you out from behind and getting aggressive when you call him out? I'm still mad about it.

There's a scene in *Avengers: Assemble*, during the Battle of New York, where Bruce Banner arrives to join the fight. Captain America says it might be time for him to get angry and turn into the Hulk. In an earlier scene, the team had wondered how Bruce could control his transformation into the big green brute, but there amongst the debris, he answers that question. 'That's my secret, Cap!' he says. 'I'm always angry.' That's me. I'm Bruce. I too am always angry. There is a simmering rage that exists within me and it boils over every time I see a dead girl's name trend. Every time I see rape in a film used to inspire men or subordinate women. Every time I see a dude tweet that they've suddenly become aware of the privilege they have for being able to walk alone home at night without fear I want to scream. REALLY, MATE? It's 2021 and you've just realised this? Was #MeToo not enough of a reminder? Was the sexist history of the world not enough of a reminder? Every day, there is something new to get angry about and it makes me want to Hulk smash the patriarchy. Because it is very much our patriarchal society that is allowing this to happen. You can make misogyny a hate crime or put more police on the streets, but that's not going to make a difference if there aren't meaningful consequences. It's not going to make a dent if men don't start making it their problem to fix instead of a woman's burden to get over. Ending male violence, abuse and harassment is actually the one job I'd be happy for men to outnumber women in. Off you go, lads. Fill those roles. Run the campaigns. Take to the streets! Put hoes before bros! Convict some dicks! Be the superheroes you pay to see, who you see yourself in.

Wouldn't it be great if that happened? If all the #NotAllMen proved it by doing the work to ensure they're not actively, or even passively, engaging in the culture that keeps women down? They don't laugh at the rape jokes uttered by male comedians? They call out their guy friends who share revenge porn pictures of the last girl they slept with? They stop wolf-whistling at random women on the street? That they *actually* believe women, because the data consistently shows the prevalence of sexual assault and harassment, not the knee-jerk reaction to defend men's honour? Like that police captain in the US who minimised the murderous actions of Robert Aaron Long, the killer of eight people, six of them women of Asian descent, by saying the spree was the result of the shooter having a 'really bad day' rather than being the misogynistic extension of Anti-Asian racism. It's frustrating to admit that there is no way that women will be safer unless men make it their responsibility too. But that would mean sacrificing their power and privilege. And after thirty-four years on this planet, I've increasingly come to the conclusion that a lot of these nice guys, these 'THIS IS WHAT A FEMINIST LOOKS

LIKE' T-shirt boys, these #NotAllMen, like the idea of equality in theory more than practice. Equality means giving up some of your privilege to balance the playing field and for too many men that is not something they want to do. They don't want to be held accountable for their sexist behaviour; they'd rather reinforce the narrative that the responsibility lies with the victim.

'She can't take a joke?' 'She can't take a compliment!' 'She was asking for it!' 'Her skirt was too short!' 'Her top was too low cut!' 'She's a tease!' 'She's been around the block!' 'She got herself drunk!' 'She's not even a she!' 'She!' 'She!' 'Her!' 'Her!' There is so much scrutiny on women, especially in the legal system when sexual cases go to court and the victim's character and sex life is ripped to shreds by the defendant's lawyers, that it's a wonder that any man goes to jail for sexual assault. The recent Netflix series *Anatomy of a Scandal* focused on the very modern nuances concerning rape and consent, of when a woman might change her mind about intercourse, but the man forces her anyway. Even though the series fails its female victim of colour in favour of his white female victim and wife, it's pretty apt that the rich, white, upper-middle-class offender gets away with it. The stats certainly aren't in women's favour. From 2019–20, police recorded 55,130 rapes in England and Wales.[14] That's a massive number. It's hard not to think about how many were likely not reported, but of that 55,130 recorded cases, only 2,102 led to prosecutions with 1,439 ending in a conviction. A year earlier, there were one-third fewer rapes recorded, but double the prosecutions and convictions. Where's the justice?

There's a scene in *Crash*, the 2004 Oscar Best Picture winner, that sticks out in my mind. We see Thandiwe Newton's character molested by Matt Dillon's racist police officer while her husband watches. Later, she's in a car crash and he's the officer who rescues her. It's a redemption arc that turns this racist

---

[14] https://rapecrisis.org.uk/news/rape-convictions-fall-to-record-low-in-england-and-wales/

rapist into a hero cop that leaves a particularly bad taste compared to Kaouther Ben Hania's *Beauty and the Dogs* which refuses to give law enforcement the benefit of the doubt or a scene showing her protagonist's harrowing assault. This Tunisian-set film might be one of the most disturbing, yet poignant, reminders of how authority figures can perpetuate the worst violence towards women and protect their own as a young woman spends a long and traumatic night trying to report the police officers who gang-raped her that very same evening. It's one of the many Arab films from female film-makers, like *The Silence of the Palaces*, *Capernaum* and *Shakwa* that tackle the way women's bodies are continually subjected to the perverse brutality of men in a culture where systemic and religious patriarchal forces assert its control.

But the reality is that police brutality towards women is prevalent around the world. Last year, a report revealed that in the UK over the last four years some 2,000 claims of sexual misconduct including rape had been made against serving police officers.[15] This data came after former Metropolitan Police firearms officer, Wayne Couzens (who was nicknamed 'The Rapist' by co-workers because he made women feel uncomfortable) was convicted of the kidnapping, rape and murder of thirty-three-year-old Sarah Everard as she walked home at night. In 2022, the Independent Office for Police Conduct (IOPC) shared a report that detailed horrific messages shared by Met police officers about hitting and raping women. 'I would happily rape you . . . if I was single', one male officer texted a female officer. 'If I was single I would happily chloroform you.'[16] Rape culture is rooted in every facet of our supposedly civilised society and

---

[15] Sharman, Jon, '2,000 police officers accused of sexual misconduct in past four years' (11 October 2021) https://www.independent.co.uk/news/uk/home-news/police-sexual-misconduct-uk-b1935993.html

[16] Dodd, Vikram, 'Met officers joked about raping women, police watchdog reveals' (1 February 2022) https://www.theguardian.com/uk-news/2022/feb/01/met-officers-joked-about-raping-women-police-watchdog-racist

like Victoria Sullivan fifty years ago, I too am sick of seeing women get raped on screen.

I do get why some women have a morbid curiosity that drives their watching of films and TV shows with this theme. We're so used to seeing ourselves victimised in real life, and maybe to some extent it offers some solace that the traumatic incidences of male violence depicted in say, *Law & Order: SVU* or Netflix true crime shows are happening to other women we can empathise with but remain distant from. Some might also offer female viewers guidance on how to avoid the worst and spot the red flags, but that does little to prevent random attacks. In a Milwaukee park, thirty-six-year-old woman Ee Lee was raped, beaten and murdered by two male assailants with nine others watching and filming it, when she was simply relaxing on a blanket in the daytime.[17] Documentaries help raise awareness about this public health crisis but allow you to engage with the subject without having to witness the heinous acts. *The Rape of Recy Taylor* examines the historical precedent set in the US – at a time when it was socially acceptable for Black women to be both racially and sexually subordinated by the dominant white class – through the experience of Taylor, her refusal to stay silent after being gang-raped by six white men and the Civil Rights movement it sparked. *The Hunting Ground* highlights the proclivity for sexual assault on US college campuses while Hogir Hirori's *Sabaya* follows the efforts of former Yazidi sex slaves to infiltrate and rescue fellow women who are still being enslaved by ISIS fighters at the dangerous al-Hawl refugee camp in Syria.

There are myriad ways in which women are targeted and some recent female film-makers have chosen to exhibit the violence head-on. Charlène Favier's *Slalom* centres a sixteen-year-old skier

---

[17] McCloskey, Jimmy, 'Boys, 15 and 17, "filmed themselves raping and killing woman, 36, who was relaxing in park"' (11 February 2021) https://metro.co.uk/2021/02/11/boys-15-and-17-filmed-themselves-raping-killing-woman-36-at-park-14067686/

who is groomed by her coach. The French director sensitively depicts the sexual exploitation; it's not gratuitous but it is no less excruciating to watch. Similarly, Jennifer Fox's *The Tale* is a biographical drama about her own sexual relationship with Bill, a forty-year-old running coach, when she was thirteen, which she only began to understand was statutory rape when she was older. A title card at the end of the film reassures viewers that the rape scene between Bill and thirteen-year-old Jennifer used a body double in her place, but it is no less agonising to sit through. Even actor Jason Ritter struggled to film the scene. 'Several times he had to turn away and go in another room, and I know he cried,' said Fox. 'It was just so brutal for him to think about how horrible this really was.'[18] There's a debate to be had about whether a film-maker needs to show a rape so explicitly for the weight of it to be felt. I understand the urge to elicit strong reactions in audiences, but as someone who considers herself an emotionally-led critic, it can be utterly draining. The rape scene in *Boys Don't Cry* is upsetting, but director Kimberley Peirce used test screenings and recut it '100 times' to get it to a shape where the feedback was no longer it's 'too long and too brutal':

> I would read these questionnaires and what I eventually realized was if the real rape is brutal and long, the movie version has to be brutal and long but not so brutal and long that it brutalizes you. There's an art to capturing the potency of the experience. Very early on, it was clear to me, I did not want to contribute to the pornography of violence. I did not want to recreate violence against any human being, in particular, a transperson in such a way that it denigrates the original person or the audience. That only encourages more violence. The important thing to

---

[18] Lenker, Maureen Lee, 'Jennifer Fox had to use her real name in *The Tale* so people would believe the story' (25 May 2018) https://ew.com/tv/2018/05/25/jennifer-fox-had-to-use-her-real-name-in-the-tale-so-people-would-believe-the-story/

know is when I create violence on screen, even though I have good intentions, I know it's possible that I could make something pornographic. Therefore, I have to test myself. So we kept screening and I kept cutting it down until the miracle day when the questionnaires said 'I don't like rape. I don't like this rape. But I know you've done the best job you can.' They were saying they didn't look away. So now it's just long enough.[19]

I remember watching Jennifer Kent's *The Nightingale*, a rape-revenge thriller set in 1825-Tasmania and feeling sick afterwards. The first rape scene highlights the way victims might disassociate during the act. The camera closes in on Clare (an ex-Irish convict, now maid, mother and wife) as she tearfully accepts the assault by British officer Hawkins by focusing her attention on the fire opposite. That was a walk in the park compared to what followed. The second assault lasts three and a half minutes and sees Clare being punched in the head, laid down by Hawkins in front of her husband and brutally raped as he screams and she cries. Her husband is killed, Hawkins offers Clare to his second-in-command and as he rapes her, her crying baby's neck is broken by another soldier who launches the child at a wall to silence it. Aboriginal woman Lowana is later introduced – whose purpose seems to solely illustrate the native women were kept as sex slaves too – and she is soon raped and shot in the back. It's a film that prioritises the traumatic experience of a white woman and her need for vengeance over that of the indigenous population. Clare forces Aboriginal guide Billy to help her, which only makes the violence towards Lowana more unbearable and jarring to witness. 'For a film so focused on colonial violence against women,' writes critic Larissa Behrendt, 'the perfunctory and superficial interrogation

---

[19] Reddish, David, '"Boys Don't Cry" at 20: director Kimberly Peirce reflects on a classic' (29 September 2019) https://www.queerty.com/boys-dont-cry-20-director-kimberly-pierce-reflects-classic-20190929

of how that dynamic plays out for Aboriginal women is a serious flaw that plays into a colonial cinematic tradition.'[20] I was nodding along reading Angelica Jade Bastién's critical essay on the purpose of rape scenes in response to the film:

> It would behoove film-makers to ask themselves what they want audiences to feel in these moments. What am I trying to say about rape beyond the fact that it is a vicious, soul-crushing act? How can I visually communicate trauma in ways that don't revel in brutality for brutality's sake? Are these scenes better served by inventive metaphor?[21]

These are important questions that need to be asked because there is no doubt that cinema should continually examine and reassess cultural and social norms that have informed the human experience. BBFC president Patrick Swaffer says classification was updated from 2014 in its 2019 guidelines to reflect the evolving attitudes towards sexual threat and sexual violence after a consultation found people requesting 'certain depictions of rape, in particular, should receive a higher rating.'

In order to raise awareness of the insidiousness of sexual violence and challenge ingrained misogynistic behaviours, we need film-makers, artists, writers, journalists, to tackle it head on through media and make us feel uncomfortable as well as entertained. But finding a balance between grim reality and artistic licence should be considered, as Bastién says, 'without heaping new trauma on audience and actors.' Especially when we factor in the intersectional perspectives of who is telling these stories beyond a cis, white and heterosexual gaze.

---

[20] Behrendt, Larissa, 'The Nightingale review – ambitious, urgent and necessarily brutal. But who is it for?' (20 August 2019) https://www.theguardian.com/film/2019/aug/20/the-nightingale-review-ambitious-urgent-and-necessarily-brutal-but-who-is-it-for

[21] Bastién, Angelica Jade, 'What Does It Mean for a Rape Scene to Be "Done well"?' (9 August 2019) https://www.vulture.com/2019/08/rape-scenes-movies-nightingale-classic-hollywood.html

Chapter 18

'Wow you're very exotic looking. Was your dad a G.I.?'

– The Office (2006)

I WAS AT A 2021 'women in film' breakfast event at Picturehouse Central in London one weekday morning chatting to some, you know, women in film, when I felt a tap on my side and the words, 'Hi, Corrina.' I looked at the white woman quizzically. We'd met and spoken at another function, but she'd mistaken me for another critic and now we had an awkward situation in front of us.

'It's Hanna, actually,' I said with a smile, 'we've met before, how are you?'

She looked slightly embarrassed, pointed to my hair and said, 'Oh, sorry, I was confused by your curly hair, it looks just like Corrina's.'

It doesn't; I have larger, looser curls and hers are smaller and tighter due to her Jamaican heritage.

'Don't worry,' I chuckled, 'we mixed-race people all look the same!'

I don't think she liked my joke because she soon extricated herself from the conversation. Oh well! It's not the first time someone has mistaken me for someone else. I was at the MOBO Awards one year as a guest and when I was walking down the red carpet into Wembley Arena, someone started shouting,

'Lisa Maffia, Lisa Maffia!' I looked around hoping to spot the So Solid Crew star myself until, alas, I realised the guy was actually shouting at me. After hosting a Q&A panel for *The Essex Serpent* at the Radio Times TV Festival, the cabbie who took me home told me he loved me in 'that Bristol show' *The Outlaws* and I have to assume he mistook me for Anglo-Indian Portuguese actress Rhianne Barreto and not Christopher Walken.

False attribution is a common occurrence for people of colour by white people because of an 'own-race bias'[1] especially in mostly white-occupied spaces. Look no further than Hollywood award shows. When Daniel Kaluuya won the Best Actor Oscar for *Judas and the Black Messiah*, he was asked by a white journalist how he enjoyed being 'directed by Regina' King. He hadn't. That was nominee Leslie Odom Jr in *One Night in Miami*. It had to be a South African journalist, didn't it? During a 2015 Golden Globe nomination announcement Latinas America Ferrera and Gina Rodriguez were mixed up when the official Twitter account tagged Rodriguez in a picture featuring Ferrera who was one of the presenters. The very same year a different type of racial insensitivity occurred when Rashida Jones, the daughter of Black music legend Quincy Jones and Jewish model Peggy Lipton, was questioned by TNT's red-carpet station reporter Danielle Demski, who said, 'You look like you've just come off an island or something. You're very tan, very tropical.' Jones politely responded, 'I mean, you know, I'm ethnic.'

I've never felt so triggered watching a red-carpet pre-show. Jones having to explain her ethnicity is something every Black, Indigenous and Person of Colour (BIPOC) has had to do in their life. But when you're mixed there's a different tension.

---

[1] Hourihan, Kathleen L., Aaron S. Benjamin and Xiping Liu, 'A cross-race effect in metamemory: Predictions of face recognition are more accurate for members of our own race' (2 July 2012) National Library of Medicine, https://www.ncbi.nlm.nih.gov/pmc/articles/PMC3496291/

Discrimination in terms of colourism and featurism has fuelled a side of the beauty industry that promises to deliver Eurocentric looks. Products like skin lightening cream popular in India and cosmetic surgery like rhinoplasty in the Middle East to streamline aquiline noses. Palestinian-American model Bella Hadid recently spoke about her regrets over not keeping the 'nose of her ancestors' by having surgery at fourteen.[2] I had similar insecurities over my nose and glad my parents, at least, never supported those types of thoughts. Thandiwe Newton has in recent years lamented the fact that she might have been cast in roles that could have gone to darker-skinned actresses such as 2013's *Half of the Yellow Sun* where she plays an Igbo woman. 'I was perceived in so many different ways, and it was always about the individual who was perceiving. It was very much on the spectrum of "is she Black enough, or is she too Black?"' she told *Vulture* in 2020:

> Nowadays, there is regret for me. I recognize how painful it is for dark-skinned women, particularly, to have to deal with being substituted or overlooked. For example, you watch *Queen & Slim*. I look at Jodie [Turner-Smith]. Or, you look at Lupita [Nyong'o]. To see a woman of colour, to see that dark skin, that beautiful chocolate skin, my mother's skin, onscreen . . . It's holy. I do see so clearly why there's been so much deep disappointment.'[3]

There was uproar when Afro Latina Zoe Saldana used skin-darkening makeup when playing Nina Simone in a 2016 biopic, as well as a prosthetic nose, instead of just casting a darker-skinned Black woman, and she rightly apologised.

---

[2] Haskell, Rob, 'Bella From the Heart: On Health Struggles, Happiness, and Everything In Between' (15 March 2022) https://www.vogue.com/article/bella-hadid-cover-april-2022

[3] Jung, Alex, 'Thandie Newton Is Finally Ready to Speak' (7 July 2020) https://www.vulture.com/article/thandie-newton-in-conversation.html

Darker-skinned actresses have also struggled to secure leading roles compared to their male counterparts who can be more readily positioned as interracial love interests opposite white women than the other way round. The image of Viola Davis snogging Liam Neeson in *Widows* shouldn't be radical, but it really subverted that colourist position and positioned dark-skinned women as desirable. *Bridgerton* season one was recently criticised because it presented a more positive depiction of its mixed characters compared to its darker-skinned characters. At the same time these actors' very Blackness has also come into question. I was once a guest on a panel discussing screen representation of sex and when the Netflix series was brought up, one Black panellist said these actors 'weren't really Black.' I didn't know what to say. This wasn't the first time I'd heard such a concerning statement. That light-skinned privileges negate any sort of racial prejudice you might experience or a claim to that non-white identity. 'You're marooned,' Irish-Ethiopian actress Ruth Negga told me. 'You feel like your identity is front and center of something that is some sort of abstract argument and you're there going, "I'm a fucking human being!"'[4] It creates an uncomfortable implication of a 'pick one' ultimatum which people often pick for you. Or it can make you feel like you are less than a whole person.

'Half-caste' was a common label I used to describe myself in my youth, but after studying John Agard's poem of the same name in secondary school I no longer felt comfortable wearing that label: 'I close half-a-eye, consequently when I dream, I dream half-a-dream, an when moon begin to flow, I half-caste human being, cast half-a-shadow.'[5] It was the first time I had really dealt with racism specific to my existence in

4 Flint, Hanna, 'Ruth Negga Takes Center Stage' (31 March 2022) https://www.townandcountrymag.com/leisure/arts-and-culture/a39427166/ruth-negga-lady-macbeth-interview/
5 Agard, J. (2004). Half-Caste. United Kingdom: Hodder & Stoughton.

an English class. There was only me and one other girl who were mixed in the room in an overwhelmingly white school, but it gave me critical language and biting metaphors to understand why I should never let myself be called that ever again. It was as much a racist slur as being called a mongrel: something I'd been called too. Yet, as a teenager, I still couldn't divorce myself from those self-loathing, internalised racist feelings that I needed to pass for white to be more accepted. I was self-conscious and it's not surprising given the invisibility I felt at school. '[Mixed race-kids] feel that they are not recognised in the curriculum, that teachers don't know what language to use, that they don't have many champions who can take their experiences to a wider audience,' Bradley Lincoln, Multiple Heritage Project founder, said in 2011. 'A lot of them feel under pressure to choose one [racial] identity to the exclusion of the other, for a number of reasons – peer pressure, family relationships, schools misunderstanding. They have had to deal in silence with having their identity negated by a range of institutions and public bodies. They need the support to be able to self-define.'[6]

More so in American cinema has this tension, for mixed women especially, passing for white been explored because segregation and miscegenation laws remained in place into the twenty-first century. The 'tragic mulatto' came to prominence in the late nineteenth century, a character who might at first be accepted into white society by denouncing their Blackness, but end up in a worse place by the end of the story. Abolitionist literature popularised this trope which Donald Bogle suggests is because Black mulattos were desirable as they were 'the closest to the white ideal' and its origin in white supremacist fears of racial mixing and to create even more of a stigma concerning interracial sexuality.[7] The tragic mulatto transferred

---

[6] https://www.theguardian.com/society/raceforchange/story/0,,2187827,00.html

[7] Bogle, Donald, *Toms, Coons, Mulattoes, Mammies, and Bucks: An Interpretive History of Blacks in American Films*.

271

to the silver screen in the films of Black film-maker Oscar Micheaux and was famously the subject of the 1934 movie *Imitation of Life* based on Fannie Hurst's novel of the same name. Fredi Washington starred as Peola, the light-skinned daughter of a dark-skinned Black housemaid and cook Delilah (Louise Beavers). She grows up in a household where white business owner Bea (Claudette Colbert) and her daughter Jessie (Rochelle Hudson) profit off Delilah's labour. Her proximity to whiteness influences her rejection of her Blackness in favour of passing.

The film kills off that part of her identity symbolically by having Delilah die from a broken heart because of her daughter's final renouncement. Peola's subsequent remorse, however, ensures that the message doesn't condone this form of racial erasure, but empathises with the turmoil of living through in a racist world where their existence is treated as taboo. Director John Stahl, Donald Bogle writes, 'must have sensed that [Washington] might bring something to the role that was not necessarily written into the script – and that she might give the character an emotional truth by drawing on some of her own professional tensions and disappointments.'[8] The film had to go through several edits because of the Production Code Administration and rules prohibiting certain presentations of racial themes. 'Hurst's novel dealing with a partly colored girl who wants to pass as white violates the clause covering miscegenation in spirit, if not in fact!'[9] PCA head Joseph Breen wrote in response to the project when Universal submitted it for approval. 'The Code,' Charles Lawrence Gray suggests also, 'sought to erase or revise the actual history in which white slave owners took advantage of black women who then gave

---

[8] Bogle, Donald, *Bright Boulevards, Bold Dreams: The Story of Black Hollywood*.

[9] PCA, Imitation file, memo re "Material Submitted to This Office But Not Scheduled For Immediate Production," April 2, 1934. https://www.colorado.edu/gendersarchive1998-2013/1998/05/01/picturizing-race-hollywoods-censorship-miscegenation-and-production-racial-visibility#n11

birth to mulatto children.'[10] So interracial relations between non-white and white characters was forbidden and part of why Washington failed to get many roles after the film's release as she couldn't be cast as a romantic lead. That and because, unlike Peola, she proudly identified with her Black heritage and refused to hide it like Rita Hayworth and Merle Oberon would. 'I have never tried to pass for white and never had any desire to do so . . . Perhaps I have been able to show in the new picture how a girl might feel under the circumstances but I am not showing how I feel myself.'[11]

Washington felt that Peola 'didn't want to be white. She wanted white opportunities, the very same changes at life as her white best friend', which makes me think she would have relished the opportunity to play Clare Kendry in Rebecca Hall's *Passing*. Adapted from Nella Larsen's 1929 novel of the same name, which came out of the Harlem Renaissance that the actress was embedded in, Clare, played by Ruth Negga, is a woman choosing to pass as white as the wife of a racist white husband. She re-enters the Black world, seeking excitement, through a rekindled friendship with her childhood friend Irene, portrayed by Tessa Thompson, who is a prominent figure in their Black society. While her death at the end is tragic, she is not a typical 'tragic mulatto', as Claudia Tate points out: 'The conventional tragic mulatto is a character who 'passes' and reveals pangs of anguish resulting from forsaking this other Black identity. Clare reveals no such feelings: in fact, her psychology is inscrutable.'[12]

---

[10] Gray, Charles Lawrence, 'In Plain Sight: Changing Representations of "Biracial" People in Film 1903–2015' (2016) http://epublications.marquette.edu/dissertations_mu/682

[11] Quoted in Petty, M. J. (2016). Stealing the Show: African American Performers and Audiences in 1930s Hollywood. United States: University of California Press. P. 167

[12] Tate, Claudia, 'Nella Larsen's Passing: A Problem of Interpretation' (1980) *Black American Literature Forum,* https://doi.org/10.2307/2904405

Washington's casting as Peola was refreshing because of how often these roles were filled by white actors and continued to be in the decades after. She should have been cast as Julie in *Showboat* but Universal wanted Helen Morgan to remain in the role she originated on Broadway and later, the 1956 remake saw Ava Gardner cast over Lena Horne. Irish Catholic Jeanne Crain played a tragic mulatto in *Pinky* while Susan Kohner, who was Irish-Mexican on her mother's side, Austrian-Jewish on her father's, appeared in the 1959 *Imitation of Life* remake as a version of Peola, still with a Black mother. Zita Johann played the half-Egyptian damsel in the original version of *The Mummy* and Rachel Weisz's Evie was the same mix in the blockbuster remake. In Westerns of the 1950s, '60s and '70s, film-maker Greg Pak describes a 'Half Breed Hero' trope where white-Native American characters 'inspires identification as he actively resists white racism.'[13] Although he admits, 'it's hard to watch the films without being painfully aware that almost every "Half Breed Hero" was played by a white actor (Jeffrey Hunter, Elvis Presley, and Steve McQueen, to name just a few).' More recently, Angelina Jolie played Mariane Pearl, whose parents were Dutch-Jewish and Afro-Chinese-Cuban, in *A Mighty Heart*; Emma Stone played Allison Ng in *Aloha*, a character with Chinese and Hawaiian heritage; while Marion Cotillard appeared as Talia al Ghul in *The Dark Knight Rises* despite the comic book character being of Chinese and Arab ancestry. No wonder we are called white.

There are fewer cases where monoracial ethnic minorities have played mixed characters though they do exist. Black-British actress Marianne-Jean Baptiste played the daughter of Brenda Blethyn in Mike Leigh's *Secrets & Lies*, one of the greatest movies ever made. Lana Condor takes the lead as mixed Asian-American teen Lara Jean in Netflix's *To All The*

---

[13] Pak, Greg, '"Mulattoes, Half-Breeds, and Hapas": Multiracial Representation in the Movies', https://www.pbs.org/mattersofrace/essays/essay4_mulattoes.html

Boys I Loved Before series, but as someone who was adopted from Southeast Asia by white American parents you can expect she has an understanding of the dual heritage experience. Jeymes Samuel's recent all-Black homage to the Spaghetti Western *The Harder They Fall* was a satirical subversion of the whitewashed genre that has always erased Black people from the West, but it was criticised for casting Zazie Beetz as a character loosely based on the dark-skinned historical figure Stagecoach Mary. Yet there was pretty much silence on the fact that most of the real-life characters being depicted were of mixed Native American, Black and white ancestry and being played by non-mixed Black actors. LaKeith Stanfield portrayed a character whose heritage is in his name, Cherokee Bill, and Idris Elba as Rufus Buck who was a half-Black, half-Creek Indian outlaw. Is it positive representation if you are erasing minorities in the process?

If mixed actors do get cast, it's predominantly because of their racial ambiguity. Certainly, towards the tail end of the twentieth century and after the millennium, when multiculturalism was being more openly championed and people identifying as mixed rose in numbers, that was increasingly the case. It didn't matter what your racial background was, as long as you looked the right type of ethnic the casting director wanted in their film you were golden. Naomi Scott's casting in *Princess Jasmine* as an Arab princess, Rosario Dawson playing Roxana, a Middle Eastern princess in *Alexander*, while Fred Armisen has played every type of ethnicity because of his German, Korean and Venezuelan mix, from Barack Obama to Mohamed bin Salman. Zendaya might be the highest profile mixed actress in the world right now thanks to roles in *The Greatest Showman*, the Spider-Man franchise and *Euphoria*, but none of these roles have grappled with her identity. Admirably she has talked about not taking roles that might be better suited to darker-skinned actors. 'I am Hollywood's acceptable version of a Black girl and that has to change,' she said in 2018. 'We're vastly too beautiful and

too interesting for me to be the only representation of that.'[14]
But as Chani in *Dune*, a character in the book that was coded
as white and Bedouin Arab, the film-makers have decided
Arab people don't fit within their vision of this future.

Vin Diesel is the ultimate poster child for this sort of 'ethnically ambiguous' type of casting. The American actor, whose
mother is white and absent father's ethnicity unknown, even
made a 1995 short film called *Multi-Facial*, about his frustrating
experience trying to find work. It was seen by Steven Spielberg
and influenced his casting in *Saving Private Ryan*. Diesel has
since gone on to lead the *Fast & Furious* franchise as well as
other blockbuster films like *Pitch Black* series and *xXx* films
with little attempt to bolster his backstory with anything definitive, which seems fair considering he doesn't know it himself.
For a long time, no one realised that Keanu Reeves had Chinese-
Hawaiian heritage because his characters often fit within
American archetypes: Bill, the stoner dude in the *Bill & Ted*
franchise, Johnny Utah, the quarterback turned FBI agent in
Point Break, Jack Craven, the cop in *Speed* and Kevin Lomax,
the Deep South lawyer in *The Devil's Advocate*. Dean Cain
famously played Superman in the TV series but like Reeves,
his Japanese heritage was mostly unknown, and his career has
been defined by white American roles.

Raceless characters played by mixed actors can mean that
it is up to the audience to 'make an appraisal, whether
conscious or unconscious, regarding the character's racial identity'.[15] Colourblind casting is an extension of racelessness. In
Jessica Swales' WW2 film *Summerland*, the sole focus is placed
on the taboo lesbian relationship between Gemma Arterton's
writer Alice Lamb and Gugu Mbatha-Raw's Vera thus skirting
the additional stigma of race. In *Normal People*, writer Maz

[14] https://www.bbc.co.uk/news/newsbeat-43879480

[15] Gray, Charles Lawrence, 'In Plain Sight: Changing Representations of
"Biracial" People in Film 1903–2015' (2016) https://epublications.marquette.
edu/cgi/viewcontent.cgi?article=1693&context=dissertations_mu

Do points out that most of the antagonists that were white on the page changed on screen: British-Portuguese-Indian actor Sebastian de Souza 'as a student who defends Nazis under the spurious guise of "free speech"' Zimbabwean-Swedish actor Lancelot Mcubi as a BDSM-fan photographer and Vietnamese-French actress Aoife Hinds as the girlfriend of the lead who you are absolutely not rooting for. 'She may not be a Nazi sympathiser or abuser like the other new PoC characters orbiting the protagonists but ultimately you end up disliking her too,' says Do.[16]

When Rashida Jones was cast as Karen Filippelli in *The Office* she is given no real background. Her Italian surname, picked by writer Greg Daniels as a nod to a white exec, has people, even today, boxing her in as a white character with Southern European features. When I watched the series, I simply read her as Italian and African-American and I wouldn't be surprised if other people thought the same. 'Karen's white co-workers secretly debated if she was black, Italian, Filipina, or biracial,' notes Joshua K. Wright. 'In her white male co-workers' eyes, there was something more exotic and appealing about her as a Filipina than a black woman.'[17] There's a scene when Karen first meets Steve Carell's Michael Scott. 'Wow you're very exotic looking,' he says. 'Was your dad a G.I?' *Parks & Recreation* would similarly utilise this reductive and exoticised punchline. Amy Poehler's Leslie once tells Jones's character Anne, 'Your ambiguous ethnic blend perfectly represents the dream of the American melting pot.' I'm sure the writers thought that they were doing something subversive here, but they only Othered her instead.

Mexican-American actress Jessica Alba played a hip hop dancer in *Honey* and a stripper in *Sin City* and found it difficult

---

[16] Do, Maz, 'A review of all the "other people" in Normal People' (21 May 2020) https://gal-dem.com/a-review-of-all-the-other-people-in-normal-people/

[17] Wright, Joshua K., *"Wake Up, Mr. West": Kanye West and the Double Consciousness of Black Celebrity.*

to fit in casting boxes. 'They couldn't figure out my ethnicity,' Alba said. 'I would always go out for "exotic." They were like, "You're not Latin enough to play a Latina, and you're not Caucasian enough to play the leading lady, so you're going to be the 'exotic' one." Whatever that was.'[18] One third of people within the Latinx community identify themselves as mixed, according to a 2015 study by the Pew Research Center, yet film and TV rarely reflects that. Rather than writing her identity into her roles, Alba's was erased by omission. When she was cast as Sue Storm, the actress was given blonde hair and her brother Johnny Storm was played by white actor Chris Evans, so her whiteness to many was assumed in lieu of any racial identifiers in the script. But her appearance added to her appeal. 'The fact that you can't be sure who they are is part of their seductiveness,' casting agent Melanie Ross said in a piece on the rise of 'ethnically ambiguous' labels in the *Guardian* in 2004.[19] You got to love how confident film industry types were about this fetishisation, but that is exactly the sort of treatment we've been getting for years. Jennifer Beals' breakthrough role in 1985 film *Flashdance* managed to obscure any racial identification other than exotic through the fact that she was a welder by day and a dancer by night. She would play a tragic mulatto in Carl Franklin's *Devil in a Blue Dress* and mostly found that film roles have wanted to typecast in either that role or a raceless other. 'Somehow my story wasn't there,' she said in 2005:

> I was too young to start reading Faulkner. I hadn't seen *Imitations of Life* so I wasn't aware that I was supposed to be this insane, over-sexed tragic mulatto gal. I mean certainly, my otherness sometimes was so palpable it was a wonder that anyone could see me. I was that invisible.

[18] Alba, Jessica, discusses her ethnicity (9 February 2017) http://www.popsugar.com/latina/Jessica-Alba-Her-Ethnicity-Video-43132591

[19] Arlidge, John, 'Forget black, forget white. EA is what's hot' (4 January 2004) https://www.theguardian.com/uk/2004/jan/04/britishidentity.race

> And certainly, when society fails to tell your story there is
> an unspoken message that the story is not worth telling.[20]

Alas, the movie *Hanna* is not based on my childhood, so I've
yet to see a film that captures my experience. I bought a DNA
test in 2020 to make me feel less ambiguous in my identity.
North Africa is a pretty diverse region, centuries of colonisation
will do that to a place, and given how often I'm mistaken for
being Lebanese or Spanish or South Asian I thought it was
about time I got a definitive answer. Turns out, I'm very diverse.
34.4% Tunisian, 1.3% Nigerian, 5.5% Middle Eastern, 33.7%
Celtic and 25.1% Iberian. That last number has me thinking
I had a few Moorish ancestors settled in Portugal. Or a
Carthaginian in Spain, maybe. As an Ancient history fan, Dad
has long liked the idea of me being a descendent of Hannibal
and, you know, I do love elephants. The lack of English is
certainly amusing. The one place I've lived my entire life and
it doesn't even register in my DNA. (I guess we know who I
won't be supporting next World Cup. Just kidding! Well, let's
see who qualifies.) I read the results several times over and felt
this sense of relief. I shed a few tears. So much of my past has
felt like a mystery and every time someone asks where I'm
from, where I'm *really* from, it's an unwelcome reminder that
to many people I don't fully belong here. I carry the shame of
abandoning that side of myself to assimilate and my mind has
been fraught with anxiety over who I am allowed to be. But
the results offered a road map to explore everywhere I come
from and scientific proof of what I see in the mirror. Though
even today I still feel like a racial imposter for not being raised
with access to all my cultures and I have to justify my heritage
as mixed and not white.

I remember having a conversation with one of my Black female
critic friends in the US, one of many we've had about racial

---

[20] https://www.youtube.com/watch?v=nD3FTUsTBPM&ab_channel=
JenBealsOnline

representation in cinema as well as opportunities for women of colour in film. She told me she thought I was white when we first met whereas she describes herself as light-skinned despite the fact she very clearly passes 'the brown paper bag test'[21]. I was surprised by the racial distinction she gave herself and honestly, a bit frustrated with the one she gave me. Only in recent years, with the internet, has my racial ambiguity been questioned and mostly by trolls trying to silence me talking on matters of diversity. I felt like Rashida Jones when her sister Kidada suggested she was white-passing compared to herself. '"Passed"? I had no control over how I looked,' she told *Glamour*:

> This is my natural hair, these are my natural eyes! I've never tried to be anything that I'm not. [. . .] I want to say: 'Do you know how hurtful that is to somebody who identifies so strongly with half of who she is? If you're obviously Black, White people watch their tongues, but with me they think they can say anything. When people don't know 'what' you are, you get your heart broken daily.[22]

Passing didn't prevent the racial abuse or the fetishisation I've encountered. Race is in the eye of the beholder and mostly defined by a black and white binary. So if we don't have an appearance within those narrow parameters, they are more easily delineated as white or white-passing. That and there are increasing cases of white women employing beauty treatments to make themselves look ambiguous which means that people like myself, like Rashida Jones on that red carpet, are lumped in the same barrel. This flattening can also manifest outside of whiteness. If a person's genetic mix stems from two or more ethnic minority groups, then the dominant aesthetic features

---

[21] A colourism term in African-American oral history to describe a discriminatory practice in which an individual's skin tone is compared to the colour of a brown paper bag.

[22] Jones, Rashida, 'Magazines: Glamour Scans' (2005) http://rashidajones. blogspot.com/2009/04/magazines-glamour-scans-2005.html

can limit them to one too. Yara Shahidi is famous for her roles in the series *Black-ish* and spin-off *Grown-ish* as Zoey Johnson, but identifies as African-American and Iranian:

> Being someone that is half-Black and half-Iranian and proud of both sides, it gave me a community of people that identify as Blackish. Because so many times, if you are of any race, there is a certain feeling of this meter of like, 'How Black am I? How Iranian am I?' and it's hard when you're both to feel as though you can coexist as both and be fully both.[23]

Salma Hayek identifies as a 'Mexican-Arab in America'[24] – Mexican of Spanish descent on her mother's side and Lebanese on her father's – but neither actresses have been able to explore the Middle Eastern side of their heritage on screen. Save for the animated film *The Prophet*, based on the book by Kahlil Gibran, which Hayek produced and was the only Arab voice in a cast of mostly white actors including Liam Neeson, John Krasinski and Hollywood's favourite Middle Easterner (despite not being so) Alfred Molina. The black and white paradigm of racial discourse continues to be restrictive.

Colour-conscious casting would go a long way to improve our understanding of these expansive experiences. It's what made Negga's casting in both *Loving* and *Passing* so powerful as well as Gugu Mbatha-Raw's in *Belle* and *Beyond the Lights*. Their identity is front and centre rather than being a quirky or exotic character trait. *East is East* is one of the few British films capturing the tensions in a British-Indian family and Jimi Mistry's central performance was a major part in landing those complex emotions concerning identity and assimilation. 'My

---

[23] Bergado, Gabe, 'Yara Shahidi Opens Up About Being Biracial' (7 April 2017) https://www.teenvogue.com/story/yara-shahidi-opens-up-being-mixed-race

[24] Mullally, William, 'Salma Hayek discusses her Lebanese heritage, political correctness' (11 November 2021) https://www.arabnews.com/node/1965901/lifestyle

father is from India, my mother from Northern Ireland and I have two younger sisters, so I was bang on for Tariq,' Mistry said. 'I had had exposure to the Indian side of my family, but I considered myself very British. My mum would say I was quite strong-minded and rebellious. I don't think a part has ever fitted me so perfectly.'[25]

Being ethnically ambiguous functions as the character equivalent of empty calories. I wish writers would make more effort to build these characters from a place of inclusion for all. We'd have fewer situations where actors are being denounced as passing for white, or promoting colourism, if screen images of ethnicity didn't reinforce a racial hierarchy that solely presented multicultural inheritance through aesthetic markers.

If Alana Haim can get cast in *Licorice Pizza* by Paul Thomas Anderson because she 'looks like a girl from the Valley; she talks like a girl from the Valley; she is a girl from the Valley,' then that sort of specificity in casting should be afforded to actors dubbed ethnically ambiguous. Obviously, we won't see that in a PTA film any time soon; love the guy, but even his wife Maya Rudolph hasn't had any roles in his films tailored to her Black-Jewish heritage. 'Meeting other mixed kids has always affected me,' Rudolph once said 'It was like a part of a secret society.'[26] Please let your hubby in on the secret, Maya! But I too have had so many conversations with people over the years, especially those in the film industry, and while there hasn't been a consensus, there is a simmering frustration about screen representation. We deserve better than ticking diversity boxes so film-makers can give themselves a pat on the back for doing the bare minimum. For a very long time, I didn't have a handle on who I am, but now I do, I'd prefer if cinema wasn't a part of telling me otherwise.

[25] Pelley, Rich, 'How we made East Is East' (20 September 2021) https://www.theguardian.com/culture/2021/sep/20/how-we-made-east-is-east

[26] Weaver, Caity, 'How Maya Rudolph Became the Master of Impressions' (14 September 2018) https://www.nytimes.com/2018/09/14/magazine/maya-rudolph-snl-amazon-forever.html

Chapter 19

'"Heinous bitch" is the term used most often.'

– 10 Things I Hate About You (1999)

A FILM WRITER FRIEND once told me that during an interview for a job he dropped my name as a writer he would want to commission. Oh that's nice of him, I thought. But he wasn't finished. The man who interviewed him knew who I was and apparently in response to my name said 'she's intense' and it wasn't meant as a compliment. I laughed. Most women know the connotation associated with being called 'intense'. It falls under the pejorative umbrella of gendered descriptors alongside 'feisty', 'intimidating', 'bossy', 'abrasive' and 'shrill'. 'Intense' suggests I am too forceful in the way I express myself and opinions. Assertive men are categorised as bold and assured, but assertive women are considered aggressive, hysterical even, and when you're an outspoken woman of colour that label is used far more frequently. He says 'intense'; I say 'strong'. Of course I am. I was raised by a woman whose job was to speak up for others in a working environment where her gender, class and educational background could be (c)overtly used to keep her in her place. She taught me to respect myself and others by claiming my space and not mincing my words. As I've gotten older, I've found the confidence to follow her lead as well as the strong female leads I'd spent three decades watching.

As a kid who got into play fights as much as I played dress up, and managed to break a few bones[1] along the way, seeing the girls taking names, kicking ass and looking cute was my favourite type of series to watch. *Kim Possible*, *The Powerpuff Girls* and *Totally Spies* provided smart, powerful and funny crime-stopping teenagers able to thwart baddies around the globe and still do their homework. *Totally Spies* even had a girl of colour in its trio through sporty Alex who I loved, yet her changing ethnicity over the years, from Chinese to Afro-Latina, does little to position her as more than tokenism. Spinelli in *Recess* was the toughest kid on the playground, who didn't let gender norms dictate how she acted, and what can I say about Mulan that hasn't already been said? Well, there was this one time I was at the oldest Confucian temple in Chengdu where we were dressed up in traditional robes and given a bow and arrow to shoot a target and when my sharpshooting impressed one of the masters, he said I reminded him of Mulan. I may or may not have involuntarily broken into 'I'll Make a Man Out of You' in response.

In live-action, *Buffy the Vampire Slayer* would similarly position a teen girl as a proudly femme heroine. One of the most relatable strong female leads of her era, Buffy Summers tries to balance her regular life with her supernatural destiny to prevent demons, vampires and monsters from achieving hell on earth and I would watch this religiously after *The Simpsons* on BBC Two each week. I idolised Buffy. A cool but not cool girl who loved fashion, going out but didn't have to be the smartest person in the room because her nerdy BFF and lesbian witch Willow was right there. As a slayer, Buffy was powerful, strategic, tough, agile and deadly capable in combat. Her capacity for empathy and her vulnerability were never treated as weaknesses.

---

[1] I still break bones: I once had a metal plate fitted to repair my right thumb after breaking it due to falling down the stairs at The Box nightclub. Coincidentally Idris Elba was there and he kindly gave me ice for my thumb.

She stood up for people, was both a protector and in need of protecting and it's the way the writers and Sarah Michelle Gellar delivered her very human, internal conflict between instinct, emotion and intellect that has seen her become an iconic Strong Female Character™ beloved by more than just cis straight white girls like herself.

Yet the term Strong Female Character™ (SFC) has earned a controversial reputation nowadays because its ubiquity encompasses any female character with rich motivations, flaws, quirks and emotional depth. She can range from *A Fantastic Woman*'s Marina to *Widows*' Veronica, *Satin Rouge*'s Lilia to *Jezebel*'s Julie Marston. An all-time fave is *10 Things I Hate About You*'s Kat. In this teen comedy, based on Shakespeare's play *The Taming of the Shrew*, Kat is written both literally and figuratively as an SFC, made clear in a scene between her and her guidance counsellor Ms Perky after she's kicked out of class. Kat's blunt criticism of the English syllabus for only teaching books written by the likes of Ernest Hemingway 'an abusive alcoholic misogynist' instead of Sylvia Plath, Charlotte Bronte or Simone de Beauvoir does not go down well with two male characters. Joey, her classmate and ex throws some sexist insults her way while her frustrated teacher Mr Morgan makes the point that she's a middle-class white girl who doesn't get to co-opt school oppression when he's unable to teach a book written by 'a Black man'. He's right to call her out: a bit of a white feminist is our Kat. Get Octavia E. Butler and Alice Walker on the curriculum! Sending her to the office while letting Joey remain in class is also a bit unfair. But it's a perfect example of the patriarchal order that Kat is so keen to reject and the next scene establishes how her nonconformist, feminist ideals are at odds with the status quo:

MS PERKY

I hear you were terrorising Mr Morgan's
English class again.

285

KAT

Expressing my opinion is not a terrorist action.

MS PERKY

The way you expressed your opinion to Bobby
Ridgeway?
By the way his testicle retrieval operation
went quite well if you're interested.

KAT

I still maintain that he kicked himself in the balls.

MS PERKY

The point is Kat. [points at mug] Cat!
People perceive you as somewhat –

KAT

Tempestuous?

MS PERKY

'Heinous bitch' is the term used most often.

KAT

That Kat sees the term 'heinous bitch' as a badge of honour
is exactly why I love her. She doesn't care what people think
or say and that gives her power as a woman both intellectually
and physically. It's easy to stereotype her as an angry feminist,
but writers Kirsten Smith and Karen McCullah gave her depth
beyond her nineties riot grrl playlist. Kat's strong-willed attitude, sardonic humour, rebellious and fighting nature is part
of an attempt to combat the deep melancholy she carries. The
loss of her mother, the misogyny of her father and the psychological violence of Joey dumping her after pressuring her into
having sex. It was her first time and she's put up impenetrable

walls to protect herself from feeling vulnerable. The film's plot revolves around the idea of 'taming' her but it ultimately reveals that all she needed was a romantic partner willing to treat her as his equal, not his prize.

For better and for worse, the last fifty years has seen the SFC become synonymous with action heroines because of a literal interpretation of the word 'strong'. She leads stories, fights her own battles and has become an antidote to the more common damsel in distress. I'm a slut for superheroes and an unapologetic fan of the action genre, so love nothing more than sitting back and watching imposing, independently-minded women cause chaos or save the day in equal measure. I get a rush of antici-pation when Nice drags her boot across the floor in *Hotel Artemis* then pulls a knife out ready to fight in her sultry red evening gown: 'don't cross my line' she says. They mistakenly do. I live vicariously through the exploits of Wanda Maximoff and Harley Quinn, two women with iffy moral compasses whose behaviour fluctuates from heroic to villainous depending on the stakes. I've sat countless times in quiet awe, observing the nonchalant ease with which Jen Yu dispatches a restaurant full of men in *Crouching Tiger, Hidden Dragon*. I stressed and cried with Katniss Everdeen as she tries to survive a battle to the death against more privileged and better trained foes in *The Hunger Games*. I could watch on loop the domestic fight scene between The Bride and Vernita Green in *Kill Bill Vol. 1* and still feel the sharp change in temperature when Vernita's daughter comes home from school. I cackle every time the acerbic Charli Baltimore in *The Long Kiss Goodnight* reclaims the language of toxic masculinity and fires it back at the dude whose stupid enough to get in her face.

MALE ASSASSIN

Hey, princess. You want some company?

CHARLI

No, thanks. I'm saving myself for when I get raped.

This type of SFC has evolved over the years with film-makers responding to the gender politics of the time, but would we ever use the phrase 'Strong *Male* Character'? It's already assumed they will be strong: superpowers or not. Unless you're Steve Coogan in *The Parole Officer* who needs to eat emergency bags of crisps to combat his hypoglycaemia. Of the top grossing films of 2019, female protagonists were more common in horror, dramas and comedies, according to Women and Hollywood, while action was the least common for women to work in, relative to men, in the top 500 grossing films of that same year.[2] Before the seventies, Jeffrey A. Brown writes, the action heroine was typified by 'the femmes fatale of 1930s and 1940s film noir, the spunky tomboys of the 1950s teen films and the leather clad mod heroines of 1960s television programs like *The Avengers* and *Honey West*.'[3] Donny lass Diana Rigg's Emma Peel in the British spy series certainly walked so Scarlett Johansson's Black Widow could run. In fact, after the series aired, Marvel Comics changed Black Widow's costume to a black catsuit to match. In 1972, the first issue of Gloria Steinem's *Ms.* magazine was published with 'Wonder Woman for President' on the cover and the superhero in a call-to-action pose. The mag wanted to reclaim the Amazonian princess after several years of her being reduced to a sexless 'female James Bond' type at odds with the feminist philosophy of her inventor William Moulton Marston. She soon became an icon of second-wave feminism as an SFC who was given back her lasso, bracelets and strength of a hundred men alongside the compassion of one woman, making her the ultimate protector. A few years later Lynda Carter would originate the heroic role on screen in the *Wonder Woman* TV series, making her an even bigger sex symbol, and the cinematic SFC from the seventies

---

[2] Women and Hollywood, '2019 Statistics', https://womenandhollywood. com/resources/statistics/2019-statistics/

[3] Brown, Jeffrey A., *Dangerous Curves: Action Heroines, Gender, Fetishism, and Popular Culture*.

onwards became as much about her physical attributes as her physical skill.

The hypersexual avatar of feminised violence originated with Pam Grier, the 'Godmother of Blaxploitation'. She became cinema's defining figure of Black female empowerment after graduating from 'chicks in chains' movies to become the first African-American woman to lead an action movie in films like *Coffy*, *Foxy Brown*, *Sheba*, *Baby*, among others. Where compassion underscores Wonder Woman's actions, Grier's characters limit this feeling to only their loved ones and Black working-class community, while exhibiting a raging passion for violent justice against the corruptive powers of the white patriarchal world. She didn't have superpowers, just a tenacious urge to carry out glorious vengeance. It was a far cry from the typical maids, cooks and other service roles Black women had more regularly been seen in; the voluptuous Grier did her own stunts, and looked hot AF taking on drug dealers and crooks with brutal abandon. 'Her film persona was based on aggression towards men and an unabashed exploitation of her body,' writes Rikke Schubert. 'Mixed with the action were always rapes, beatings, torture, kinky femme fights, sex, anything to expose that incredible flesh.' And Grier didn't mind; she requested the nudity. 'I am where I am because I took those tough roles,' she said in 1976. 'If I had held out for those sweet, pretty, demure parts I'd still be waiting.'[4]

A far more vanilla and less vigilante version of Grier's Blaxploitation heroines would be depicted in seventies series like *Police Woman*, *Charlie's Angels* and *The Bionic Woman* where the leading ladies are given orders by men and objectified in ways that don't seem entirely necessary to the plot. Carrie Fisher's Leia – inspired by *Flash Gordon*'s Dale and Princess Aura as well as Clara de la Rocha, a colonel in the

---

[4] Grier, Pam, 'Grier's Fighting the "Piece of Meat" Image' (25 June 1976) https://www.newspapers.com/newspage/143838976/

Mexican Revolution, in the hair department – debuted in 1977 as a tenacious SFC with agency, the ability to fight and fend for herself despite the dangerous consequences, but by 1983's *Return of the Jedi*, *Star Wars* creator George Lucas had turned her into a sexual fantasy by making her a slave to the crime boss Jabba the Hutt and putting her in that infamous gold bikini. 'I went from the only female in that series, and it wasn't a real sexual character, to all of a sudden, boom,' Fisher said in 2015, adding a year later. 'I hated wearing that outfit and I couldn't wait to kill [Jabba].'[5] And we loved watching you do it, Carrie. Shame it took thirty-two years for the *Star Wars* franchise to give a woman the lead, but Rey ushered in even more SFCs in the franchise and with the *Ahsoka Tano* series, starring Rosario Dawson, we finally get a female lead who breaks the white brunette mould.

Back in 1979, *Alien* would subvert this sexually objectified version of the SFC with the iconic Ellen Ripley, a character originally written as a man with all the gendered traits remaining intact. Sigourney Weaver exhibits a less typically feminised aesthetic, with short hair and a slim frame who is courageous, strategic, quick-thinking and unemotional, unlike her hysterical female shipmate Lambert. Ripley represents the type of SFC that author Carina Chocano bristles at. 'They refer to the old-fashioned "strong, silent type", a type that tolerates very little blubbering, dithering, neuroticism, anxiety, melancholy or any other character flaw or weakness that makes a character unpredictable and human.'[6] Yet, for all the masculinity Ripley is afforded in the original film, she's still battling a female alien enemy in the sequel and a maternal trait is subsequently added to her, ever more explicitly as the franchise continues. The SFC

[5] *Daily News*, http://www.nydailynews.com/entertainment/movies/fisher-leia-slave-costume-didn-pretty-article-1.2452630

[6] Chocano, Carina, 'Tough, Cold, Terse, Taciturn and Prone to Not Saying Goodbye When They Hang Up the Phone' (1 July 2011) https://www.nytimes.com/2011/07/03/magazine/a-plague-of-strong-female-characters.html

can always find herself with kids to protect, from Gena Rowlands in *Gloria* to Taraji P. Henson in *Proud Mary*, because god forbid she could exhibit empathy without needing a child to bring it out.

From *The Terminator* to *T2: Judgment Day*, Linda Hamilton, as Sarah Connor, begins as a sort of Virgin Mary type-SFC destined to give birth to John Connor (Edward Furlong), the messianic resistance leader who will save mankind from extinction by artificial intelligence Skynet. She transforms from a damsel-in-distress into a muscular fighter better able to protect him. She's physically strong and ripped to look at, countering the soft, skinny standard for women on screen. Sarah sacrifices her ability to love to remain laser-focused on her mission, seeing John as less of a son and more of a moral duty. She's more weapon than woman, but the one time she lets her guard down and shows affection towards her son is when she couldn't kill Miles Dyson (Joe Morton), the scientist who invented Skynet, after seeing his young son crying. Sarah bursts into tears then tells John that she loves him, which gender studies critic Susan Jefford suggests is as if 'her admission of failure at being a tough combatant releases her to have the feelings of a mother.'[7] From then on, she becomes less integral to the plan and like Kyle Reese in the original, Dyson and Arnie's masculine-coded T-800 sacrifice themselves to save the day because that's what men do. [Pause for salute.] When Sarah returns in *Terminator: Dark Fate*, yay, she's allowed to be old, but she becomes even more of the grumpy male action trope and lets John die on her watch within the first few minutes of the movie. You had one job, Sarah! One job! It also begs the question: what was the bloody point of the franchise if the robot overlords could just keep sending terminators back in time, to kill the new saviour? OK, moving on.

Across the world in Hong Kong, action heroines have a much more storied history with Angela Mao Ying (*Hapkido*),

---

[7] Jeffords, Susan, *Hard Bodies: Hollywood Masculinity in the Reagan Era.*

Hsu Feng (*A Touch of Zen*) and Cheng Pei-pei (*Come Drink with Me*) among the most celebrated actresses exhibiting their phenomenal swordplay and martial art skills against men in period settings. By the eighties and nineties, the more contemporary 'Girls with Guns' subgenre was popularised by films with some stunning original titles like *Iron Angels*, *Killer Angels*, and, *Angel Terminators* which saw a team of SFCs working and fighting together. The OG film was *Yes, Madam* starring Michelle Yeoh in only her second film opposite Scottish martial arts fighter Cynthia Rothrock, as a couple of no-nonsense cops teaming up to beat down crime lords and high-kick the patriarchy with mad stunts and fight choreography to rival Jackie Chan's frenetic kung fu output. They wear their hair short, their bodies covered up with the tracksuit sleeves rolled up in true eighties fashion to deliver some monumental pounding of men that truly raised the bar for what kind of fighting SFCs could get up to. Fantasy series *Xena: Warrior Princess* was influenced by the female fighters of Hong Kong cinema, whose agility, speed and acrobatic ability was as formidable as her sword and chakram skills. Yes, this Ancient Greek SFC carried a Persian weapon in a series built on a melting pot of myths and legends from across the world. There wasn't a week I didn't tune in to her spin-off series on Channel 5 after Lucy Lawless was introduced as an evil-warlord-turned-warrior-do-gooder in *Hercules: The Legendary Journeys*, traversing Ancient Greece with her female sidekick-turned-soulmate, Gabrielle. Xena provided some much-needed explicit queer iconography in the genre after *Red Sonja* pretty much demonised lesbianism in 1985 through its female antagonist evil Queen Gedren. It passed the Bechdel Test, but at what cost? Xena also bucked the trend for action heroines always being the only woman in the room. I loved the revisionist CBBC series *Maid Marian and Her Merry Men* because it taught me from an early age that I could be the leader of the pack and stand up against 'tyranny, injustice, cruelty to animals and stuff'. Still, she was the only gal in the gang, with the other significant female character being Rotten Rose who she was pitted against constantly because of course girls can't get on.

Atsuko Tanaka's Major Motoko Kusanagi in *Ghost in the Shell*, Jennifer Garner's Sydney Bristow in *Alias*, Scarlett Johansson's Natasha Romanoff in Marvel, and Anne Parillaud's Nikita were the lone SFCs in a man's world whose sex appeal is just as deadly as their combat skills. Major's cyborg body, her shell, is that of the female ideal which she strips of clothing when carrying out her missions. A lingerie-clad Sydney with a riding crop seduces her way into the private room of her target. Black Widow has spent the last ten years running around in a catsuit and only recently got to step out on her own to fight against and with other women. Nikita locks and loads a sniper rifle in her cherry-patterned underwear to do a hit and later runs around in a little black dress during an iconic restaurant shootout. All but one has been medically-altered and/or manufactured for violent action suggesting their original female bodies weren't up to the challenge and more easily controlled as with *Serenity*, *Ultraviolet* and the *Dark Angel* TV series too. You don't see Ethan Hunt being genetically altered to do espionage or The Rock's Hobbs when he is literally taking down a helicopter with his bare hands. At least Steve Rogers was pumped with super soldier serum before having the audacity to hold on to a flying chopper.

The mostly white and lithe female assassin continues to be a pretty popular occupation for the SFC, but after *La Femme Nikita*, Luc Besson delivered one of my favourites, a contract-killer-in-training through Natalie Portman's Mathilda in *Leon*. She's a complicated, vulnerable twelve-year-old girl trying to grow up too quickly after witnessing the murder of her neglectful parents and beloved brother. She wants bloody retribution but also likes to play dress up. She's sexually precocious, romantically attaching herself to the eponymous hitman who thankfully never reciprocates her affection. It still projected sexual maturity onto a young girl and Portman would suffer the consequences. 'I was so excited at 13 when the film was released and my work

and my art would have a human response,' she said in 2018. 'I
excitedly opened my first fan mail to read a rape fantasy that
a man had written me.'[8] According to a 2016 study analysing
films from 1960 to 2014, female characters are far more likely
to be sexualised than male characters: 'one in three (29%)
female characters are portrayed in "revealing clothing"
(compared to 7% of male characters), and one in four (26%)
appear partially or fully naked during the film (compared to
9% for male characters).'[9] Angelina Jolie was arguably the first
bona fide blockbuster SFC, lending her enviable beauty, brains
and body to her string of roles in the original *Tomb Raider*
films, *Gone in Sixty Seconds*, *Mr & Mrs Smith*, *Wanted* and *Salt*,
yet she rarely got to share the screen or a scene with another
woman. Jolie really was the blueprint for the action babe who
appealed to all genders. If you didn't want to be her, you were
aroused by her and men didn't mind watching her brutalise
other men because she looked fuckable doing it. While not in
'their traditional exhibitionist role,' Mulvey's thesis on Visual
Pleasures still applies here as these SFCs 'are simultaneously
looked at and displayed, with their appearance coded for strong
visual and erotic impact so that they can be said to connote
to-be-looked-atness.' That was certainly the case with the
Charlie's Angels films starring Cameron Diaz, Lucy Liu and
Drew Barrymore and Kate Beckinsale's *Underworld* franchise.
From 2000, hypersexualised female action leads became more
common[10] which might also have something to do with how
many comic book characters were being brought to life on the
big screen. Female superheroes were drawn in skimpy outfits
that clung to their ridiculously proportioned, voluptuous figures.

---

[8] https://www.youtube.com/watch?time_continue=139&v=tXWHO14c88c

[9] Heldman, Caroline, Laura Lazarus Frankel and Jennifer Holmes, '"Hot,
Black Leather, Whip": The (De)evolution of Female Protagonists in Action
Cinema, 1960–2014' (2016) *Sexualisation, Media, and Society*, https://
journals.sagepub.com/doi/full/10.1177/2374623815627789

[10] Ibid.

'The women superheroes are super-female in their appearance, and the men are super male,' says Pamela Boker. 'But the concepts of femininity and masculinity, as cultural categories and aggressiveness are all but eliminated.'[11]

In 2005, *Elektra* embodied this with her hard body, red corset and matching pants as the first female Marvel superhero to get her own movie. You better believe I was in the cinema opening weekend. I even bought the DVD (which I still have), because I was a teen starved for female-led heroics and the superhero bar was pretty much in hell after *Catwoman*. The male writers of that DC Comics film really did Halle Berry dirty with its beauty industry baddie storyline. 'They thought a female story couldn't be a badass saving the world from some natural disaster that threatened mankind,' Berry told me. 'We were limited to just saving women from their faces cracking off.'[12] Elektra isn't just a cold, robotic assassin but has a heart and even after coming back from the dead is willing to put her life on the line again to save a father and daughter. 'Despite oozing star quality, Garner struggles to rise above the limitations of the script,' said critic Helen O'Hara. 'While she's able to play with a few character quirks, such as her obsessive-compulsive fruit arranging, and excels in the fight scenes, she's not given a single witticism, so seriously does the film take her plight.'[13] I couldn't take the scene seriously when she's fighting against white sheets and a gust of wind that kept blowing her long hair in her face. I think that might just be my biggest action genre pet peeve. Please either shave a woman's hair off, a la G.I. Jane and *Mad Max: Fury Road's* Furiosa, or give women hairbands like director Cathy Yan and writer Christina Hodson do for the ladies in *Birds of Prey*. Harley Quinn giving

---

[11] Boker, Pamela S., 'America's women superheroes: Power, gender, and the comics'. Mid-Atlantic Almanac 2 (1993): 107–18

[12] My interview with Berry for *Empire* magazine, December 2021.

[13] O'Hara, Helen, 'Elektra Review' (1 January 2000) https://www.empireon-line.com/movies/reviews/elektra-review/

Black Canary a hair tie personally felt like the biggest win for female representation in the action genre in its entire history.

When female writers and directors have been involved, the SFC has fared far better. With *Thelma & Louise*, Callie Khouri gave a massive middle finger up to male violence by repurposing the road trip for female enjoyment, self-discovery and empowerment. Susan Sarandon and Geena Davis's best friends become outlaws drinking, shooting and fucking their way to freedom. The end scene is an iconic moment of feminist cinema. Instead of handing themselves in, together they choose to speed off the edge of a cliff into a canyon. Death offers the freedom they will never have in life, but by having their rebellion frozen in mid-air it cements this moment of liberation in cinematic history. Put that on a poster, baby! While she does play second fiddle to Neo in the Wachowski siblings' *The Matrix* trilogy, Trinity still has agency, is a formidable fighter, a calming presence and is able to die heroically for the cause. When she's brought back in *The Matrix: Resurrections* she and Neo are firmly established as the two sides of the same Chosen One coin and it's rather beautiful. Krysten Ritter's *Jessica Jones*, created by Melissa Rosenberg, gets to claim the stereotypical male role of a private investigator as well as be an utter mess. She has unresolved trauma and self-loathing, a drinking habit, a slutty attitude, a grungy wardrobe, and a sarcastic sense of humour making her superstrength the least interesting thing about her.

Patty Jenkins' *Wonder Woman* and *Captain Marvel*, written by co-directors Anna Boden and Ryan Fleck with Geneva Robertson-Dworet, proved that the strongest weapon in these women's arsenal was not their superpowers but their humanity. Brie Larson's mightiest hero got the benefit of being written with a sense of humour, unlike poor Elektra. Lashana Lynch's Maria Rambeau was given a purpose beyond just being the emotional anchor for her superpowered best friend and able to use her regular pilot skills to save a host of lives. Rambeau's daughter, Monica, is played by Teyonah Parris in the *WandaVision* series with her beautiful natural afro hair and curvier figure intact. It's her grief that grounds her character's motivation towards an emotional pact with the chaos being that is Scarlet Witch creating a way out for them both. The Rambeaus, along with *Black Panther*'s Dora Milaje, Gamora, Valkyrie and MJ show there is more to Black SFCs. They represent the diversity of personalities, skills and aims beyond how their male counterparts might expect them to function.

The SFC trope is an imperfect beast continuously reshaped by powers rarely interested beyond their bottom line. I can get on board with the criticism about her commodification as a performative female empowerment statement. Big studios pushing badass women with feminist zingers when their own corporate culture continues to see intersectional under-representation of women on and off screen is not a great look. Where the wealth gap between the boss and the lowest rank of employee is a gulf despite the hundreds of millions, sometimes billions, their tentpole releases rake in. I've rankled at the faux feminist nods delivered in such films as *X-Men: Dark Phoenix*, *Men in Black: International* and *Avengers: Endgame* that reminded us these franchises have long championed male characters at the expense of female. I'd prefer a course-correction by broadening the opportunities for female leads in complex roles, played by under-represented women, written by women for films directed by women, not tokenistic gestures that amount to 'our bad!' And don't get me started on the completely unnecessary final scene in *The 355* when, after avoiding making any overt feminist statements, the girl gang of spies awkwardly get together to deliver a basic bitch equivalent of 'fuck the patriarchy!' to the bad guy who got away with it. It still makes me cringe.

But there's no denying that the SFC fosters a sense of power in a world that often makes women feel powerless. It's empowered me into action, like the time at uni I headbutted my ex mid-argument outside a nightclub when he wouldn't let me go. More recently, a male staff member at my council-owned gym walked into the spa during a women's only period. After refusing to leave, I made a complaint and it was suggested if

I kicked up a fuss the women's only space would be removed. So I kicked up an even bigger fuss with the council; they upheld my complaint, gave their staff fresh training and gave me a free month. Even in the humdrum of everyday life I feel more confident moving through the world without needing to appease fragile masculinity. Seeing strong women claim their space, take on the proverbial man and live to tell the tale has been a reassuring, albeit inconsistent, image to witness. And, given the trope more frequently manifests in the most popular cinema genre right now, this authoritative positioning of women might just offer the average female cinemagoer the same sort of solace. Or at the very least, provide inspiration for younger generations who no longer have to be raised on movies that teach us women require men to rescue them.

She could be physically weak but still courageous, like *Encanto*'s Mirabel or *Heathers*' Veronica. Her strength of character can be shown through success as well as failure like Turquoise in *Miss Juneteenth*. 'The best Strong Female Characters,' writes Tasha Robinson, 'are the physically and emotionally weak ones. Characters who have a lot to overcome to become heroes are the bravest and most inspirational.'[14] We deserve more than stock action babes, gender-swapped movies and rebooted franchises that don't do enough to establish female leads outside of the male shadows of the originals. An exception might actually be *Bumblebee*, written by Christina Hodson, whose teen lead Charlie, a far cry from the sexualised sidepieces of the previous *Transformers* films, brings earnest warmth to proceedings and earns back much of the lost faith in the franchise. Not enough films are being written or greenlit that explore these endless possibilities and complexities of what it is to be a woman. She should be pushed to explore intersectional realms of being beyond what she currently is. Or she will never persist.

[14] Robinson, Tasha, 'With Star Wars' Rey, we've reached Peak Strong Female Character' (19 December 2015) https://www.theverge.com/2015/12/19/10626896/star-wars-the-force-awakens-rey-mary-sue-feminist

Acknowledgements

To Mum, Dad, Karim and Nick – I wouldn't be the person I am today without our blended family. I love you all unconditionally.

I want to thank all of my wonderful friends who have cheered me on during this writing endeavour. Corin and Cecile for reading my early bits and providing the kind words I needed to hear when I was feeling my most anxious. Thank you, Candice, Dominic, Rachel and Justin for your solace, writing and work advice. And to Parisa, Chloe, Jade, Lilah, Colette, Obi, Lucy, Amon, Clarisse, Coryn, Eva, Sophie, Nikki and Leila for the moral support and social distraction when I needed to feel human again. Russell, thank you for the love and for introducing me to the Nintendo Switch.

Thank you to my editor Kwaku for getting me entirely and helping to cut back on my propensity to waffle. Ross for copy-editing and proofing. To Dave, Candida, Vidisha, Grace and the Footnote team, thank you for all the positive reinforcement during this rather intense journey! Thank you to my agent Rukhsana for having my back, patiently explaining the process to an author newbie, and answering my random texts even when I didn't realise it was your day off. Sorry about that!

Thank you to Nikesh Shukla for sending me a text asking if I ever thought about writing a book. I had but never felt the confidence to pursue the idea until you suggested it and helped me get going. *Kamala Harris voice* We did it, Nik!

And to all the film-makers of the world, thank you for the movies. Well, some of them.

Post-credits Scene

So I GET A TEXT from my editor Kwaku on the first day of my holiday, the first since before lockdown, suggesting I add some closing thoughts to the book after the last chapter and my eyes bulged. We were already trying to whittle down the 100,000 words I wrote, now they want me to add in more?! But they felt it might be good to offer my final thoughts, like Jerry Springer, and so in lieu of a piece to camera, here's a few musings.

Writing this book has been an experience like no other, as a writer and a human being. Passing a critical eye on your own life as well as movies can be a triggering quest, especially when others factor into your life story so far, so it's been a journey for all the people I care about too. Sometimes it's been overwhelming the feelings it's brought up but ultimately it's offered a catharsis of sorts and lifted a lot of emotional weight. It feels good to share and my hope is that anyone reading this might find some big or small comfort in my words.

I wrote this book in 2.5 months and some chapters were harder to write than others. I might have disassociated at some point! I even went through a break up during the final editing process which, well, was not ideal timing! So if you love it, you can marvel at my thought-provoking insight. If you hate it, well, I wrote it in 2.5 months, give me a break!

There are so many films I would have loved to have included and that was one of the toughest parts of the process: how to reflect the diversity of storytelling over the last 100 years and lack thereof. But as I've only been on the planet for 34 years, I let myself off. There is always the next book and so much of my life yet to be told and experienced. So many more films to watch and to be made. And one thing I can guarantee is that I will never run out of things to say, and neither will the Movies.

Bibliography

Articles & Interviews

Alba, Jessica, discusses her ethnicity (9 February 2017) http://www.popsugar.com/latina/Jessica-Alba-Her-Ethnicity-Video-43132591

Al Jazeera, 'Palestine Remix: Destroyed Palestinian Villages', https://interactive.aljazeera.com/aje/palestineremix/maps-and-data-visualisations.html

Amnesty International UK, 'Online abuse of women widespread in UK', https://www.amnesty.org.uk/online-abuse-women-widespread

Arjun, Sajip, 'Much Apu about nothing' (27 October 2017) https://www.telegraph.co.uk/tv/0/much-apu-nothing-calling-simpsons-racist-misses-point/

Arlidge, John, 'Forget black, forget white. EA is what's hot' (4 January 2004) https://www.theguardian.com/uk/2004/jan/04/britishidentity.race

Barnhardt, Adam, 'Moon Knight Director Takes Shot at Dwayne Johnson's Black Adam' (22 March 2022) https://comicbook.com/dc/news/moon-knight-director-takes-shot-dwayne-johnsons-black-adam/

Bastién, Angelica Jade, 'What Does It Mean for a Rape Scene to Be "Done well"?' (9 August 2019) https://www.vulture.com/2019/08/rape-scenes-movies-nightingale-classic-hollywood.html

BBC News, 'American Sniper film "behind rise in anti-Muslim threats"' (25 January 2015) https://www.bbc.co.uk/news/entertainment-arts-30972690

BBC News, 'Brie Larson wants more diversity among film critics' (15 June 2018) https://www.bbc.co.uk/news/newsbeat-44495537

Beat, 'New research shows eating disorder stereotypes prevent people finding help', https://www.beateatingdisorders.org.uk/news/beat-news/eating-disorder-stereotypes-prevent-help/

Behrendt, Larissa, 'The Nightingale review – ambitious, urgent and necessarily brutal. But who is it for?' (20 August 2019) https://www.theguardian.com/film/2019/aug/20/the-nightingale-review-ambitious-urgent-and-necessarily-brutal-but-who-is-it-for

Bergado, Gabe, 'Yara Shahidi Opens Up About Being Biracial' (7 April 2017) https://www.teenvogue.com/story/yara-shahidi-opens-up-being-mixed-race

Berkvist, Robert, 'Omar Sharif, 83, a Star in "Lawrence of Arabia" and "Doctor Zhivago," Dies' (10 July 2015) https://www.nytimes.com/2015/07/11/movies/omar-sharif-a-star-in-dr-zhivago-dies-at-83.html

Beydoun, Khaled A., 'It doesn't matter that an Arab will play Aladdin' (19 July 2017) https://www.aljazeera.com/opinions/2017/7/19/it-doesnt-matter-that-an-arab-will-play-aladdin

Brameso, Charles, 'Claire Denis on *High Life*' (13 September 2018) https://www.vulture.com/2018/09/claire-denis-on-putting-juliette-binoche-in-a-fuckbox.html

Buchanan, Kyle, 'The Toughest Scene I Wrote' (17 December 2014) https://www.vulture.com/2014/12/finding-obvious-childs-perfect-fartcry-balance.html

Buckley, Cara, 'Male Critics Are Harsher Than Women on Female-Led Films' (17 June 2018) https://www.nytimes.com/2018/07/17/movies/male-critics-are-harsher-than-women-on-female-led-films-study-says.html

Burnham, Bo, Spirit Awards acceptance speech (25 February 2019) https://www.youtube.com/watch?v=IHHLiS0tttU

Campbell, Denis, 'Record numbers of women reach 30 child-free in England and Wales' (27 January 2022) https://www.theguardian.com/lifeandstyle/2022/jan/27/women-child-free-30-ons

Chocano, Carina, 'Tough, Cold, Terse, Taciturn and Prone to Not Saying Goodbye When They Hang Up the Phone' (1 July 2011) https://www.nytimes.com/2011/07/03/magazine/a-plague-of-strong-female-characters.html

Daily News, http://www.nydailynews.com/entertainment/movies/fisher-leia-slave-costume-didn-pretty-article-1.2452630

Das, Lina, 'I felt raped by Brando' (19 July 2007) https://www.dailymail.co.uk/tvshowbiz/article-469646/I-felt-raped-Brando.html

Dichiara, Tom, 'NATALIE PORTMAN SAYS HER "BLACK SWAN" MASTURBATION SCENE IS "SO DISGUSTING"' (30 November 2010) https://www.mtv.com/news/2438013/natalie-portman-black-swan-masturbation-scene/

Do, Maz, 'A review of all the "other people" in Normal People' (21 May 2020) https://gal-dem.com/a-review-of-all-the-other-people-in-normal-people/

Dodd, Vikram, 'Met officers joked about raping women, police watchdog reveals' (1 February 2022) https://www.theguardian.com/uk-news/2022/feb/01/met-officers-joked-raping-women-police-watchdog-racist

Ebert, Roger, 'Aladdin' (25 November 1992) https://www.rogerebert.com/reviews/aladdin-1992

Ebert, Roger, *Frenzy* (1 January 1972) https://www.rogerebert.com/reviews/frenzy-1972

Emami, Gazelle, 'The *Not Without My Daughter* Problem' (11 January 2016) https://www.vulture.com/2016/01/not-without-my-daughter-problem.html

End Violence Against Women, 'Major new YouGov survey for EVAW: Many people still unclear what rape is' (6 December 2018) https://www.endviolenceagainstwomen.org.uk/major-new-survey-many-still-unclear-what-rape-is/

Evans, Diana, '"I'm Taking Back What's Mine": The Many Lives Of Thandiwe Newton' (4 April 2021) https://www.vogue.co.uk/news/article/thandiwe-newton-interview

Ferme, Antonio, 'Sean Young Says Her Career Was Derailed by Ridley Scott, Oliver Stone, Warren Beatty and Others'

(22 March 2021) https://variety.com/2021/film/news/sean-young-ridley-scott-oliver-stone-warren-beatty-1234935883/

Flint, Hanna, 'Gerard Butler praises Geostorm's diversity, thinks Gods of Egypt "whitewash" backlash was "too much"' (20 October 2017) https://uk.movies.yahoo.com/gerard-butler-praises-geostorms-diversity-thinks-gods-egypt-whitewash-backlash-much-095603184.html

Flint, Hanna, 'Ruth Negga Takes Center Stage' (31 March 2022) https://www.townandcountrymag.com/leisure/arts-and-culture/a39427166/ruth-negga-lady-macbeth-interview/

Flint, Hanna, 'Sliding Doors is turning 21 and is still as relevant as ever – here's why' (2019) https://www.stylist.co.uk/life/sliding-doors-rerelease-gwyneth-paltrow-peter-howitt-inter-view-exclusive/264965

Foundas, Scott, '"Exodus: Gods and Kings" Director Ridley Scott on Creating His Vision of Moses' (25 November 2014) https://variety.com/2014/film/news/ridley-scott-exodus-gods-and-kings-christian-bale-1201363668/

Fox, David J., 'Disney Will Alter Song in "Aladdin"' (10 July 1993) https://www.latimes.com/archives/la-xpm-1993-07-10-ca-11747-story.html

Freer, Ian, 'EMPIRE ESSAY: Singin' In The Rain Review' (26 January 2006) https://www.empireonline.com/movies/reviews/empire-essay-singin-rain-review/

Friedman, Stewart D., 'How Our Careers Affect Our Children' (14 November 2018) https://hbr.org/2018/11/how-our-careers-affect-our-children

Gerish, Devika, '"He's All That" Review: Much Ado About Nothing' (27 August 2021) https://www.nytimes.com/2021/08/27/movies/hes-all-that-review.html

Goop, 'Viva la Vulva', https://goop.com/gb-en/wellness/relationships/the-upside-of-a-crush-even-if-youre-in-a-committed-relationship/

Gray, Charles Lawrence, 'In Plain Sight: Changing Representations of "Biracial" People in Film 1903–2015' (2016) http://epublic-ations.marquette.edu/dissertations_mu/682

Greco, Patti, 'The *To-Do* List Director Maggie Carey on Casting Connie Britton and Aubrey Plaza's Masturbation Scene' (23 July 2013) https://www.vulture.com/2013/07/to-do-list-director-maggie-carey-interview.html

Gregory, Andrew, 'One in four women experience domestic abuse before 50 – study' (16 Feb 2022) https://www.theguardian.com/society/2022/feb/16/one-in-four-women-experience-domestic-abuse-before-50-study

Grier, Pam, 'Grier's Fighting the "Piece of Meat" Image' (25 June 1976) https://www.newspapers.com/newspage/143838976/

Handy, Bruce, 'Cinema: The Force Is Back' (10 February 1997)

Hans, Simran, 'Desiree talks comedy, her web series and the success of Appropriate Behaviour' (6 April 2016) https://network.bfi.org.uk/news-and-features/on-first-features/appropriate-behaviour-desiree-akhavan

Haskell, Rob, 'Bella From the Heart: On Health Struggles, Happiness, and Everything In Between' (15 March 2022) https://www.vogue.com/article/bella-hadid-cover-april-2022

Hayek, Salma, 'Harvey Weinstein Is My Monster Too' (13 December 2017) https://www.nytimes.com/interactive/2017/12/13/opinion/contributors/salma-hayek-harvey-weinstein.html?

Hooks, Bell, 'Cultural Criticism & Transformation' (1997) https://www.mediaed.org/transcripts/Bell-Hooks-Transcript.pdf

Horton, Adrian, 'He's All That review – Netflix's dull TikTok teen remake lacks charm' (27 August 2021) https://www.theguardian.com/film/2021/aug/27/hes-all-that-review-netflixs-dull-tiktok-teen-remake-lacks-charm

Irish Examiner, 'Beyonce warns against her maple syrup diet' (16 August 2006) https://www.irishexaminer.com/lifestyle/arid-30272483.html

Jones, Monique, '"A Wrinkle In Time" Spoiler Review: A Heartbreaking Misfire With A Powerful Burden' (12 March 2018) https://www.slashfilm.com/556838/wrinkle-in-time-spoiler-review/?utm_campaign=clip

Jones, Rashida, 'Magazines: Glamour Scans' (2005) http://rashida-jones.blogspot.com/2009/04/magazines-glamour-scans-2005.html

Jung, Alex, 'Thandie Newton Is Finally Ready to Speak' (7 July 2020) https://www.vulture.com/article/thandie-newton-in-conversation.html

Kacala, Alexander, 'How Hollywood heartthrobs and Steven Spielberg helped make a drag queen cult classic' (3 September 2020) https://www.today.com/popculture/how-steven-spielberg-made-film-wong-foo-cult-classic-t190808

Kael, Pauline, 'Talking Out of Turn #4: Pauline Kael (1983)' (26 November 2010) https://www.criticsatlarge.ca/2010/11/talking-out-of-turn-4-pauline-kael-1983.html

Kaufman, Charlie, 'Screenwriters' Lecture' (30 September 2011) https://www.bafta.org/media-centre/transcripts/screenwriters-lecture-charlie-kaufman

Khazan, Olga, 'Why Straight Men Gaze at Gay Women' (8 March 2016) https://www.theatlantic.com/health/archive/2016/03/straight-men-and-lesbian-porn/472521/?utm_campaign=the-atlantic&utm_medium=social&utm_source=facebook&fbclid=IwAR0CtpbxHWFMrx7yk-NoYcLbNiCGHjItgrgu9ixETF6UW9nqfvpXJD38wLc

Kiang, Jessica, '"Mainstream" review: Internet Fame Eats Itself in Gia Coppola's Satire' (5 September 2020) ://variety.com/2020/film/reviews/mainstream-review-gia-coppola-1234759713/

Killingsworth, Matthew A. and Daniel T. Gilbert, 'A Wandering Mind Is an Unhappy Mind' (12 November 2010) http://www.sciencemag.org/content/330/6006/932.abstract

Kim, Kristen Yoonsoo, 'The Woman Behind *Raw*, the Horror Movie So Scary It Makes Audiences Pass Out' (12 March 2017) https://www.gq.com/story/raw-julia-ducournau

Komar, Marlen, 'The Sneaky History Of Why Women Started Shaving' (14 December 2016) https://www.bustle.com/articles/196747-the-sneaky-manipulative-history-of-why-women-started-shaving

Kuntz, Tom, 'Word for Word. A Scholarly Debate; Rhett and Scarlett: Rough Sex Or Rape? Feminists Give a Damn' (19 February 1995) https://www.nytimes.com/1995/02/19/weekinreview/word-for-worda-scholarly-debate-rhett-scarlett-rough-sex-rape-feminists-give.html

Leadbeater, Alex, 'Producer Dan Lin Interview: Aladdin' (11 September 2019) https://screenrant.com/dan-lin-interview-aladdin-producer/

Lenker, Maureen Lee, 'Jennifer Fox had to use her real name in *The Tale* so people would believe the story' (25 May 2018) https://ew.com/tv/2018/05/25/jennifer-fox-had-to-use-her-real-name-in-the-tale-so-people-would-believe-the-story/

Loughrey, Clarisse, 'Deadpool 2 interview: Zazie Beetz on why Domino embraces armpit hair' (18 May 2018) https://www.independent.co.uk/arts-entertainment/films/features/deadpool-2-domino-armpit-hair-zazie-beetz-interview-cast-a8354601.html

Louis, William Roger, 'The Great Middle East Game, and Still No Winner' (27 August 1989) https://www.nytimes.com/1989/08/27/books/the-great-middle-east-game-and-still-no-winner.html

Maas, Sofie Cato, 'The Gaze of Shame: A Conversation with Catherine Breillat' (21 October 2019) https://mubi.com/notebook/posts/the-gaze-of-shame-a-conversation-with-catherine-breillat

McCloskey, Jimmy, 'Boys, 15 and 17, "filmed themselves raping and killing woman, 36, who was relaxing in park"' (11 February 2021) https://metro.co.uk/2021/02/11/boys-15-and-17-filmed-themselves-raping-killing-woman-36-at-park-14067686/

McDowell, Edwin, '"Exodus" in Samizdat: Still Popular and Still Subversive' (26 April 1987) https://www.nytimes.com/1987/04/26/books/exodus-in-samizdat-still-popular-and-still-subversive.html?smid=url-share

McNab, J.M., '"The Mummy" Is Not A "Perfect Film," It's Racist Garbage' (21 March 2022) https://www.cracked.com/

article_33077_the-mummy-is-not-a-perfect-film-its-racist-garbage.html

Montreal Gazette, 'Famous Silent Screen Vamp Theda Bara Dies of Cancer' (8 April 1955) https://news.google.com/newspapers?id=qYEtAAAAIBAJ&pg=7227,1426917&dq-=arab-death+theda-bara&hl=en

Moss, Rachel, 'This Is How Many Times A Year Women Masturbate, Compared To Men' (16 August 2021) https://www.huffingtonpost.co.uk/entry/how-often-do-men-and-women-masturbate_uk_611a2f5ee4b0454ed70f7b27

Mullally, William, 'Salma Hayek discusses her Lebanese heritage, political correctness' (11 November 2021) https://www.arabnews.com/node/1965901/lifestyle

Newman, Andrew Adam, 'Sometimes, Even Women Need a Smoothly Shaved Face' (9 June 2015) https://www.nytimes.com/2015/06/11/fashion/sometimes-even-women-need-a-smoothly-shaved-face.html

Newton, Steve, 'Horror in Vancouver: 16-year-old Alicia Silverstone talks The Crush' (7 March 2014) https://www.straight.com/blogra/17751/horror-vancouver-16-year-old-alicia-silverstone-talks-crush

New York Times, 'Arab-Americans Protest "True Lies"' (16 July 1994) https://www.nytimes.com/1994/07/16/movies/arab-americans-protest-true-lies.html

NPR, 'Forget The Temptress Rep: Here's The Real Cleopatra' (25 April 2010) https://www.npr.org/2010/04/25/126195946/forget-the-temptress-rep-heres-the-real-cleopatra

O'Hara, Helen, 'Elektra Review' (1 January 2000) https://www.empireonline.com/movies/reviews/elektra-review/

Olsen, Mark and Ehsanipour, Asal, 'How Halle Berry channeled her childhood trauma in directorial debut, "Bruised"' (21 December 2021) https://www.latimes.com/entertainment-arts/awards/story/2021-12-21/halle-berry-netflix-bruised-envelope-podcast-interview

Pak, Greg, '"Mulattoes, Half-Breeds, and Hapas": Multiracial Representation in the Movies', https://www.pbs.org/matter-sofrace/essays/essay4_mulattoes.html

Pelley, Rich, 'How we made East Is East' (20 September 2021) https://www.theguardian.com/culture/2021/sep/20/how-we-made-east-is-east

Perthen, Amanda, 'Minister for Fitness's "secret" Tunisian husband' (18 February 2007) https://www.pressreader.com/uk/the-mail-on-sunday/20070218/282093452273077

Petersen, Anne Helen, '"Eating disorders are for white girls."' (16 June 2021) https://annehelen.substack.com/p/eating-disorders-are-for-white-girls?s=r

Petty, M. J., Stealing the Show: African American Performers and Audiences in 1930s Hollywood. (United States: University of California Press, 2016)

Reddish, David, '"Boys Don't Cry" at 20: director Kimberly Peirce reflects on a classic' (29 September 2019) https://www.queerty.com/boys-dont-cry-20-director-kimberly-pierce-reflects-classic-20190929

Ricci, Christina, interview on *The Graham Norton Show* (21 January 2017) https://www.youtube.com/watch?time_continue=167&v=_wnEwtCk3Ng&feature=emb_title&ab_channel=BBC

Ringwald, Molly, 'What About "The Breakfast Club"?' (6 April 2018) https://www.newyorker.com/culture/personal-history/what-about-the-breakfast-club-molly-ringwald-metoo-john-hughes-pretty-in-pink

Robinson, Tasha, 'With Star Wars' Rey, we've reached Peak Strong Female Character' (19 December 2015) https://www.theverge.com/2015/12/19/10626896/star-wars-the-force-awakens-rey-mary-sue-feminist

Rottenberg, Josh, 'The Real Don Jons: How online porn has affected a generation' (26 September 2013) https://ew.com/article/2013/09/26/real-don-jons-porn/

Roxborough, Scott, 'Cannes: "Nymphomaniac" Producer Reveals Graphics Are Used in "Groundbreaking" Sex Scenes' (20 May 2013) https://www.hollywoodreporter.com/movies/movie-news/cannes-nymphomaniac-producer-sex-scenes-525666/

Rubin, Rebecca, 'Film Criticism Continues to Be Dominated by Men, Study Shows' (24 May 2022) https://variety.com/2022/film/news/film-critics-male-female-study-1235276110/

Ryzik, Melena, 'Shooting Film and TV Sex Scenes: What Really Goes On' (26 February 2015) https://www.nytimes.com/2015/03/01/movies/shooting-film-and-tv-sex-scenes-what-really-goes-on.html?_r=0

Serrill, Michael S., 'Tunisia Punishing the Pious' (12 October 1987)

Shapiro, Lily, 'In Conversation: Mary Harron' (22 April 2020) https://www.vulture.com/2020/04/mary-harron-american-psycho-in-conversation.html

Sharman, Jon, '2,000 police officers accused of sexual misconduct in past four years' (11 October 2021) https://www.independent.co.uk/news/uk/home-news/police-sexual-misconduct-uk-b1935993.html

Shyamalan, M. Night, *Wired* interview (23 July 2021) https://www.youtube.com/watch?v=ltC3VTAwGXM

Sinha-Roy, Piya, 'A whole new world: First look at Guy Ritchie's live-action remake of Disney's magical classic *Aladdin*' (19 December 2018) https://ew.com/movies/2018/12/19/aladdin-first-look-ew-cover-story/

Sullivan, Victoria, 'Does "Frenzy" Degrade Women?' (30 July 1972) https://archive.nytimes.com/www.nytimes.com/library/film/073072hitch-frenzy-comment.html

United Nations, 'Peace, dignity and equality on a healthy planet', https://www.un.org/en/global-issues/population

Zavamed, 'How Realistic is Sex on Screen', https://www.zavamed.com/uk/sex-on-screen.html

Watts, Naomi and David Lynch interview (17 April 2020) https://www.youtube.com/watch?v=e_BjbaBEyb4&ab_channel=Josip%C4%90olo

Weaver, Caity, 'How Maya Rudolph Became the Master of Impressions' (14 September 2018) https://www.nytimes.com/2018/09/14/magazine/maya-rudolph-snl-amazon-forever.html

Welkos, Robert W., 'More of This … Less of This?' (6 May 1993) https://www.latimes.com/archives/la-xpm-1993-05-06-ca-31955-story.html

Women and Hollywood, '2019 Statistics', https://womenand-hollywood.com/resources/statistics/2019-statistics/

Journal Articles

Abderrahmene, Bourenane, 'Authenticity and Discourses in Aladdin' (1992) *Journal of Arab & Muslim Media Research*, https://www.researchgate.net/publication/344682480_Authenticity_and_discourses_in_Aladdin_1992

Allen, Jeanne Thomas, 'The Representation of Violence to Women: Hitchcock's "Frenzy"' (1985) *Film Quarterly*, https://online.ucpress.edu/fq/article-abstract/38/3/30/40491/The-Representation-of-Violence-to-Women-Hitchcock?redirectedFrom=fulltext

Anderson, Lisa, Jill-Marie Shaw and Linda McCargar, 'Physiological effects of bulimia nervosa on the gastrointestinal tract' (1997) https://downloads.hindawi.com/journals/cjgh/1997/727645.pdf

Bachmann, Gideon, 'Review: Exodus by Otto Preminger' (1961) *Film Quarterly*.

Berrios, German E. and Lazare Rivière, 'Madness from the womb' (2006) National Library of Medicine, https://pubmed.ncbi.nlm.nih.gov/17146991/

Boker, Pamela S., 'America's women superheroes: Power, gender, and the comics'. Mid-Atlantic Almanac 2 (1993): 107–18

Butler, Judith, 'Sex and Gender in Simone de Beauvoir's Second Sex' (1986) *Yale French Studies*, https://www.jstor.org/stable/2930225?origin=crossref

Caporale, Marzia M., 'The Semiotics of Change: Re-writing the Female Body in Contemporary Tunisian Cinema' (2014) *Dalhousie French Studies*, https://www.jstor.org/stable/43487467

Copelin, David, '"F" is for Farid' (1989) *Cinéaste*, https://www.jstor.org/stable/23803059?read-now=1&refreqid=excelsior

%3Ab8d9c93f7878defea8f5b1771f890df6&seq=2#page_scan_tab_contents

Courtney, Susan, Picturizing Race: Hollywood's Censorship of Miscegenation and Production of Racial Visibility through Imitation of Life (1998), https://www.colorado.edu/gendersarchive1998-2013/1998/05/01/picturizing-race-hollywoods-censorship-miscegenation-and-production-racial-visibility#n11

Crowdus, Gary, 'Lawrence of Arabia: The Cinematic (Re) Writing of History' (1989) *Cinéaste*, https://www.jstor.org/stable/41687645.

Heldman, Caroline, Laura Lazarus Frankel and Jennifer Holmes, '"Hot, Black Leather, Whip": The (De)evolution of Female Protagonists in Action Cinema, 1960–2014' (2016) *Sexualisation, Media, and Society*, https://journals.sagepub.com/doi/full/10.1177/2374623815627789

Hourihan, Kathleen L., Aaron S. Benjamin and Xiping Liu, 'A cross-race effect in metamemory: Predictions of face recognition are more accurate for members of our own race' (2 July 2012) National Library of Medicine, https://www.ncbi.nlm.nih.gov/pmc/articles/PMC3496291/

Javorsky, Emilia, 'Race, Rather than Skin Pigmentation, Predicts Facial Hair Growth in Women' (May 2014) *Journal of Clinical and Aesthetic Dermatology*, https://www.ncbi.nlm.nih.gov/pmc/articles/PMC4025516/

McNabney, Sean M., Krisztina Hevesi and David L. Rowland, 'Effects of Pornography Use and Demographic Parameters on Sexual Response during Masturbation and Partnered Sex in Women' (2020) *International Journal of Environmental Research and Public Health*, https://www.mdpi.com/1660-4601/17/9/3130/htm

Scheiner, Georganne, 'Look at Me, I'm Sandra Dee: Beyond a White, Teen Icon' (2001) *Frontiers: A Journal of Women Studies*, https://muse.jhu.edu/article/12013.

Shaheen, Jack G., '"The Gladiator": How in the World Did Bad Arabs Happen to This Roman on His Way to the Forum?' (14 August 2000) https://www.wrmea.org/000-august-september/

the-gladiator-how-in-the-world-did-bad-arabs-happen-to-this-roman-on-his-way-to-the-forum.html

Sharif, Omar, and Miriam Rosen, 'The Making of Omar Sharif: An Interview' (1989) *Cinéaste,* https://www.jstor.org/stable/23803061

Subramanian, Janani, and Jorie Lagerwey, 'Food, Sex, Love, and Bodies in "Eat Pray Love" and "Black Swan"' (2013) *Studies in Popular Culture,* https://www.jstor.org/stable/23610149

Tate, Claudia, 'Nella Larsen's Passing: A Problem of Interpretation' (1980) *Black American Literature Forum,* https://doi.org/10.2307/2904405

Thompson, S.H. and K. Hammond, 'Beauty is as beauty does: body image and self-esteem of pageant contestants' (September 2003) National Library of Medicine, https://pubmed.ncbi.nlm.nih.gov/14649788/

Williams, Linda, 'Cinema and the Sex Act' (2001) *Cinéaste,* https://www.jstor.org/stable/41689431

Books

Agard, John, *Half-Caste* (United Kingdom: Hodder & Stoughton, 2004)

Aldington, Richard, *Lawrence of Arabia: A Biographical Enquiry* (New York, 1976).

Beauvoir, Simone de. The Second Sex. (United Kingdom, Vintage, 2011).

Bogle, Donald, *Bright Boulevards, Bold Dreams: The Story of Black Hollywood* (New York, 2005).

Bogle, Donald, *Toms, Coons, Mulattoes, Mammies, and Bucks: An Interpretive History of Blacks in American Films* (New York, 2004).

Brown, Jeffrey A., *Dangerous Curves: Action Heroines, Gender, Fetishism, and Popular Culture* (Jackson, 2011).

Hedren, Tippi, *Tippi: A Memoir* (New York, 2016).

Herzig, Rebecca M., *Plucked: A History of Hair Removal* (New York, 2016).

Hooks, Bell, *Reel to Real: Race, Sex, and Class at the Movies* (Abingdon, 1996).

Jeffords, Susan, *Hard Bodies: Hollywood Masculinity in the Reagan Era* (New Brunswick, 1994).

Masri, Safwan M., *Tunisia: An Arab Anomaly* (United States, Columbia University Press, 2017).

McGilligan, Patrick, *Alfred Hitchcock: A Life in Darkness and Light* (New York, 2003).

Moon, Krystyn R., *Yellowface: Creating the Chinese in American Popular Music and Performance, 1850s–1920s* (Rutgers University Press, 2005). http://www.jstor.org/stable/j.ctt5hjb1x.

Morris, Benny, *Israel's Border Wars, 1949–1956: Arab Infiltration, Israeli Retaliation, and the Countdown to the Suez War* (Oxford, 1997).

Mulvey, Laura, *Visual Pleasure and Narrative Cinema* (London, 2016)

Nolen-Hoeksema, Susan, *Women Who Think Too Much: How to Break Free of Overthinking and Reclaim Your Life* (London, 2003).

Rosewarne, Lauren, *Periods in Pop Culture: Menstruation in Film and Television* (Washington DC, 2012).

Saadawi, Nawal El, *The Essential Nawal El Saadawi: A Reader* (United Kingdom, Zed Books, 2013).

Said, Edward W., *Orientalism* (United Kingdom, Penguin Modern Classics, 2003, 1995).

Segal, Lynne, *Straight Sex: Rethinking the Politics of Pleasure* (London, 2015).

Slimani, Leïla, *Sex and Lies* (London, 2020).

Totman, Sally, *How Hollywood Projects Foreign Policy* (United Kingdom, Palgrave Macmillan, 2009).

Wright, Joshua K., *"Wake Up, Mr. West": Kanye West and the Double Consciousness of Black Celebrity* (Jefferson, 2022).

Reports

Choueiti, Marc, Stacy L. Smith, Katherine Pieper and Ariana Case, 'Gender and Race/Ethnicity of Film Reviewers Across 100 Top Films of 2017' (June 2018) https://assets.uscannenberg.org/docs/cricits-choice-2018.pdf

Hecker, Kaplan & Fink, 'NCAA External Gender Equity Review' (2 August 2021) https://kaplanhecker.app.box.com/s/6fpd51gxk9ki78f8vbhqcqh0b0o95oxq

Khan, Al-Baab, Dr. Katherine Pieper, Stacy L. Smith, Marc Choueiti, Kevin Yao and Artur Tofan, 'Missing & Maligned: The Reality of Muslims in Popular Global Movies' (June 2021) https://assets.uscannenberg.org/docs/aii-muslim-rep-global-film-2021-06-09.pdf

Lauzen, Martha M., 'Thumbs Down 2018: Film Critics and Gender, and Why It Matters' (2018) https://womenintvfilm.sdsu.edu/wp-content/uploads/2018/07/2018_Thumbs_Down_Report.pdf

Office for National Statistics, 'Nature of sexual assault by rape or penetration, England and Wales: year ending March 2020' (18 March 2021) https://www.ons.gov.uk/peoplepopulation-andcommunity/crimeandjustice/articles/natureofsexualassa ultbyrapeorpenetrationenglandandwales/yearendingmarch2020

UCLA, 'Hollywood Diversity Report' (2021) https://socialsciences.ucla.edu/wp-content/uploads/2021/04/UCLA-Hollywood-Diversity-Report-2021-Film-4-22-2021.pdf

Williams, Linda, 'Film Bodies: Gender, Genre, and Excess' (1991) *Film Quarterly,* https://online.ucpress.edu/fq/article-abstract/44/4/2/39822/Film-Bodies-Gender-Genre-and-Excess?redirectedFrom=fulltext

Trailers
3 Generations trailer, https://www.youtube.com/watch?v=maUZLJaHhcg

Documentary Films
Shaheen, Jack G., *Reel Bad Arabs: How Hollywood Vilifies a People* (2006).

Social Media
Evangelista, Chris, Twitter feed (16 June 2021) https://twitter.com/cevangelista413/status/1405241777125212163?s=20&t=vVqtEJLbRAZ8IXJ8fubU6w

Bilge, Ebiri, Twitter feed (16 June 2021) https://twitter.com/
BilgeEbiri/status/1405247690364047360?s=20&t=vVqtEJLb
RAZ8IXJ8fubU6w

Rogen, Seth, Twitter feed (18 August 2017) https://twitter.com/
Sethrogen/status/898369963836231682

Websites

Disney Princess Fandom (Esmerelda), https://disneyprincess.
fandom.com/wiki/Esmeralda

Forebears, 'Zammel surname', https://forebears.io/surnames/
zammel